Mastering Smalltalk Programming

From Basics to Expert Proficiency

Contents

Introduction

Smalltalk is a highly influential and dynamic object-oriented programming language that has made significant contributions to the field of computer science. Developed in the 1970s at Xerox PARC by Alan Kay and his colleagues, Smalltalk introduced numerous innovations that have shaped modern programming languages and development practices. Its design emphasizes simplicity, uniformity, and direct manipulation of objects, making it a powerful tool for both beginners and experienced developers.

The purpose of this book, "Mastering Smalltalk Programming: From Basics to Expert Proficiency," is to provide a comprehensive guide to mastering the language. This book is structured to take readers from the basics of Smalltalk programming to advanced topics, ensuring a deep understanding of core concepts and best practices. Each chapter builds on the previous one, covering essential topics in a logical progression.

The book begins with an exploration of Smalltalk's history, its development, and the key figures who contributed to its creation. Readers will gain insight into the philosophy and goals that guided the language's design, as well as the key features and innovations introduced by Smalltalk. This background is crucial for appreciating the context in which Smalltalk emerged and its lasting impact on the programming world.

Setting up the Smalltalk programming environment is the next step. This book provides detailed instructions for choosing the right Smalltalk distribution, downloading and installing it, and navigating the integrated development environment (IDE). This chapter aims to ensure a smooth start for readers, allowing them to focus on learning the language without unnecessary hurdles.

Following the setup, the book delves into the basic syntax and structure of Smalltalk programs. Readers will learn how to create their first Smalltalk programs, understand basic data types, use variables and constants, perform arithmetic operations, and handle strings and characters. This foundational knowledge is essential for writing and understanding Smalltalk code.

A significant portion of the book is dedicated to exploring object-oriented principles in Smalltalk. Concepts such as objects, messages, classes, instances, inheritance, polymorphism, encapsulation, and metaclasses are covered in detail. Understanding these principles is crucial for leveraging the full power of Smalltalk's object-oriented capabilities.

Classes and methods are fundamental constructs in Smalltalk, and this book provides comprehensive coverage of their definition, usage, and organization. Topics include instance variables, class variables, method definition syntax, method overriding, method categories, and the differences between class methods and instance methods. This knowledge is essential for effective class and method design in Smalltalk.

Control structures and collections are also explored in depth. Readers will learn about conditional statements, loops, and iteration, as well as how to handle various collection types such as arrays, dictionaries, and sets. Advanced topics such as block closures and nested collections are also covered, providing a thorough understanding of control structures and collections in Smalltalk.

For those looking to extend their knowledge further, the book covers advanced collection types and streams. This includes sorted collections, weak collections, custom collections, and various stream operations. Practical examples and performance considerations are provided to help readers apply these concepts effectively.

Graphics and user interface programming in Smalltalk are also addressed, with chapters dedicated to basic drawing operations, creating and handling windows, event handling, building user interfaces, and customizing UI components. This section is essential for readers interested in developing interactive and visually appealing applications.

Concurrency and parallelism are critical topics in modern programming, and this book provides an introduction to processes, threads, synchronization, shared resources, parallel processing patterns, and asynchronous programming in Smalltalk. Understanding these concepts is crucial for building responsive and efficient applications.

Finally, testing and debugging are covered extensively. The book introduces readers to writing test cases, using the SUnit framework, running and managing tests, setting breakpoints, inspecting variables, tracing code execution, handling exceptions, and using logging for debugging. These skills are vital for maintaining and improving the quality of Smalltalk applications.

Throughout this book, readers will find detailed explanations, practical examples, and best practices to help them master Smalltalk programming. Whether you are a beginner starting with the basics or an experienced developer looking to deepen your knowledge, this book aims to be a valuable resource for learning and mastering Smalltalk.

Chapter 1

Introduction to Smalltalk and Its History

Smalltalk, born in the 1970s at Xerox PARC, is a pioneering object-oriented programming language developed by Alan Kay and his team. Renowned for its simplicity and groundbreaking features, Smalltalk introduced concepts like live coding environments, which have heavily influenced modern programming languages. This chapter explores its origins, evolution, and the philosophy that shaped its creation, and further examines its lasting impact on the software development industry and the numerous dialects that emerged over the years.

1.1 The Origins of Smalltalk

Smalltalk was conceived in the 1970s by Alan Kay and his team at Xerox Palo Alto Research Center (PARC). The goal was to create a programming language and environment that embodied the principles of object-oriented programming (OOP), promoting modularity, ease of understanding, and reuse of code. This section delves into the historical context, motivations, and pioneering work that led to the creation of Smalltalk.

Alan Kay, influenced by the ideas of Ivan Sutherland's Sketchpad and Simula, the first object-oriented programming language, envisioned a computing environment where children could explore and learn programming intuitively. Kay's early work, combined with the innovations at Xerox PARC, aimed to create a "personal dynamic medium," a precursor to modern graphical user interfaces (GUIs) and integrated development environments (IDEs).

Historical Context

The 1970s were a period of significant innovation in computer science. At Xerox PARC, researchers were developing technologies that would ultimately shape the future of computing, including Ethernet, laser printing, and the Alto personal computer. This environment fostered interdisciplinary collaboration and cross-pollination of ideas, essential for the birth of Smalltalk.

Motivations

Kay's motivation stemmed from his belief in the power of computing as a medium for creative thought and communication. He aimed to create a system where users could manipulate objects on the screen directly and intuitively. This vision was inspired by Seymour Papert's LOGO language, which emphasized learning through doing. For Kay, the ultimate goal was to build a system that was so simple that a child could use it to create complex programs.

Development Process

The initial version, known as Smalltalk-72, was more of a proof of concept than a fully-fledged language. It introduced the idea of objects as the fundamental building blocks of the system. Each object could encapsulate data and behavior, responding to messages sent to it by other objects. This model was a radical departure from the procedural programming paradigms dominant at the time.

In subsequent iterations—Smalltalk-74 and Smalltalk-76—Kay and his colleagues refined these concepts. They introduced a clearer syntax and semantics for message passing and object creation. The environment also began to take shape, incorporating the iconic overlapping window interface, which allowed users to interact with multiple objects simultaneously.

```
Object subclass: Rectangle [
    | width height |

    width: anInteger [
        width := anInteger.
    ]

    height: anInteger [
```

```
        height := anInteger.
    ]

    area [
        ^width * height.
    ]
]
```

The above code demonstrates the creation of a Rectangle class in Smalltalk, showcasing the simplicity and elegance of the language. The subclass method is used to define a new class, with width and height as instance variables. Methods such as width: and height: are used to set these variables, while the area method calculates the area of the rectangle.

Smalltalk-80

The most influential version, Smalltalk-80, solidified many of the ideas from earlier versions and included a comprehensive development environment. This version introduced the Model-View-Controller (MVC) paradigm, which became a cornerstone of GUI design. The environment allowed live coding, where changes to the code could be made and tested immediately, supporting rapid prototyping and iterative development.

Algorithm 1: Creation and interaction with Circle objects in Smalltalk

Data: Initialization and user inputs
Result: Creation and interaction with Smalltalk objects

```
Object subclass: Circle [ | radius |
radius: anInteger [ radius := anInteger. ]
circumference [ (2 * 3.14 * radius). ] ]
Function PrintCircumference(myCircle, otherCircle)
    | circleArray |
    circleArray := Array with: myCircle with: otherCircle.
    circleArray do: [:each | Transcript show: each
      circumference; cr. ]
```

The algorithm above presents an example of creating and interacting with Circle objects in Smalltalk. It creates instances of the Circle class, sets their radius, and calculates their circumferences, outputting the results to the Transcript.

The success of Smalltalk-80 led to its widespread adoption and influence. The language and its principles became a touchstone for later OOP languages like Objective-C and Java. Smalltalk's live coding environment, rich libraries, and powerful development tools laid the groundwork for modern IDEs and interactive programming experiences. The contributions of Alan Kay and his team at Xerox PARC thus marked a significant milestone in the history of computer science, steering the trajectory of software development towards the ubiquitous use of object-oriented programming.

1.2 The Development and Evolution of Smalltalk

The development of Smalltalk commenced in the 1970s at Xerox PARC (Palo Alto Research Center). The pioneering efforts by the research group led by Alan Kay, including prominent figures such as Dan Ingalls, Adele Goldberg, and others, were instrumental in shaping the language. Their primary objective was to create a robust tool conducive to education and powerful enough for complex software engineering tasks. Thus, Smalltalk was designed to exemplify the principles of object-oriented programming (OOP).

```
"Example of a simple Smalltalk method"
Object subclass: MyObject [
    MyObject >> sayHello [
        Transcript show: 'Hello, world!'.
    ]
]
```

This code snippet is a fundamental example where MyObject is a subclass of Object, and the sayHello method sends the string 'Hello, world!' to the system transcript.

Smalltalk-72 marked the initial iteration, characterized by a minimalistic syntax highly reliant on message passing. The subsequent versions, notably Smalltalk-74 and Smalltalk-76, introduced enhancements in language structure and performance. A major breakthrough was achieved with Smalltalk-80, the first version to be released outside of Xerox PARC. It was designated as the standard reference for the language, providing a comprehensive environment including development tools and a rich class library.

```
"Initialization of the Smalltalk environment"
SmalltalkImage current [
    initialize [
        "Perform initialization tasks"
        Transcript clear.
    ]
]
```

In Smalltalk-80, the concepts of "everything is an object" and the encompassing message-passing mechanism became more refined. The introduction of the Model-View-Controller (MVC) architectural pattern within Smalltalk-80 had a profound impact on software design architectures. The MVC pattern segregates the application logic (Model), user interface (View), and user input (Controller), fostering a modular and cohesive approach to software development.

The evolution continued with various adaptations and optimizations. The compilations of Smalltalk, such as Squeak, VisualWorks, and Pharo, each contributed unique elements to the language ecosystem. Squeak, for example, leveraged a highly portable and nearly entirely Smalltalk-implemented virtual machine. This portability widened Smalltalk's compatibility with different computing platforms.

```
"Creating a simple morph in Squeak"
Morph new openInWorld.
```

Later developments expanded Smalltalk's scope and capability. VisualWorks, a descendant of Smalltalk-80, introduced a new level of performance and a refined graphical user interface framework. Pharo, a modern evolution, focused on creating an open-source, highly integrated environment prioritizing both agility and adeptness for professional developers and researchers.

A significant innovation during the development phase was the Just-in-Time (JIT) compilation, dramatically improving the execution speed of Smalltalk programs. This technique allowed dynamic compilation of bytecode into machine code, only when necessary, optimizing performance without a trade-off in the flexibility.

```
Smalltalk virtual machine improvements led to enhanced performance metrics:
- Bytecode to machine code compilation: 5-20x speed increase.
- Reduced memory footprint from optimized object memory management.
```

Throughout its development, Smalltalk's emphasis on a live programming environment—an interactive workspace where developers can test, inspect, and modify the code instantaneously—was revolutionary. This feature significantly impacted developer productivity and provided a model adopted by various modern IDEs.

The continued evolution of Smalltalk is marked by its dialects, each addressing different user needs while maintaining the core object-oriented principles. These dialects demonstrate Smalltalk's adaptability across diverse domains, from education to industrial applications.

1.3 Influential Figures in the Smalltalk Community

The development and evolution of Smalltalk owe much to the visionary contributions of several key individuals. Their innovative ideas and relentless efforts have not only shaped Smalltalk but have also had a lasting impact on the field of computer science. This section delves into the achievements and influence of these figures.

Alan Kay: Often regarded as the father of Smalltalk, Alan Kay's work at Xerox PARC in the early 1970s was instrumental in the creation of the language. Kay introduced the concept of object-oriented programming (OOP) with a focus on creating an environment that was both user-friendly and capable of simulating any real-world process. His idea of "everything is an object" revolutionized programming paradigms and influenced many subsequent languages.

Dan Ingalls: As a key collaborator of Alan Kay, Dan Ingalls made significant contributions to the development of the Smalltalk-76 and Smalltalk-80 systems. Ingalls was responsible for many of the innovative features in Smalltalk, including the concept of bitblt (a block transfer operation for raster graphics) and the development of the Smalltalk virtual machine. His work on efficient memory management and real-time garbage collection remains foundational in the field.

Adele Goldberg: Adele Goldberg was a major figure in the Smalltalk community, contributing to both its development and advocacy. Goldberg co-authored several seminal works on Smalltalk, including "Smalltalk-80: The Language and Its Implementation." Her efforts in education, especially through the creation of the "LearningWorks" project, fostered a broader understanding and appreciation of Smalltalk among computer science students and professionals alike.

Ted Kaehler: Known for his work on the educational application of Smalltalk, Ted Kaehler was instrumental in developing the concept of "scripting" within the Smalltalk environment. His contributions to the design of user-friendly interfaces helped make Smalltalk more accessible to non-programmers, thus broadening its reach and applicability.

John Maloney: John Maloney played a pivotal role in the development of Squeak, an open-source Smalltalk environment. Squeak extended the capabilities of original Smalltalk, introducing multimedia features and a rich development environment that made it suitable for a wide range of applications. Maloney's vision and technical expertise significantly advanced Smalltalk's usability and functionality.

Andreas Raab: A prominent figure in the Squeak and Croquet projects, Andreas Raab's contributions to virtual reality applications and 3D graphics in Smalltalk environments were groundbreaking. His work on Morpic, a visual interface framework, allowed developers to create complex graphical user interfaces with ease.

Ward Cunningham: While best known as the inventor of the wiki, Ward Cunningham was also an influential member of the Smalltalk community. His work focused on software design patterns and best practices within Smalltalk, leading to the development of techniques such as the CRC (Class-Responsibility-Collaboration) cards, which are now widely used in software design.

David N. Smith: As the creator of the IBM Smalltalk environment, David N. Smith contributed significantly to the commercialization and industrial use of Smalltalk. His work made Smalltalk a viable option for enterprise applications, extending its influence beyond academia and research.

Kent Beck: An advocate of Test-Driven Development (TDD) and Extreme Programming (XP), Kent Beck's methodologies were deeply influenced by his work with Smalltalk. His approaches to software development emphasized iterative design, testing, and collaboration, principles that resonate with the dynamic nature of Smalltalk programming.

```
Object subclass: #Person
    instanceVariableNames: 'name occupation'
    classVariableNames: ''
    poolDictionaries: ''
    category: 'MyCategory'

Person>>initialize
    name := 'Unnamed'.
    occupation := 'Unknown'.

Person>>setName: aName
    name := aName.

Person>>setOccupation: anOccupation
    occupation := anOccupation.

Person>>display
    ^'Name: ', name, ' Occupation: ', occupation.

"Creating an instance and using the Person class"
| person |
person := Person new.
person setName: 'Alan Kay'.
person setOccupation: 'Computer Scientist'.
Transcript show: person display. "Outputs: Name: Alan Kay Occupation: Computer
    Scientist"
```

Transcripts of historical interviews, publications, and personal accounts further illustrate the collaborative nature of Smalltalk's development. The following exemplifies a typical output from executing the code:

```
Name: Alan Kay Occupation: Computer Scientist
```

These influential figures collaborated to create a programming language and environment that embodies the principles of simplicity, flexibility, and powerful abstraction. Their collective efforts pioneered the development of user-friendly interfaces and dynamic, live coding environments that have continued to influence modern software development practices.

1.4 Philosophy and Goals of Smalltalk

Smalltalk was conceived with a strong philosophical foundation and set of goals centered around creating an intuitive, user-friendly, and robust programming environment. Alan Kay and his team at Xerox PARC aimed to revolutionize the way programming languages interacted with both developers and the system they programmed. They envisioned a language that was not just a tool for coding, but an immersive environment fostering creativity, learning, and evolution of ideas.

1. Uniformity and Simplicity

One of the core philosophies of Smalltalk is uniformity. The language is built upon the idea that everything is an object, including numbers, characters, and even classes themselves. This object-centric model promotes an elegant uniformity, minimizing the conceptual load for the programmer. By ensuring that operations and interactions are consistently handled through message passing between objects, Smalltalk eliminates the need for special cases or complex syntax rules found in other languages.

```
Object subclass: #Person
    instanceVariableNames: 'name age'
    classVariableNames: ''
    poolDictionaries: ''
    category: 'Examples'.
```

In the snippet above, creating a new class Person follows the same consistent syntax and semantics applied across the entire language.

2. Interactivity and Immediate Feedback

Smalltalk's live coding environment is a direct manifestation of the emphasis on interactivity and immediate feedback. The development environment is designed to be highly interactive, allowing programmers to experiment in real-time. This feature was radical at the time of its inception and has since become a hallmark of effective programming environments.

Developers can modify code and see the effects instantaneously without compiling the entire application. This approach supports a higher level of experimentation and iterative development.

```
Transcript show: 'Hello, World!'.
5 + 3.
(Point x: 10 y: 20) display.
```

By executing the code snippets in a workspace, developers instantly observe the output, enhancing their understanding and debugging capabilities.

```
Hello, World!
8
(Point x: 10 y: 20)
```

3. Human-Centric Design

Another guiding principle of Smalltalk is its human-centric design. Alan Kay envisioned computing as an aid to human thinking and creativity. Smalltalk's syntax and semantics are designed to be readable and writable by humans, focusing on clarity and expressiveness. The language encourages a style that reads like natural language, making code easier to understand and maintain.

```
aPerson := Person new.
aPerson name: 'John Doe'.
```

The method `name:` reads naturally, resembling the way humans communicate, which lowers the cognitive barrier to learning and using the language.

4. Educational Impact and Accessibility

From its inception, Smalltalk was designed to be an educational tool. Alan Kay's vision included making computing power accessible to children and non-experts, embodying the idea of computing as a new medium for thought. This led to a language and environment that not only professional programmers could use but also learners at various levels could grasp.

Tools like the Smalltalk Browser offer an intuitive interface for navigating classes, methods, and hierarchical structures—facilitating understanding and exploration of the codebase.

5. Innovation and Evolution

Smalltalk was intentionally designed to foster innovation and support the evolution of both individual programs and the language itself. The Smalltalk environment is conducive to exploratory programming, enabling rapid prototyping and iterative refinement of ideas. Its dynamic typing system allows flexibility, while reflective capabilities enable the language to adapt and extend itself.

The concept of "image-based" persistence, where the entire system state (including code, objects, and runtime context) is saved and restored, underscores the environment's adaptability. This mechanism not only streamlines development but also encourages developers to take risks and experiment without fear of irreversible consequences.

6. Decoupling and Modularity

Smalltalk promotes decoupling and modularity through its object-oriented design. Objects encapsulate state and behavior, communicating via well-defined interfaces. This separation of concerns allows for greater modularity, making systems easier to maintain, extend, and adapt.

```
Person>>name
    ^name

Person>>name: aName
    name := aName

Person>>age
    ^age

Person>>age: anAge
    age := anAge
```

In this example, accessor methods encapsulate the name and age attributes, demonstrating how Smalltalk objects manage their own state.

The philosophy and goals of Smalltalk have had a profound impact on the development of subsequent programming languages and environments. Its emphasis on simplicity, uniformity, interactivity, human-centric design, educational accessibility, innovation, and modularity continues to influence modern programming practices and tools. This foundation has ensured that Smalltalk remains a significant and respected language in the software development community.

1.5 Key Features and Innovations

Smalltalk is heralded for numerous features and innovative concepts that played a pivotal role in the advancement of computing. These features not only underscore its historical significance but also illuminate its profound impact on modern programming paradigms.

First and foremost, Smalltalk embodies the pure object-oriented programming paradigm. Every entity in Smalltalk, from control structures to primitive data types, is an object. These objects communicate exclusively through the use of messages, making the mechanism simple yet powerful. This approach provides consistency and uniformity within the language.

```
anObject doSomething.
```

In the above code snippet, anObject receives the message doSomething. This concept ensures encapsulation and reinforces the separation of concerns, as each object maintains its own state and behavior.

One of Smalltalk's defining features is its integrated development environment (IDE). Smalltalk introduced the concept of a live coding environment, where developers can inspect, modify, and test the system on-the-fly without needing to stop and recompile. This interactive experience is facilitated by several tools integrated into Smalltalk's IDE:

- **Inspector**: Allows examination and manipulation of object instances at runtime.
- **Debugger**: Provides a powerful tool for identifying and resolving issues in running code.
- **Workspace**: An interactive area to write and execute arbitrary Smalltalk expressions.

Smalltalk's emphasis on immediacy and interactivity significantly accelerates the development cycle, fosters experimentation, and reduces the latency between code writing and code execution.

The language also introduces a dynamic typing system. Unlike statically typed languages where variable types are declared explicitly, Smalltalk leverages runtime type identification. This flexibility simplifies code and enhances rapid prototyping. However, it requires more robust testing frameworks to mitigate potential runtime errors.

```
| aVariable |
aVariable := 5.
aVariable := 'Hello World'.
```

In the above listing, aVariable initially holds an integer value, then is reassigned to a string, exemplifying Smalltalk's dynamic typing.

Another hallmark of Smalltalk is its metaprogramming capabilities, largely facilitated by its concept of metaclasses. In Smalltalk, every class is an instance of a metaclass, providing a reflective system that allows the program to inspect and modify its own structure and behavior.

```
Object subclass: #ExampleClass.
ExampleClass class.
```

In this case, ExampleClass is an instance of a metaclass, enhancing the language's flexibility and dynamism.

Furthermore, Smalltalk champions a simple yet powerful syntax. The language's concise and human-readable syntax reduces cognitive load, making the code more accessible and maintainable. Smalltalk syntax typically follows the format:

```
Object messageSelector: argument1 with: argument2.
```

This simplicity extends to control structures, which are implemented as message sends. For example, Smalltalk handles conditional execution using the ifTrue: ifFalse: message pattern.

```
aBoolean ifTrue: [ "Block of code to execute if true" ] ifFalse: [ "Block of code to
    execute if false" ].
```

Smalltalk's garbage collection system is another notable innovation. Automatic memory management eliminates the complexity and errors associated with manual memory allocation and deallocation, thus reducing the potential for memory leaks and other related issues.

Lastly, the language embraces the concept of block closures. Blocks are anonymous functions or lambda expressions encapsulated within square brackets, enablings flexible and reusable control constructs.

```
block := [ :x | x + 1 ].
block value: 5. " => 6 "
```

In this example, block is a block closure that takes one argument and returns the argument incremented by one.

Smalltalk's innovations extend beyond the mere syntactical and structural elements. Its influence is evident in numerous modern programming languages that adopted object-orientation, dynamic typing, integrated development environments, and reflective capabilities.

1.6 The Impact of Smalltalk on Modern Programming Languages

Smalltalk's influence on modern programming languages is both profound and extensive. As a pioneering object-oriented programming (OOP) language, Smalltalk's introduction in the 1970s initiated a paradigm shift in the software development industry. The core principles and innovations introduced by Smalltalk have permeated numerous contemporary programming languages. This section explores these influences in detail, focusing on language features, development practices, and the evolving landscape of coding environments.

Object-Oriented Programming: Smalltalk was one of the first languages to implement the concept of objects, encapsulating both data and behaviors. This encapsulation promotes modularity and reuse of code. Modern programming languages such as Java, C#, Python, and Ruby have embraced and extended these object-oriented principles. In Java, for example, the encapsulation of data and methods within classes directly parallels Smalltalk's object model. Similarly, languages like Python and Ruby emphasize ease of use and dynamic typing, akin to the flexible nature of Smalltalk.

```
class Greeter:
    def __init__(self, name):
        self.name = name

    def greet(self):
        print(f"Hello, {self.name}!")
```

Python's syntax for defining classes and creating instances shows clear inspiration from Smalltalk's design philosophy. The simplicity and readability are reminiscent of the original Smalltalk environment.

Live Coding and Development Environments: One of Smalltalk's most innovative features was its live coding environment. This interactive approach to software development, allowing changes to be made and tested in real-time, influenced the development environments of several modern languages. The Integrated Development Environments

(IDEs) for languages like JavaScript, such as Node.js and React Native, prominently feature live reloading capabilities. Additionally, Python's interactive mode and IPython notebooks offer dynamic experimentation that mirrors Smalltalk's live coding environment.

```
// Using React Native's live reload feature
import React from 'react';
import { Text, View } from 'react-native';

const App = () => {
  return (
    <View>
      <Text>Hello, world!</Text>
    </View>
  );
};

export default App;
```

This JavaScript example showcases the impact of Smalltalk's live coding model. Changes to the code can be visually observed immediately, as seen in frameworks like React Native.

Virtual Machines and Runtime Environments: Smalltalk was designed to run on a virtual machine (VM), which managed the abstraction between hardware and software. This concept has been foundational for other languages such as Java and C#, which rely on the Java Virtual Machine (JVM) and Common Language Runtime (CLR), respectively. These VMs provide platform independence, a feature first realized in Smalltalk.

Garbage Collection: The automatic memory management introduced by Smalltalk, known as garbage collection, has become a staple in many modern languages. This feature, which relieves programmers from manually managing memory allocation and deallocation, is implemented in languages such as Java, Python, JavaScript, and Ruby. The fundamental principles of garbage collection algorithms, initially explored within Smalltalk, have evolved and diversified, but the core philosophy remains deeply rooted in Smalltalk's legacy.

Reflection and Introspection: Reflection, the ability of a program to inspect and modify its own structure and behavior at runtime, was a defining characteristic of Smalltalk. This powerful feature supports dynamic typing and late binding, and is integral to languages such as Python, Ruby, and Java. In Java, the Reflection API allows code to manipulate objects, classes, and methods dynamically.

```
import java.lang.reflect.Method;

public class ReflectionExample {
```

```
    public static void main(String[] args) {
        try {
            Class<?> cls = Class.forName("java.util.ArrayList");
            Method method = cls.getDeclaredMethod("size");
            Object instance = cls.newInstance();
            System.out.println("Size: " + method.invoke(instance));
        } catch (Exception e) {
            e.printStackTrace();
        }
    }
}
```

This Java code demonstrates the capability to inspect and manipulate the properties of an object at runtime, a clear derivation from Smalltalk's reflective capabilities.

Design Patterns: The idea of design patterns, popularized by the *Gang of Four* book, has roots in the Smalltalk community. The use of design patterns to solve recurrent problems in software design is now a fundamental concept in software engineering. Common patterns such as Singleton, Observer, and Model-View-Controller (MVC) were all either initially discovered or heavily utilized in Smalltalk environments.

```
public class Singleton {
    private static Singleton instance;

    private Singleton() {}

    public static Singleton getInstance() {
        if (instance == null) {
            instance = new Singleton();
        }
        return instance;
    }
}
```

The Singleton pattern, encapsulated in this Java example, exemplifies a design approach that originated in Smalltalk programming practices.

Influence on Scripting Languages: The ease of use and flexibility of Smalltalk have directly influenced the advent of scripting languages. Both Python and Ruby inherit Smalltalk's philosophy of being highly readable and straightforward, aiming to be easily accessible to new programmers while powerful in advanced application.

Ruby, for instance, borrows from Smalltalk's object model, providing every piece of data with their own methods, while Python emphasizes clear, readable code which is a hallmark of Smalltalk's design ethos.

Thus, the legacy of Smalltalk is deeply entrenched in the fabric of modern programming languages. The innovative concepts introduced by Smalltalk have not only been preserved but also have evolved to drive the development of contemporary languages. This continuity underscores the enduring influence of Smalltalk on the field of computer science.

1.7 Smalltalk Dialects and Variants

Smalltalk, though originally conceived as a singular programming language, has spawned a variety of dialects and variants since its inception. These variants are largely compatible with the core principles of Smalltalk but have diverged to accommodate different needs, platforms, and preferences of their respective communities. Understanding these dialects not only provides insight into the flexibility and adaptability of Smalltalk but also highlights the innovations introduced by each variant.

Smalltalk-80 is widely considered the standard-bearer for Smalltalk dialects. Developed at Xerox PARC, it laid the foundation for many subsequent versions. Smalltalk-80 introduced the infamous MVC (Model-View-Controller) architectural pattern and a robust environment for interactive development. Its image-based persistence paradigm, where the entire system state is saved and restored from a single file, remains a hallmark of Smalltalk environments.

Squeak is an open-source implementation of Smalltalk that emerged from the efforts of several of the original Smalltalk-80 developers, including Alan Kay. Squeak is noted for its portability and multimedia capabilities, including support for sound, graphics, and various input devices. The following example demonstrates how to create a simple graphical object in Squeak:

```
ellipse := EllipseMorph new.
ellipse bounds: (0@0 corner: 100@100).
ellipse color: Color red.
World addMorph: ellipse.
```

The execution of this code will generate an ellipse morph in the Squeak world, graphically demonstrating the live, interactive nature of the environment.

Dolphin Smalltalk is another influential dialect, particularly in the Windows operating system milieu. Dolphin is appreciated for its modern GUI and integration with Windows APIs. Its lightweight and responsive development environment align well with the needs of commercial and enterprise applications.

GNU Smalltalk offers a slightly different approach by focusing on script-based execution of Smalltalk code rather than the traditional image-based method. This makes GNU Smalltalk suitable for users who are more accustomed to text-based scripting languages. A simple script in GNU Smalltalk may look like this:

```
Object subclass: Person [
    | name age |

    Person class >> newName: n age: a [
        ^self new initializeName: n age: a.
    ]

    initializeName: n age: a [
        name := n.
        age := a.
    ]
    printDetails [
        'Name: ', name, ' Age: ', age printString.
    ]
].
p := Person newName: 'Alice' age: 30.
p printDetails.
```

When run, this script outputs:

```
Name: Alice Age: 30
```

Pharo is a modern open-source Smalltalk environment that has gained significant traction due to its active community and robust support for modern software development practices. Pharo places a strong emphasis on continuous integration, testing, and integrated development environments. Inside Pharo, tools like the Refactoring Browser and Moose platform for software and data analysis are widely used. Below is an example of a class definition in Pharo:

```
Object subclass: Book [
    | title author year |

    Book class >> title: t author: a year: y [
        ^self new initializeTitle: t author: a year: y.
    ]

    initializeTitle: t author: a year: y [
        title := t.
        author := a.
        year := y.
    ]

    printDetails [
        String streamContents: [:s |
            s nextPutAll: 'Title: '; nextPutAll: title; nl;
            nextPutAll: 'Author: '; nextPutAll: author; nl;
            nextPutAll: 'Year: '; nextPutAll: year printString].
```

```
    ]
].
b := Book title: 'The Art of Smalltalk' author: 'John Doe' year: 2022.
b printDetails.
```

Outputs:

```
Title: The Art of Smalltalk
Author: John Doe
Year: 2022
```

The VisualWorks dialect is another longstanding and commercially viable version of Smalltalk. Initially developed by ParcPlace Systems, it offers a comprehensive suite for enterprise-level application development, boasting an advanced integrated development environment (IDE), cross-platform capabilities, and a vast library of reusable components.

Finally, *Amber Smalltalk* represents the convergence of Smalltalk with modern web technologies. By compiling Smalltalk code to JavaScript, Amber allows developers to leverage the expressive syntax and dynamic capabilities of Smalltalk within the web browser environment. This makes it an interesting choice for web application developers.

Each dialect carries the essence of Smalltalk's core philosophy while extending its capabilities, tooling, and applicability to different aspects of software development. Understanding these variants is crucial for both appreciating the versatility of Smalltalk and for selecting the appropriate toolset for particular project needs.

1.8 Community and Ecosystem

The Smalltalk community is characterized by its collaborative spirit and commitment to advancing the language and its applications. This community has played a crucial role in the evolution and sustenance of Smalltalk, fostering a thriving ecosystem that supports both educational and professional endeavors.

The ecosystem surrounding Smalltalk encompasses various tools, libraries, frameworks, and platforms that enhance the development experience. The combination of a dedicated community and rich ecosystem ensures that Smalltalk remains relevant and accessible to developers of all levels.

Open-Source Projects and Contributions

The open-source ethos is deeply embedded within the Smalltalk community. Numerous open-source projects have been initiated and are actively maintained by enthusiasts and practitioners. Some of the notable open-source dialects include Squeak, Pharo, and GNU Smalltalk. Each of these dialects has its own set of features and optimizations tailored to specific use cases and preferences.

- **Squeak:** An open-source Smalltalk implementation with a strong focus on educational and multimedia applications. It is known for its powerful development environment and active community contributions.
- **Pharo:** A modern open-source Smalltalk environment, Pharo focuses on research and industrial applications. It offers advanced features like a just-in-time (JIT) compiler and an agile development environment.
- **GNU Smalltalk:** Unlike other dialects that emphasize graphical interfaces, GNU Smalltalk is designed for scripting and command-line use. It is suitable for users who prefer minimalistic and script-driven development.

Collaboration and knowledge sharing are facilitated through platforms such as GitHub, where developers can contribute to existing projects or initiate new ones. Version control systems play a pivotal role in managing these contributions, ensuring that enhancements and bug fixes are systematically incorporated.

Education and Learning Resources

The Smalltalk community prioritizes education and continuous learning. There are extensive resources available for learners at various stages in their programming journey. These resources include online tutorials, documentation, forums, and dedicated educational platforms.

- **Online Tutorials and Documentation:** Websites like Squeak.org and Pharo.org provide comprehensive guides and documentation. These resources cover basic syntax, advanced features, and best practices.
- **Forums and Discussion Groups:** Platforms such as the comp.lang.smalltalk newsgroup, Stack Overflow, and dedicated Slack channels enable community members to seek help, discuss ideas, and share experiences.

- **Educational Platforms:** Projects like Morphic in Squeak and interactive Smalltalk workspaces offer an immersive learning environment where users can experiment and learn through hands-on coding.

Conferences and Events

Community-driven conferences and events are vital for networking, knowledge exchange, and collaboration. Notable events include Smalltalks, the international Smalltalk conference, and Pharo Days.

- **Smalltalks:** This annual conference gathers enthusiasts, researchers, and industry professionals to present their work, discuss innovations, and explore future directions in Smalltalk development.
- **Pharo Days:** Focused on the Pharo community, this event showcases the latest advancements, use cases, and research in the Pharo environment.

These events often feature workshops, hackathons, and keynote presentations from leading figures in the Smalltalk community. They provide a platform for newcomers to interact with veterans, fostering a sense of camaraderie and collaborative spirit.

Industry Adoption and Professional Development

Smalltalk's adoption in industry spans various domains, including finance, healthcare, and telecommunications. Organizations leveraging Smalltalk benefit from its object-oriented architecture, which enhances maintainability and scalability.

Case studies highlighting successful Smalltalk implementations demonstrate its efficacy in solving complex problems. Examples include banking systems, where Smalltalk's robust framework ensures transactional integrity and real-time processing capabilities.

Professional development opportunities abound within the Smalltalk ecosystem. Certification programs, training workshops, and mentorship initiatives are available for those seeking to deepen their expertise.

```
"Example of a simple Smalltalk class definition and method implementation"
Object subclass: #Person
    instanceVariableNames: 'name age'
    classVariableNames: ''
    poolDictionaries: ''
    category: 'Community-Ecosystem'.
```

```
Person>>initialize
    name := ''.
    age := 0.

Person>>name: aName age: anAge
    name := aName.
    age := anAge.

Person>>displayPerson
    ^ 'Name: ', name, ' Age: ', age printString.
```

As illustrated in the code example, defining classes and methods in Smalltalk is straightforward, further contributing to its usability in various professional settings.

The cohesive integration of community initiatives, educational resources, and practical applications continues to solidify Smalltalk's position as a valuable and enduring programming language.

1.9 Real-World Applications of Smalltalk

Smalltalk, with its innovative object-oriented paradigm and dynamic environment, has been successfully deployed in various real-world applications. These applications span across different domains including finance, education, healthcare, and customer relationship management (CRM).

One prominent example is in the financial sector. In the early 1990s, the financial services company "JP Morgan" adopted Smalltalk to develop its derivative trading systems. The language's ability to handle complex financial models and its robustness in managing real-time transactions made it an ideal choice. Smalltalk's dynamic typing and reflective capabilities allowed rapid adaptability to the fast-evolving financial market requirements.

In the healthcare domain, notable usage can be observed in the development of Clinical Information Systems (CIS). For instance, "Patient Care Information Systems" (PCIS) was implemented using Smalltalk to manage patient data, ensuring real-time access and updates to critical medical records. The interactive development environment of Smalltalk facilitated quick iterations and refinements, improving system efficiency and reliability.

Education has also benefitted significantly from Smalltalk, particularly through the creation of various educational tools and simulations. The etoys system, built on the Squeak Smalltalk environment, is an excellent example. Etoys provides an interactive platform for children to learn programming concepts by creating simulations and games. Its visual programming interface, leveraging the simplicity and flexibility of Smalltalk, makes it accessible to young learners, fostering computational thinking and creativity.

Moreover, Smalltalk's influence can be seen in the domain of telecommunications. Projects such as the "Telecom Billing System", developed by the company "Vantive Corporation", utilized Smalltalk for its billing and customer service applications. Vantive leveraged Smalltalk's capabilities to handle complex customer interactions and large datasets, ensuring streamlined billing processes and efficient customer service management.

Another domain where Smalltalk proved its mettle is in CRM systems. The VASCO project by ParcPlace Systems developed a CRM application using VisualWorks, a Smalltalk environment. This system was able to integrate various customer service processes seamlessly, thanks to Smalltalk's robust object-oriented architecture, leading to improved customer satisfaction and operational efficiency.

Below is a sample Smalltalk code snippet used in a CRM application to illustrate handling of customer data:

```
Customer := Object subclass: [
    | name email |
    Customer class >> newNamed: aName email: anEmail [
        ^ self new initializeNamed: aName email: anEmail
    ]

    Customer >> initializeNamed: aName email: anEmail [
        name := aName.
        email := anEmail.
    ]

    Customer >> displayDetails [
        ^ 'Name: ', name, ' Email: ', email.
    ]
]

"Creating a new customer"
newCustomer := Customer newNamed: 'John Doe' email: 'john.doe@example.com'.
Transcript show: newCustomer displayDetails.
```

Execution of the code results in:

```
Name: John Doe Email: john.doe@example.com
```

In addition to these domains, Smalltalk's versatility has enabled its adoption in various research projects and academic studies. One such project is the "OPERA" (Object-oriented Programming Environment for Research and Application Development) project, where Smalltalk served as a primary tool for developing and prototyping academic software systems aimed at exploring new computational models and methodologies.

The continued relevance of Smalltalk in these applications underscores its robust architecture and the significant advantages derived from its dynamic and reflective nature. Despite the emergence of newer programming languages, Smalltalk's simplicity and powerful object-oriented features continue to make it a viable option for various complex and mission-critical systems across multiple industries.

1.10 Current Trends and the Future of Smalltalk

In recent years, the Smalltalk programming language has experienced a revival within various niches of the software development industry. This renewal is driven by several key trends and advancements. A thorough analysis of current trends reveals three significant areas where Smalltalk continues to evolve and attract interest: the modernized development environments, the integration with contemporary technologies, and the sustaining active community. Additionally, exploring the future of Smalltalk offers insight into how it is poised to adapt and remain relevant in an ever-changing technological landscape.

Modernized Development Environments: Improving the development experience, several modern Smalltalk environments have been developed, which provide advanced features to developers. Noteworthy among these are Pharo, Squeak, and Amber. These environments introduce enhancements such as improved debugging tools, rich user interfaces, and seamless interaction with other programming languages.

Pharo, a highly active Smalltalk environment, presents an innovative IDE that includes tools like the GTSpotter for introspective browsing, advanced inspecting techniques, and improved memory management. Squeak, another prominent Smalltalk environment, continuously evolves with innovations in multimedia and education-oriented features. Amber brings Smalltalk to the web by allowing direct integration with JavaScript, showcasing the language's flexibility.

Integration with Contemporary Technologies: Smalltalk's ability to interface with contemporary technologies ensures its continued relevance. Binding Smalltalk with modern systems includes foreign function interfaces (FFIs), which allow the invocation of external libraries and APIs. This integration capability extends Smalltalk's utility to work alongside mainstream languages such as Python, Java, and C++.

To elucidate, consider a Smalltalk program that calls a C library function using FFI:

```
cLib := Smalltalk.FFIExternalLibrary libraryNamed: 'libc'.
printfFunc := cLib ffiFunctionNamed: 'printf' types: #(void*).
printfFunc callWithArguments: ('Hello, World!\n' asExternalData).
```

This example demonstrates how Smalltalk can harness existing libraries and systems, thereby expanding its application domains.

Sustaining Active Community: The Smalltalk community remains vibrant and dedicated, contributing to the development and maintenance of various dialects and libraries. The Pharo consortium, for instance, actively develops the language and its ecosystem, with regular releases that reflect contemporary software needs. The community-driven OpenSmalltalk project ensures that core implementations like Squeak receive updates and are kept compatible with modern platforms.

Community events, conferences, and user groups perpetuate a dynamic exchange of knowledge and innovation. These gatherings facilitate collaboration and inspiration, ensuring Smalltalk's principles and practices continue to evolve.

Future Prospects: The future of Smalltalk is characterized by its potential to adapt and integrate with emergent technologies. The flexibility and simplicity of Smalltalk make it well-suited for areas like the Internet of Things (IoT) and Artificial Intelligence (AI). The ongoing development of minimalist Smalltalk kernels such as MicroSqueak aims to bring Smalltalk into resource-constrained environments like embedded systems and microcontrollers.

In AI, the development of domain-specific Smalltalk dialects tailored to machine learning or data analysis platforms can foster novel implementations that leverage Smalltalk's interactive and exploratory programming strengths.

Furthermore, educational initiatives using Smalltalk can cultivate interest among new generations of programmers. Given its original design philosophy prioritizing simplicity and ease of use, Smalltalk serves as an excellent tool for introducing students to object-oriented programming concepts and interactive programming environments.

As Smalltalk continues to evolve and adapt to modern requirements, it remains a powerful and versatile tool in the programmer's toolkit. The ongoing modernization efforts, the cross-pollination with contemporary technologies, and the vibrant community all signal a promising trajectory for Smalltalk, ensuring its continued influence and application in the future technological landscape.

Chapter 2

Setting Up Your Smalltalk Environment

This chapter provides detailed guidance on selecting and installing a Smalltalk distribution, configuring the development environment, and navigating the integrated development environment (IDE). Readers will learn how to set up a workspace, use essential tools like the Smalltalk Workspace and Transcript, manage projects, understand version control basics, and troubleshoot common installation issues, ensuring a smooth start to their Smalltalk programming journey.

2.1 Choosing the Right Smalltalk Distribution

Choosing the appropriate Smalltalk distribution is a crucial initial step in setting up your Smalltalk programming environment. Deciding on a distribution that aligns with your goals will enhance your productivity and learning experience. This section discusses the various Smalltalk distributions available, highlighting their unique features and use cases, to facilitate an informed decision.

The three major distributions recommended for different purposes and levels of expertise are **Pharo**, **Squeak**, and **GNU Smalltalk**:

- **Pharo**: Pharo is highly regarded for its modern approach to Smalltalk programming. It offers a cohesive and powerful integrated development environment (IDE) and is designed to support contemporary software engineering practices. Pharo is ideal for beginners due to its comprehensive documentation and active community. Additionally, it supports advanced users with powerful tools such as the Moose analysis platform and the Roassal visualization engine. Pharo is updated frequently, ensuring access to the latest features and bug fixes.
- **Squeak**: Squeak is an open-source implementation of Smalltalk with a strong emphasis on multimedia and educational use. It retains the original ethos of Smalltalk, offering a rich, playful, and versatile platform. Squeak's Etoys system is particularly beneficial for educators and learners, allowing the creation of interactive learning projects. Although the environment may seem less intuitive for absolute beginners, it is highly extensible and well-suited for experimental and research purposes.
- **GNU Smalltalk**: GNU Smalltalk takes a more traditional approach by focusing on scripting and command-line interactions. It is suitable for users who prefer writing Smalltalk scripts and integrating them with other applications. GNU Smalltalk can be an excellent choice for experienced programmers familiar with Unix-like systems and those who require seamless integration into various development workflows.

Key Factors to Consider:

When choosing a Smalltalk distribution, there are several factors to evaluate to ensure the distribution meets your specific needs:

- **Community and Support**: Active communities provide valuable resources such as forums, mailing lists, and real-time chat channels that can be crucial for gaining insights and troubleshooting issues. Pharo boasts a vibrant and helpful community, while Squeak and GNU Smalltalk also have dedicated user bases that can assist newcomers.
- **Documentation and Learning Resources**: Well-documented distributions with abundant learning resources, including tutorials, guides, and code examples, can accelerate the learning process. Pharo excels in this area with accessible and well-maintained documentation, making it especially suitable for beginners.

- **IDE and Tooling**: The effectiveness of the integrated development environment (IDE) and available tools can significantly impact productivity. Pharo and Squeak provide graphical environments that streamline tasks from code writing to debugging and refactoring. GNU Smalltalk, on the other hand, caters to users who prefer text-based scripting and integration with other command-line tools.

- **Extensibility and Ecosystem**: Evaluate the ecosystem of packages and extensions available for each distribution. Pharo offers a rich array of libraries and frameworks that extend its functionality, making it suitable for a wide range of applications from web development to data visualization.

- **Platform Compatibility**: Ensure the distribution is compatible with your operating system. While most distributions support all major platforms, minor variations in installation procedures and performance optimizations may influence your choice.

Example Installation Commands:

For users opting for Pharo, the installation process is straightforward. Pharo provides a unified installer that simplifies setup. Below is an example of how to install Pharo on a Unix-like system:

```
curl https://get.pharo.org | bash
./pharo-ui
```

This set of commands downloads the latest Pharo image and opens the Pharo IDE. For Squeak, the installation can be performed by downloading the appropriate image from the official Squeak website and running it with the Squeak virtual machine:

```
wget https://files.squeak.org/5.3/Squeak5.3-19435-64bit/Squeak5.3-19435-64bit
     -202003021730-Linux.zip
unzip Squeak5.3-19435-64bit-202003021730-Linux.zip
./squeak.sh
```

GNU Smalltalk installation follows a traditional package manager route available on most Unix-like systems. Here is an example command to install GNU Smalltalk:

```
sudo apt-get install gnu-smalltalk
gst
```

Running `gst` starts the GNU Smalltalk interpreter, enabling script execution and interactive development.

Understanding these distributions' distinguishing features and installation steps will empower you to choose the one that best aligns with your educational and project needs, ensuring a productive and engaging Smalltalk programming experience.

2.2 Downloading and Installing Smalltalk

Given the diversity of Smalltalk distributions available, it is essential to select the version that is most appropriate for your needs. Commonly used distributions include Squeak, Pharo, and VisualWorks. Each of these has its strengths and may cater to different use cases. In this section, we will provide a detailed example using Pharo, a modern and widely-used Smalltalk environment. The principles, however, will be applicable to other distributions with minor adjustments.

1. Choosing Your Smalltalk Distribution

Pharo offers extensive support and documentation, making it a suitable choice for most users. To embark on your journey, we will focus on Pharo, which can be downloaded and installed relatively straightforwardly.

2. Downloading Pharo

Navigate to the [Pharo website](https://pharo.org/download) to download the latest stable release. Ensure you select the appropriate version for your operating system (e.g., Windows, macOS, Linux). The website typically offers a graphical installer or a zip/tar archive.

3. Installing Pharo on Various Operating Systems

Windows Installation:

1. Download the installer executable (.exe file) from the Pharo website. 2. Once the download is complete, double-click the executable to start the installation process. 3. Follow the on-screen instructions, which will guide you through agreeing to the license, selecting the installation directory, and confirming installation. 4. Once the installation is complete, launch Pharo from the start menu or desktop shortcut.

macOS Installation:

1. Download the disk image (.dmg file) from the Pharo website. 2. Open the .dmg file to mount it. 3. Drag the Pharo application to the Applications folder. 4. Once the application is copied, eject the disk image. 5. You can now launch Pharo from the Applications folder.

Linux Installation:

1. Download the .zip or .tar archive from the Pharo website. 2. Extract the downloaded archive to a directory of your choice. This can be achieved using the following command in the terminal (replace <file-name> with the name of the downloaded file):

```
tar -xvf <file-name>.tar.gz
```

3. Navigate to the extracted directory and locate the executable file. 4. Make the file executable (if necessary) with the command:

```
chmod +x ./pharo
```

5. Run the executable by typing:

```
./pharo
```

4. Initial Launch and Configuration

Upon launching Pharo for the first time, you will be greeted by the image file loading, which stores the state of your environment. Pharo uses an image-based model, meaning the entire state of the system, including all objects, classes, and running processes, is stored in a file.

Pharo.image is the default image file loaded when you start Pharo. You might also see Pharo.changes, which logs all changes made to the image.

5. Verifying the Installation

To ensure the installation process was successful, perform a simple verification. Open the Pharo environment and execute a fundamental Smalltalk expression. In the Pharo IDE, navigate to the World menu, select Workspace, and enter the following Smalltalk code:

```
Transcript show: 'Hello, Pharo!'; cr.
```

To execute this code, highlight it and press Cmd+D (macOS) or Ctrl+D (Windows/Linux). The output should be visible in the Transcript window:

```
Hello, Pharo!
```

This output confirms that the Pharo installation is functioning correctly.

6. Directory Structure

Understanding the directory structure of the installation is important:

- Pharo.image - The main image file that encapsulates the state of the Smalltalk environment.
- Pharo.changes - Logs all modifications to the image.
- pharo - The executable file.
- sources - Contains source code for the initial system, invaluable for debugging.
- vm/ - The virtual machine files necessary for running Pharo.

Careful management of these files ensures that your Smalltalk environment remains stable and responsive.

7. Updating Pharo

Periodically updating Pharo is crucial to taking advantage of new features and bug fixes. Within the Pharo environment, updates can be managed through the System menu:

```
System > Software Update > Update Pharo
```

Executing the update from within the environment ensures that you stay abreast of the latest improvements and developments.

Through these steps, you will have successfully downloaded, installed, and initialized your Smalltalk environment using Pharo, enabling you to proceed with the development and exploration of Smalltalk.

2.3 Getting Started with the Smalltalk Environment

Before diving into writing and running Smalltalk code, it is essential to become familiar with the integrated development environment (IDE) provided by your chosen Smalltalk distribution. The IDE is the primary interface for coding, debugging, and managing Smalltalk projects. Most Smalltalk distributions, such as Squeak, Pharo, and Cincom Smalltalk, offer a powerful and feature-rich development environment. This section will guide you through the basic elements of the IDE and help you get started with your first Smalltalk session.

Launching the IDE

First, launch the IDE by running the executable associated with your Smalltalk distribution. This executable is typically named something like squeak.exe, pharo.exe, or visualworks.exe. On successful launch, you will be greeted with the IDE's main interface, which usually includes multiple components such as a Workspace, Transcript, and Browser.

Workspace

The Workspace is an essential tool in Smalltalk. It allows you to write and test small pieces of code interactively. To open a Workspace, you can typically navigate through the IDE's menu: Tools > Workspace. In the Workspace, you can write any Smalltalk expression and evaluate it. For example:

```
Transcript show: 'Hello, Smalltalk!'.
```

To evaluate this expression, highlight the code and select do it from the context menu (usually accessed via a right-click). This action will display 'Hello, Smalltalk!' in the Transcript.

Transcript

The Transcript is akin to a console or log where output from the running Smalltalk code is displayed. It is particularly useful for debugging and monitoring code execution. To open the Transcript, navigate through Tools > Transcript. The Transcript window will serve as a continual feedback mechanism for your Smalltalk development, capturing text output from expressions evaluated within the Workspace and other parts of the system.

The Browser

A crucial part of mastering the Smalltalk environment is understanding and using the Browser. The Browser provides an organized way to navigate classes, methods, and packages within the Smalltalk image. To open a class browser, you typically go to Tools > Browser. The Browser presents several panes for selecting categories, classes, protocols, and methods. It also includes an editor pane for viewing and editing method code.

In the Browser, you can create new classes and methods. For instance, to create a new class:

```
Object subclass: MyFirstClass [
    | | "class variable definitions"

    MyFirstClass class >> newMethod [
        "Method definition here"
    ]
```

```
]
```

This code snippet shows how to define a new class MyFirstClass as a subclass of Object and a method newMethod. Note that the class definition scope includes the specification of instance variables inside vertical bars.

Inspecting Objects

Another powerful feature in Smalltalk is the Inspect tool, used to examine the state of objects. You can inspect the result of any expression by highlighting the code and selecting inspect it.

```
Inspector new open.
```

This snippet creates a new Inspector instance and opens an inspector window for it. The inspector provides a view into the internal state of the object, enabling you to explore its properties and evaluate expressions in its context.

Debugging

Debugging is an integral feature provided by the Smalltalk IDE. When an error occurs, a debugger window appears, offering a detailed view of the execution stack and the opportunity to inspect variable values, execute code step-by-step, and even modify the code on-the-fly. To intentionally trigger a debugger for practice, you could use the following code:

```
Error signal: 'This is a test error'.
```

Executing this will open the debugger, allowing you to trace and resolve the issue.

By becoming adept at using these fundamental components of the Smalltalk IDE, you establish a robust foundation for effective code development, debugging, and exploration. These tools not only improve your productivity but also deepen your understanding of the Smalltalk environment and its powerful capabilities.

2.4 Setting Up a Basic Workspace

Once the Smalltalk distribution and the integrated development environment (IDE) are installed, configuring a workspace becomes the initial critical step to create and manage your projects efficiently.

A Smalltalk workspace is an area where developers can write, evaluate, and execute code interactively. This section elucidates the process of setting up a basic workspace to begin coding in Smalltalk, ensuring you have the essential tools at your disposal.

Creating a New Workspace

Upon launching the Smalltalk IDE, you can create a new workspace by navigating through the menu system. Typically, this can be done by selecting Tools > Workspace. This action will open a new window within the IDE where you can begin writing Smalltalk expressions.

Workspace is a dynamic tool, enabling real-time evaluation of code snippets without the need for creating a full program. Here is an example of how you can use the workspace for a simple arithmetic operation:

```
3 + 4.
```

To evaluate the code snippet above, simply highlight the expression and execute it using the specific command provided by your Smalltalk environment (typically Ctrl + D or a menu selection like Do it). The result will display directly within the workspace, giving instant feedback on the executed operation.

Organizing Workspace Content

A well-organized workspace is key for efficient coding and debugging. Use comments to delineate sections and provide clarity. Comments in Smalltalk are written using double quotes:

```
" This is a comment in Smalltalk "
```

When writing multiple expressions or code blocks, separate them with comments for better readability:

```
" Initialize variables "
| a b c |

a := 5.
b := 10.

" Perform calculations "
c := a + b.

" Print the result "
Transcript show: c.
```

Here, the workspace is segmented into clear sections: initialization, calculation, and output. This approach enhances readability and simplifies debugging.

Using Transcripts for Output

The Transcript is an essential tool for output operations in Smalltalk. It serves as a console or log window where you can print and inspect runtime information. Before using the Transcript, ensure it is cleared and ready for new output by executing:

```
Transcript clear.
```

Here's an example showing how to use the Transcript to display messages:

```
Transcript show: 'Hello, Smalltalk!'; cr.
```

The cr message adds a carriage return after the message, moving the cursor to the next line for subsequent outputs. This organization helps to delineate different pieces of output clearly.

Persisting Workspace Code

For long-term projects, you often need to save workspace content. Saving allows for reusability and versioning. To save the contents of your workspace, use the File menu available in the IDE, typically via File > Save as.... Choose a descriptive name for your workspace file to make future retrieval straightforward.

Workspace files are saved with a .st extension, standard for Smalltalk scripts, and can be reloaded into the IDE when needed. For example:

```
file := FileStream newFileNamed: 'myWorkspace.st'.
file nextPutAll: '3 + 4.'; cr.
file close.
```

This snippet demonstrates programmatically saving an expression to a file. It uses the FileStream class to interact with the filesystem, creating a file named myWorkspace.st and writing the expression $3 + 4$ followed by a newline character.

Evaluating More Complex Expressions

As you advance, your workspace will serve as an interactive playground for more complex Smalltalk constructs such as loops, conditional statements, and object creations. For instance, evaluating a simple loop:

```
1 to: 10 do: [:i | Transcript show: i printString; cr].
```

This expression iterates from 1 to 10, printing each number to the Transcript. The block [:i | ...] defines a parameter i which takes on the values from 1 to 10 in succession.

Algorithm 1: Iteration in Smalltalk

```
Result: Populate Transcript with numbers 1 to 10
for i = 1 to 10 do
    Transcript show: (i printString); cr;
```

Managing Multiple Workspaces

In practice, you may find it useful to maintain multiple workspace windows for different tasks or projects. Modern Smalltalk IDEs typically allow multiple workspaces to be open simultaneously, enabling you to switch contexts easily. Utilize this capability to segregate experimental code from production code, or to partition distinct project phases.

Creating and managing multiple workspaces can be done via the Window menu or through direct IDE shortcuts. Consistently label each workspace window to avoid confusion, such as "ProjectA-Testing" or "ProjectB-Utilities".

Effective workspace management is fundamental to Smalltalk programming, facilitating a clean, organized, and efficient development environment for tackling even the most intricate coding challenges.

2.5 Navigating the Smalltalk IDE

Upon initializing your Smalltalk environment, understanding and navigating the Integrated Development Environment (IDE) is crucial. The Smalltalk IDE is a powerful, feature-rich interface designed to facilitate seamless programming processes. Through the following detailed exploration, we will delve into the core components and functionalities of the Smalltalk IDE, ensuring clarity and ease of use for both novice and seasoned programmers.

Main Interface Components

The primary components of the Smalltalk IDE include the following:

- Workspace: A text editor area where code can be written, tested, and executed.
- Transcript: The console window captures output from code execution.
- Browser: It displays the system classes, methods, and categories, enabling organized code access and modification.
- Debugger: It provides tools to inspect and debug code execution line-by-line.

Workspace

The Workspace acts as a sandbox environment for directly writing and executing Smalltalk expressions. You can evaluate code snippets and perform exploratory coding. An exemplary interaction with the Workspace involves:

```
"Example Code in Workspace"
3 + 4.
(Transcript show: 'Hello, World!') displayNl.
```

To execute the above code, highlight it, right-click, and select do it or press Ctrl+D. This executes and evaluates the code, immediately reflecting changes or outputs in the Transcript.

Transcript

Analogous to a log window, the Transcript captures output from code evaluations and ensures that results and messages are chronologically displayed. Continuing from our previous example:

```
7
Hello, World!
```

These outputs confirm the arithmetic operation and the string message are correctly executed.

Browser

The Browser is central to navigating and modifying system or user-defined classes and methods. It is organized into distinct panes:

- Class Category Pane: Lists categories, aiding the classification of different classes.

- Class Pane: Displays classes within the selected category.
- Method Category Pane: Provides organization for methods into protocols.
- Method Pane: Contains the methods within the selected protocol of the class.

To access a class's methods, select the class in the Class Pane and then choose the desired method category in the Method Category Pane. Clicking a method displays its source code, which can then be read or edited directly.

Debugger
The Debugger is indispensable for identifying runtime errors. Upon encountering an error, the debugger interface automatically appears, allowing detailed inspection and interactive correction. By stepping through code, evaluating expressions dynamically, and modifying code, errors can be located and resolved efficiently. A common interaction involves:

```
"Intentional Error for Debugging"
Transcript show: (3 / 0) displayNl.
```

Executing the above code prompts a division by zero error, activating the Debugger. You can then inspect the call stack, view variable states, and precisely pinpoint the error locus.

Navigational Shortcuts
The Smalltalk IDE is equipped with numerous shortcuts to improve efficiency:

- Alt+Shift+B: Activates the class Browser.
- Ctrl+D: Executes the selected text (do it).
- Ctrl+P: Prints the selected text.
- Ctrl+I: Inspects the selected object.

These shortcuts streamline the navigation across different functionalities within the IDE, enhancing workflow productivity.

Customizing the IDE
Personalizing the workspace within the IDE allows for a tailored programming environment. Accessible through the preferences menu, options include:

- Theme: Adjusting the color theme.
- Fonts: Customizing the font type and size.
- Layout: Configuring pane layout for a spatial arrangement conducive to your workflow.

Experimenting with these settings can lead to a more comfortable and productive coding environment tailored to individual preferences.

Detailed understanding and skillful navigation of the Smalltalk IDE empower users to leverage its full potential. Mastery over these components provides a foundation for efficient and effective programming, contributing to progression towards expert proficiency in Smalltalk development.

2.6 Configuring Your Development Environment

Configuring your development environment is a crucial step to ensure seamless workflow and maximize productivity when working with Smalltalk. This section guides you through the essential configurations and settings that optimize your Smalltalk environment.

To start, launch your Smalltalk IDE. Different distributions may have varying interfaces, but they generally offer similar configuration settings. For this example, we will use Pharo, a popular Smalltalk implementation. Other distributions like Squeak or VisualWorks follow similar principles but refer to specific documentation for distribution-specific instructions.

- **Preferences and Settings**: Access the preferences by selecting Tools -> Settings Browser from the menu bar. The settings browser allows you to configure various aspects such as appearance, fonts, and system behavior.
- **Appearance**: Customize the look and feel of your IDE. This includes themes, window decorations, and fonts used within the code and interface components.
- **Key Bindings**: Set up key bindings to streamline your development process. Custom key bindings can significantly enhance your efficiency in coding and navigation.

- **Auto-Save**: Enable auto-save functionality to ensure that your work is periodically saved. This can protect against data loss due to unexpected crashes.

Below is an example Smalltalk script to modify the default font settings in Pharo:

```
TextStyle defaultFont: (TextStyle named: 'Arial' size: 14).
```

To see the immediate effect of this script, execute it in your Pharo workspace. The font in all text windows should now change to Arial with a size of 14 points.

After adjusting basic appearance settings, it's essential to set up your development tools. Smalltalk environments offer tools that facilitate smooth development cycles, such as code browsers, version control, and debuggers. Configuration involves ensuring these tools are integrated correctly.

Configuring Code Browsers: The code browser allows you to navigate, edit, and manage your Smalltalk code efficiently. Key features of the code browser include class hierarchy navigation, method searching, and inline editing.

If you wish to customize the behavior of the code browser, you can modify its settings using the following script:

```
BrowserPreferences default
    showClassComment: false;
    showMethodProtocols: true;
    save.
```

Setting Up Package Management: Package management in Smalltalk is handled via tools like Monticello in Squeak/Pharo or Store in VisualWorks. These tools allow you to version your code, collaborate with others, and manage dependencies.

Here's how you configure Monticello in Pharo:

```
(MCRepositoryGroup default addRemoteRepository: 'http://smalltalkhub.com/mc/
    Pharo/MetaRepoForPharo30/main') loadVersion: 'ConfigurationOfMetacello2.0'.
```

This command adds a remote repository to your Monticello environment and loads the specified version of a package.

Source Code Versioning: Version control is another critical setup for your development environment. In Smalltalk, Monticello serves this purpose for Pharo and Squeak. To configure Monticello for your project, ensure that you add your working and remote repositories:

```
| repo |
repo := MCHttpRepository
    location: 'http://your.repository.url'
    user: ''
    password: ''.
MCCacheRepository default addRepository: repo.
```

Monticello will now manage your project's versions.

Integrating External Tools: Smalltalk environments support a variety of external tools and plugins. To enhance functionality, you may integrate plugins for aspects such as code profiling, testing frameworks (like SUnit), and continuous integration servers.

For instance, to integrate the SUnit testing framework, you might load it via the following script:

```
Gofer new
    gemsource: 'http://ss3.gemstone.com/ss/sunit.alpha';
    package: 'SUnit';
    load.
```

This script ensures that the SUnit package is downloaded and installed, allowing you to write and execute unit tests within your Smalltalk environment.

By methodically configuring your Smalltalk environment—personalizing your workspace, setting up necessary tools, and ensuring effective version control—you lay the groundwork for a productive and efficient development process. Through these adjustments, the IDE not only adapts to your workflow but enhances it by leveraging the full potential of Smalltalk's robust development ecosystem.

2.7 Using the Smalltalk Workspace

The Smalltalk Workspace is an essential tool in the Smalltalk environment, acting as an interactive development area where you can write, evaluate, and test Smalltalk code in real-time. This utility is fundamental for experimenting with Smalltalk expressions, prototyping new code, and debugging existing code without the need to compile or run an entire application.

Opening the Workspace

To open the Smalltalk Workspace, navigate through your IDE s menu system. Typically, this is accomplished by selecting Tools or Windows, followed by Workspace. In most Smalltalk distributions, you can also use keyboard shortcuts to quickly open the Workspace.

Basic Operations in the Workspace

Once the Workspace is open, it presents you with a text area where you can type Smalltalk expressions. Here is a simple example to demonstrate basic operations:

```
"Calculating the sum of two numbers"
3 + 4. "Evaluates to 7"

"Finding the factorial of a number"
5 factorial. "Evaluates to 120"

"Defining a simple block and executing it"
[:x | x + 1] value: 5. "Evaluates to 6"
```

To evaluate these expressions, place the cursor at the end of the expression or highlight the desired text and select Do it from the context menu or use the keyboard shortcut typically associated with the evaluation, such as Ctrl + D or Cmd + D.

Inspecting Objects

In Smalltalk, any expression evaluation can result in the creation of objects, which can be inspected directly from the Workspace. Consider the following operation:

```
"Creating and inspecting an Array"
myArray := #(1 2 3 4 5).
```

To inspect the myArray object, highlight the myArray variable and select Inspect it from the context menu or use the appropriate keyboard shortcut, often Ctrl + I or Cmd + I. The inspector window will open, allowing you to examine the internal structure and state of the myArray object.

```
myArray
an Array(1, 2, 3, 4, 5)
```

Using Temporary Variables

Temporary variables in the Workspace enhance testing and experimentation by allowing you to store intermediate results and reuse them without re-evaluating the entire expression context. Here is an illustration:

```
| x y |
x := 10.
y := 20.
```

```
result := x + y. "result is 30"
```

In this scenario, result holds the sum of x and y. You can use the variable result in subsequent expressions within the same Workspace session.

Writing and Evaluating Multi-line Expressions

The Workspace allows for evaluating more complex, multi-line expressions, facilitating the development of more sophisticated code constructs. Consider the following example of a conditional statement:

```
"Multi-line if-else construct"
x := 15.
y := 25.
result := (x > y)
    ifTrue: [ 'x is greater than y' ]
    ifFalse: [ 'x is less than or equal to y' ].
"result evaluates to 'x is less than or equal to y'"
```

result will hold the evaluation based on the conditional logic applied.

Debugging in the Workspace

One of the critical advantages of the Workspace is its debugging capability. When an error occurs during the evaluation of an expression, Smalltalk provides an option to enter into a debugger. For instance, evaluating:

```
"Generating an error by dividing by zero"
result := 10 / 0.
```

This will trigger an exception, and the IDE will prompt you to start the debugger, providing an interface to investigate the error context, examine the call stack, and correct the code as needed.

Saving and Loading Workspace Content

To enhance productivity, the content of the Workspace can be saved and reloaded, ensuring that essential code snippets and temporary working sets are not lost between sessions. Use the File Out option from the context menu to export the Workspace content to a file, and File In to import previously saved content.

Below is a demonstration of saving the Workspace content:

```
"Saving Workspace content to a file"
FileStream newFileNamed: 'workspace.st' do: [:stream |
    stream nextPutAll: (Workspace content).
].
```

Conversely, loading the Workspace content can be done as follows:

```
"Loading Workspace content from a file"
(FileStream readOnlyFileNamed: 'workspace.st') contents do: [:content |
    Workspace text: content.
].
```

Integrating Workspace with the Transcript

The Transcript tool can be employed alongside the Workspace for better output visualization and logging. For example:

```
"Logging output to the Transcript"
Transcript show: 'The result is: '; show: result; cr.
```

Executing this expression in the Workspace will print the result in the Transcript window, making it easier to trace and debug outputs.

The Workspace is a powerful and versatile feature of the Smalltalk environment, playing a crucial role in facilitating interactive coding, debugging, and testing. Proper utilization of its features can significantly enhance development efficiency and code quality.

2.8 Understanding and Using the Transcript

The Smalltalk Transcript is an essential tool for outputting text, debugging, and understanding the flow of program execution. It is a global object used to display information, which can significantly aid in the development and debugging processes.

Accessing the Transcript: To use the Transcript, you first need to ensure it is open and visible within your Smalltalk environment. Most Smalltalk IDEs provide an option to display the Transcript through their menu systems. For example, in Squeak, you can open the Transcript from the World menu by navigating to Open... > Transcript.

Once the Transcript window is open, you can begin to utilize it for various output operations.

Basic Operations: The Transcript stream supports a range of operations for displaying text. The most commonly used methods are:

- show: - Outputs a string to the Transcript.
- cr: - Writes a carriage return to the Transcript.
- clear: - Clears all the current content from the Transcript.

To output text, you will generally use the Transcript show: message. This method takes a string as an argument and appends it to the end of the Transcript content.

```
Transcript show: 'Hello, Smalltalk!'.
```

After executing the above line, you will see the text Hello, Smalltalk! appear in the Transcript window. The show: method does not automatically append a newline; if you need to output lines of text, use cr between each show: call.

```
Transcript show: 'First line'; cr; show: 'Second line'.
```

This can be observed as output in the Transcript window:

```
First line
Second line
```

Clearing the Transcript: To clear all existing content from the Transcript, use the clear: method:

```
Transcript clear.
```

After executing this command, the Transcript window will be empty.

Using Transcript for Debugging: The Transcript is valuable for debugging purposes, allowing developers to print variable values and execution flows to trace the behaviors of programs. This is particularly useful in unfamiliar codebases or complex algorithms where understanding intermediate states is crucial.

Consider the following example, where we want to trace the execution flow of a loop:

```
Transcript clear.
1 to: 5 do: [:i |
    Transcript show: 'Iteration: ', i printString; cr.
].
```

Executing the above code will produce the following output in the Transcript window:

```
Iteration: 1
Iteration: 2
Iteration: 3
Iteration: 4
Iteration: 5
```

Advanced Output Techniques: For more complex output, concatenate multiple strings or variables:

```
Transcript show: 'The answer is: ', (42 * 2) printString.
```

This produces:

```
The answer is: 84
```

You can also format your output into more structured data by intelligently combining strings and performing calculations or method calls within the show: message.

Using the Transcript in Methods: Incorporating Transcript outputs within your methods helps to monitor their execution. For instance:

```
Object subclass: MyClass [
    MyClass >> myMethod [
        Transcript show: 'myMethod called'; cr.
        "Additional method code"
    ]
].
```

Calling myMethod will now leave a trace in the Transcript:

```
(MyClass new) myMethod.
```

```
myMethod called
```

Using Transcript **Wisely:** While inserting Transcript messages extensively during development is helpful, it is advisable to remove or comment out such lines in the production code to avoid unnecessary performance overhead and clutter.

Ensuring that the Transcript effectively aids development requires understanding its appropriate use and limitations. Through disciplined use, the Transcript serves as a pivotal utility in developing robust and well-understood Smalltalk applications.

2.9 Loading and Saving Projects

Loading and saving projects in Smalltalk is a fundamental aspect of managing your development workflow. This section will cover the techniques to efficiently store and retrieve your code, ensuring that your work is not only preserved, but also easily accessible for future sessions and collaboration.

To begin with, Smalltalk projects are typically managed using files that store the source code and system state. Understanding how these files interact with the Smalltalk environment is crucial for effective project management.

Saving a Project: When you save a project in Smalltalk, you are essentially capturing the current state of your environment, which includes the source code of all classes and methods, along with the state of active objects. This can be performed in several ways, depending on the specific Smalltalk distribution you are using.

Here is an example using the Pharo Smalltalk environment:

```
'MyProject' asFileReference writeStreamDo: [ :stream |
    (SmartRefStream on: stream) nextPut: (Smalltalk snapshot: true)].
```

In this example, the writeStreamDo: method is used to create a new file called MyProject.st. The SmartRefStream is then used to write the current state of the environment to this file.

Loading a Project: Loading a project involves reading the saved state from a file and integrating it back into the current Smalltalk environment. This process restores the classes, methods, and objects to their saved state.

Using Pharo Smalltalk, you can load a project with the following code:

```
'MyProject' asFileReference readStreamDo: [ :stream |
    (SmartRefStream on: stream) next].
```

In this example, the readStreamDo: method is used to open the MyProject.st file. The SmartRefStream reads the state from the file and reintroduces it into the current environment.

Exporting as a Fileout: Smalltalk also supports exporting your code as .st fileouts, which are plain text representations of your classes and methods.

```
| classes |
classes := #(MyClass1 MyClass2).
FileStream fileNamed: 'MyClasses.st' do: [ :stream |
    classes do: [ :each |
        (Smalltalk at: each) fileOutOn: stream].
].
```

In this snippet, an array of class names is specified, and the fileOutOn: method is called for each class to write its definition to the file MyClasses.st.

Loading from a Fileout: To load a project from a fileout, you will read the file and file in the contents.

```
FileStream fileNamed: 'MyClasses.st' do: [ :stream |
    | content |
    content := stream contents.
    Compiler evaluate: content.
].
```

This example reads the contents of MyClasses.st into a string and then evaluates it, effectively loading the class definitions into the environment.

Using Monticello for Version Control: Monticello is a versioning system for managing Smalltalk projects, particularly beneficial for collaborative development and tracking changes over time.

- **Saving a Version:** To save a new version of a package, you use the Monticello browser. Select the package you want to version, provide a version name, and save it to a repository.
- **Loading a Version:** To load a version, select the desired repository in the Monticello browser, browse the available versions, and load the selected version.

Here is a basic Monticello save example in code:

```
| repo package |
repo := MCHttpRepository location: 'http://www.smalltalkhub.com/mc/
    YourAccount/YourProject' user: '' password: ''.
package := MCSnapshotLoader loadFromStream: ('MyPackage' asFileReference
    readStream) description.
repo saveVersion: package.
```

This script specifies a repository location and saves the current state of MyPackage to the repository.

Efficiently loading and saving projects in Smalltalk ensures that your work can be preserved, shared, and restored with consistency. These operations are pivotal for maintaining the integrity and continuity of your development efforts.

2.10 Introduction to Version Control in Smalltalk

Version control is a fundamental aspect of modern software development, and mastering it is essential for collaborative and efficient programming. In Smalltalk, version control enables developers to manage changes to source code, collaborate with team members, and track the history of modifications. This section will cover the basics of version control within the context of the Smalltalk environment, including setting up repositories, committing changes, and collaborating with other developers.

Version control systems (VCS) are tools that help developers manage changes to their source code over time. In the context of Smalltalk, one of the most commonly used VCS is Monticello. Monticello is a versioning system specifically designed for Smalltalk, and it integrates seamlessly with most Smalltalk environments.

Monticello allows developers to:

- Track changes to packages over time.
- Collaborate with other developers by sharing changes.
- Manage different versions and branches of a project.
- Revert to previous versions when necessary.

To begin using Monticello for version control in your Smalltalk environment, follow these instructions:

- Open the Monticello Browser: This tool is typically accessible from the main tools menu in your Smalltalk IDE.
- Add a Repository: Before committing any code changes, you need to add a repository where your code versions will be stored.

Suppose you want to add a new HTTP repository. You can use the following steps in the Monticello Browser:

```
1. Open the Monticello Browser from the Tools menu.
2. Click on "+Repository".
3. Select "HTTP" from the list of repository types.
4. Enter the URL of your repository.
5. Provide your username and password if required.
6. Click "Accept" to add the repository.
```

We can create a new package or select an existing one to manage with Monticello. The following steps outline how to save your changes to the repository:

```
1. Open the Monticello Browser.
2. Select your package from the package list.
3. Click on "Save".
4. Enter a message describing the changes made.
5. Choose the repository where you want to save the package version.
6. Click "Accept" to commit the changes.
```

For instance, consider you modified a class ExampleClass within the package ExamplePackage. You would open the Monticello Browser, select ExamplePackage, and then perform the steps described above to commit your changes to the repository with an appropriate commit message, such as "Updated ExampleClass with new method foo".

Retrieving and merging code changes from the repository is essential in a collaborative environment. The Monticello Browser facilitates loading changes from the repository:

```
1. Open the Monticello Browser.
2. Select the repository from the repository list.
3. Click on "Open".
4. Select the version you want to load.
5. Click "Load" to import the changes into your local environment.
```

If conflicts occur while merging changes, Monticello provides tools to resolve these conflicts. Diff and merge tools help compare differences between versions and resolve conflicts manually if necessary.

Creating and managing branches is another powerful feature of version control. Branching allows you to explore new features or bug fixes in isolation from the main codebase.

Creating and Managing Branches in Monticello:

```
1. Open the Monticello Browser.
2. Click on "Create new branch".
3. Select the base point from which to branch off (usually the latest commit of the
      main branch).
4. Provide a branch name and description.
5. Save the branch.
```

Code integration from different branches requires careful management to ensure that all changes integrate correctly without introducing bugs. Monticello helps in comparing branch differences and merging them back when ready.

An effective workflow in Smalltalk using Monticello involves regularly committing changes, updating from the repository to get the latest changes from collaborators, and resolving any conflicts as they arise.

Additional extensions and tools, such as SqueakSource and SmalltalkHub, provide hosting for Monticello repositories and enhance collaboration by providing web interfaces for managing repositories and viewing code changes.

Understanding the basic terminology and workflow of Monticello prepares you for more advanced version control practices. This foundational knowledge ensures that you can manage your codebase effectively, collaborate with ease, and maintain a comprehensive history of your project's evolution.

2.11 Troubleshooting Common Installation Issues

When setting up a Smalltalk environment, users may encounter several common issues that can hinder installation and initial configuration. This section addresses these issues by providing troubleshooting steps and solutions. Readers can utilize these guidelines to resolve problems effectively and ensure a smooth installation process.

Disk Space and Permissions

One of the primary problems encountered during installation is related to disk space and permissions.

- Error: Not Enough Disk Space – This error indicates that there is insufficient space on the drive where the Smalltalk environment is being installed. To resolve this issue, ensure that there is adequate free space available. Typically, the installation requires several hundred megabytes to a few gigabytes of free space, depending on the Smalltalk distribution.

- Error: Permission Denied – This error occurs when the installer does not have the necessary permissions to write files or create directories. Verify that the user has administrative privileges. On Unix-based systems, using sudo with the installer command may be necessary.

Installation Package Corrupted

Corrupted installation packages can also cause issues during setup. If an installation fails with error messages indicating corrupted files, follow these steps:

- Download the package again – Corruption might occur during the download process. Download the installation package anew from the official source.

- Verify integrity – Many distributions provide checksums (SHA-256, MD5, etc.) for their packages. Compare the checksum of the downloaded file with the provided checksum to ensure integrity.

Unsupported Platform or Version

Compatibility issues are another common hurdle. The Smalltalk distribution must match the operating system and its version.

- Check platform compatibility – Confirm that the chosen Smalltalk distribution supports the operating system in use. Official documentation typically lists supported platforms.
- Update the operating system – If the OS version is outdated, consider updating it to meet the requirements of the Smalltalk distribution.

Third-Party Dependencies

Smalltalk environments may rely on third-party libraries and applications. Missing dependencies often cause installation errors.

- Check for required dependencies – Refer to the official documentation for a list of prerequisite software. Install all missing dependencies before starting the installation.
- Resolve conflicts – Conflicts with pre-existing versions of dependencies can cause issues. Ensure that installed dependencies are compatible with the Smalltalk version.

Environment Variables

Correct configuration of environment variables is crucial for the successful operation of a Smalltalk environment.

- Ensure proper paths – Verify that PATH and other relevant environment variables include the directories for the Smalltalk binaries and scripts. This enables the operating system to locate and execute them properly.

```
export PATH=$PATH:/path/to/smalltalk/bin
```

- Configure environment settings – Check the configuration settings specific to the distribution. These settings could affect the performance and behavior of the development environment.

Network Issues

Network-related issues might interfere with downloading and installing Smalltalk components.

- Check internet connectivity – Ensure stable and reliable internet access during the download and installation process.
- Configure proxy settings – In corporate or restricted network environments, configure proxy settings to allow access. Use the following command to set proxy for Unix-based systems:

```
export http_proxy=http://proxy_server:proxy_port
```

- Firewall settings – Firewalls can block necessary ports and addresses. Adjust firewall settings, if needed, to allow downloads.

Incorrect configuration or errors during Smalltalk environment setup can be remedied by systematically addressing these common issues. By carefully checking disk space, permissions, file integrity, compatibility, dependencies, environment variables, and network settings, users can resolve most encountered problems, ensuring a smoother installation experience.

Once these potential issues have been dealt with, the Smalltalk environment can be fully operational, allowing users to proceed with their programming activities without interruption or delay.

Chapter 3

Basic Syntax and First Program

This chapter covers the fundamental elements of Smalltalk programming, including basic syntax, data types, variables, constants, and arithmetic operations. Readers will learn to create their first Smalltalk program, handle strings and characters, perform basic input and output, understand code blocks, and grasp the essentials of messaging and writing simple methods. The chapter also includes guidelines on using comments and documentation effectively.

3.1 Understanding Basic Syntax

Smalltalk syntax is designed to be simple and uniform, fostering an easy learning curve while providing powerful constructs for developing complex programs. The syntax is strikingly different from languages such as C or Java, and understanding its unique structure is crucial.

Statements and Messages: Smalltalk operates exclusively through sending messages to objects. Every operation within Smalltalk is a message send. Statements in Smalltalk are sequences of expressions, each terminated by a period. Here is a basic example of a statement:

```
Transcript show: 'Hello, Smalltalk'.
```

In this line, Transcript is the receiver object, show: is the message, and 'Hello, Smalltalk' is the argument. This message prompts the Transcript to display the string 'Hello, Smalltalk'.

Expressions: Expressions in Smalltalk follow a specific structure: *receiver message*. The receiver is the object to which the message is sent. Messages can be categorized into three types: unary, binary, and keyword.

1. **Unary Messages**: Unary messages do not take any arguments and are sent to the receiver object directly. The general form is: *receiver unaryMessage*

```
3 factorial
```

Here, 3 is the receiver, and factorial is the unary message.

2. **Binary Messages**: Binary messages involve operators and are typically used for arithmetic or boolean operations. They take one argument and are denoted by symbols like +, -, *, /, etc. The syntax is: *receiver binaryMessage argument*

```
3 + 4
```

This sends the + message to the object 3 with the argument 4.

3. **Keyword Messages**: Keyword messages take one or more arguments and are denoted by colons. They are the most general form of messages in Smalltalk. The syntax is: *receiver keywordPart1: argument1 keywordPart2: argument2 ...*

```
OrderedCollection new add: 5; add: 10.
```

Here, OrderedCollection new is the receiver, add: is the first keyword message, and 5 and 10 are the arguments. The semicolon ; denotes sending more than one message in sequence to the same receiver.

Operator Precedence: Smalltalk has a straightforward rule for precedence: unary messages are evaluated first, followed by binary messages, and then keyword messages. Parentheses can be used to group expressions and override the default precedence.

```
3 factorial + 4 * 2
```

This expression is evaluated as (3 factorial) + (4 * 2) because unary messages take precedence over binary, and binary take precedence over keyword.

Block Closures: Block closures, or simply blocks, are a powerful feature in Smalltalk. They allow the encapsulation of code and act as first-class objects. Blocks are defined using square brackets:

```
[ :x | x * x ]
```

This block takes one argument x and returns x * x. Blocks can be assigned to variables and executed using the value message:

```
| square |
square := [ :x | x * x ].
square value: 4
```

This code snippet defines a block square and assigns it to a variable. The block is then executed with the argument 4, returning 16.

Assignment: Variables in Smalltalk are assigned using the colon-equals operator :=. To declare a variable, pipes | are used:

```
| a b sum |
a := 3.
b := 4.
sum := a + b.
```

This code declares three variables a, b, and sum, and assigns values to them. Note the use of the period . to terminate expressions.

Comments: Comments in Smalltalk are enclosed in double quotation marks and can be placed anywhere in the code:

```
"This is a comment"
3 + 4 "Adding two numbers"
```

Cascade Messages: Cascading allows multiple messages to be sent to the same receiver object in a sequence, using semicolons ;:

```
Transcript show: 'Hello, '; show: 'World!'.
```

This sends two show: messages to the Transcript, first with 'Hello, ' and then with 'World!'. This feature keeps the code concise and readable.

Understanding and mastering basic syntax is essential for efficient Smalltalk programming. Each construct serves a meaningful purpose contributing to the language's elegance and simplicity.

3.2 Creating Your First Smalltalk Program

Creating your first Smalltalk program involves understanding the basics of the Smalltalk environment and the structure of a Smalltalk program. In Smalltalk, everything is an object, and all interactions between objects occur through message passing. This distinctive feature greatly influences how programs are written and understood in Smalltalk.

To begin with, ensure you have a Smalltalk environment set up. Popular environments include Squeak, Pharo, and GNU Smalltalk. For this section, we will use Pharo, a modern and widely-used Smalltalk environment.

Step 1: Opening the Playground

Upon launching Pharo, you will be greeted by the main interface. To start writing your first Smalltalk program, open a Playground, which is an interactive workspace. You can do this by navigating to World Menu → Tools → Playground.

Step 2: Writing Your First Smalltalk Code

In the Playground, you can enter and execute Smalltalk code interactively. Let's start with the classic "Hello, World!" program. Type the following code in the Playground:

```
Transcript show: 'Hello, World!'; cr.
```

In this code, Transcript is an object that handles displaying text to the user. The message show: 'Hello, World!' instructs the Transcript to display the string 'Hello, World!'. The ; cr part sends the cr message to add a newline.

Step 3: Executing the Code

To execute the code, select it and then choose Do it from the right-click context menu, or use the shortcut Ctrl + D. After executing, you should see "Hello, World!" displayed in the Transcript window.

Understanding Message Syntax

Smalltalk programs consist of sequences of messages sent to objects. There are three types of messages: unary, binary, and keyword messages. Here is a brief overview using simple examples you can try in your Playground.

Unary messages are sent to an object and consist of a single method name:

```
3 factorial. "Evaluates to 6"
```

Binary messages are infix operators such as arithmetic operators:

```
3 + 4. "Evaluates to 7"
```

Keyword messages can have one or more arguments:

```
10 raisedTo: 2. "Evaluates to 100"
```

Defining a Simple Method

Smalltalk encourages defining reusable code within methods. Let's create a simple method within a class. First, define a new class named Greeter. In the Pharo workspace, execute the following code:

```
Object subclass: #Greeter
    instanceVariableNames: ''
    classVariableNames: ''
    poolDictionaries: ''
    category: 'Examples'.
```

This defines a class Greeter inheriting from Object. Next, add a method to this class to print a greeting:

```
Greeter>>sayHello
    Transcript show: 'Hello from Greeter!'; cr.
```

In the above snippet, » is used to define a method for the Greeter class. The method sayHello will print a greeting message to the Transcript.

Instantiating and Using the Greeter Class

To use the new Greeter class, create an instance of it and send the sayHello message:

```
| myGreeter |
myGreeter := Greeter new.
myGreeter sayHello.
```

Here, we declare a variable myGreeter, assign it a new instance of Greeter, and then send sayHello to myGreeter. Upon execution, the message "Hello from Greeter!" should appear in the Transcript.

This section aimed to demystify the process of creating a simple Smalltalk program. Understanding the structure and execution of Smalltalk code reveals the elegance and simplicity of this powerful, object-oriented language. Experimenting within the interactive Playground fosters hands-on learning, solidifying fundamental concepts.

3.3 Basic Data Types in Smalltalk

In Smalltalk, data types are fundamental for representing and manipulating data within a program. Unlike statically-typed languages, Smalltalk employs dynamic typing, allowing variables to hold any type of object during runtime. This section delves into the core data types in Smalltalk, highlighting their characteristics and usage.

The primary data types in Smalltalk include: Numbers, Characters, Strings, Symbols, Booleans, and Collections. Each of these data types serves specific purposes and provides a set of methods for manipulation.

Numbers: Numbers in Smalltalk are divided into several categories: integers, floating-point numbers, fractions, and scaled decimals.

- **Integers**: Represent whole numbers without fractional parts. Example of integer literals include 42, -19, and 0. Operations like addition, subtraction, multiplication, and division can be performed on integers.

```
| x y z |
x := 10.
y := 5.
z := x + y. "z is 15"
```

- **Floating-point numbers**: Represent real numbers with fractional parts. They are denoted using a decimal point. Examples include 3.14, -0.001, and 2.71. Floating-point numbers are crucial for computations requiring precision.

```
| a b c |
a := 3.5.
b := 0.5.
c := a * b. "c is 1.75"
```

- **Fractions**: Represent rational numbers as a ratio of two integers. They are created using the / operator. Example: $1/2$ or $3/4$.

```
| fraction1 fraction2 result |
fraction1 := 1/2.
fraction2 := 3/4.
result := fraction1 + fraction2. "result is 5/4"
```

- **Scaled decimals**: Provide precise decimal arithmetic and are typically used in financial applications. Example: $1.23s2$.

Characters: Characters are represented by a single character enclosed in a pair of single quotation marks. Examples include 'a', 'B', and '3'. Characters are objects of the Character class.

```
| char1 char2 char3 |
char1 := $a.
char2 := $A.
char3 := $3.
```

Strings: Strings are sequences of characters enclosed in single quotes. They can represent words, sentences, or any text data. String manipulation includes concatenation, comparison, and slicing.

```
| greeting name fullGreeting |
greeting := 'Hello, '.
name := 'Smalltalk!'.
fullGreeting := greeting, name. "fullGreeting is 'Hello, Smalltalk!'"
```

Example output:

```
fullGreeting is 'Hello, Smalltalk!'
```

Symbols: Symbols are unique, immutable strings that are typically used for identifiers or keys. They are denoted by a leading # symbol.

```
| symbol1 symbol2 |
symbol1 := #example.
symbol2 := #example.
(symbol1 == symbol2) "Evaluates to true, as both symbols are identical"
```

Booleans: Booleans represent true/false values. The Boolean class has two singleton instances: true and false.

```
| condition |
condition := true.
condition ifTrue: [ 'This block executes when condition is true' ].
```

Collections: Collections encompass data structures like arrays, lists, sets, and dictionaries. They enable the storage and manipulation of groups of objects.

- **Arrays**: Indexed collections with fixed size.

```
| array |
array := #(1 2 3 4).
array at: 1. "Returns 1 - arrays are 1-indexed"
```

- **Lists**: Linked collections allowing dynamic resizing.

```
| list |
list := List new.
list add: 'Smalltalk'.
```

```
list add: 'is'.
list add: 'great!'.
```

- **Sets**: Unordered collections of unique elements.

```
| set |
set := Set new.
set add: 'apple'.
set add: 'banana'.
set add: 'apple'. "Duplicates not added"
```

- **Dictionaries**: Key-value pairs for mapping associations.

```
| dictionary |
dictionary := Dictionary new.
dictionary at: 'name' put: 'Smalltalk'.
dictionary at: 'year' put: 1980.
```

The understanding and appropriate utilization of these basic data types form the foundation for mastering Smalltalk programming. Integrating these fundamental elements will enable building more complex abstractions necessary for advanced development tasks.

3.4 Variables and Constants

In Smalltalk, as in other programming languages, variables and constants play crucial roles in managing data within a program. A thorough understanding of how to declare, initialize, and utilize variables and constants will enable effective data manipulation and better program structure.

Variables in Smalltalk are mutable storage locations, allowing their values to change as needed during program execution. They serve as references to objects, and the data type of the object can change dynamically.

To declare and initialize a variable in Smalltalk, the assignment operator ':=' is used. Consider the following example:

```
| myVariable |
myVariable := 10.
myVariable := 'Hello World'.
```

In the example above, myVariable is first assigned the integer value 10, and subsequently reassigned the string value 'Hello World'. Smalltalk's dynamic typing allows myVariable to reference different types of objects.

Variable names in Smalltalk must begin with a lowercase letter and can contain both uppercase and lowercase letters, digits, and underscores. However, they must not begin with a digit, and it is good practice to use meaningful names to enhance code readability and maintainability.

Constants, on the other hand, are immutable storage locations with values that do not change once assigned. In Smalltalk, there is no direct syntax for declaring constants like in some other languages (e.g., the const keyword in C++). However, Smalltalk conventionally uses class variables or pool dictionaries to simulate constants.

To define a constant using a class variable, one would typically write a class method to access the constant value. For example:

```
Object subclass: MyConstants [
    MyConstants class >> pi [
        ^3.14159
    ]
]
```

In the example, we define a class MyConstants that provides a class method pi returning the value of the mathematical constant π. This approach ensures that the value of pi remains unmodified throughout the program.

Fundamentally, Smalltalk adheres to object-oriented principles, which means every variable holds a reference to an object. Assignments involve passing these references rather than copying the object itself, thereby preserving memory efficiency and data integrity. Consider the following sample code illustrating reference assignment:

```
| a b |
a := 'Smalltalk'.
b := a.
b := b , ' Programming'.
```

Here, a references the string 'Smalltalk', and b is assigned the same reference as a. When b is subsequently modified to append ' Programming', it does not affect a since b now references a new string object.

Scope of Variables in Smalltalk is determined by where they are declared. Smalltalk supports various scopes, including:

- Instance Variables: Declared in a class and accessible by all methods in that class instance.

- Class Variables: Shared among all instances of a class, providing a means to share data across different objects of the same class.
- Temporary Variables: Declared within a method or code block, having a lifetime confined to that block of code.

Temporary variables are denoted using vertical bars within a method or block:

```
aMethod [
    | tempVar1 tempVar2 |
    tempVar1 := 5.
    tempVar2 := 10.
    ^tempVar1 + tempVar2
]
```

In the method aMethod, tempVar1 and tempVar2 are temporary variables used locally within the method and discarded once the method returns the result.

Class Variables and Instance Variables are declared in the class definition and initialized upon instance or class instantiation.

```
Object subclass: Person [
    | name age |
]
Person class >> new [
    ^super new initialize
]
Person >> initialize [
    name := ''.
    age := 0.
]
```

In the class Person, name and age are instance variables. The initialize method sets their initial values when a new Person instance is created.

Efficient use and understanding of variables and constants are paramount in Smalltalk programming, allowing clear and effective data management within programs. Constants, though not directly supported as in some other languages, can be implemented through class methods to ensure values remain unchanged, embodying the principles of immutability where necessary.

3.5 Arithmetic Operations

Arithmetic operations in Smalltalk are performed using standard mathematical operators. These operations are essential for manipulating

numerical data and performing calculations within your programs. The primary arithmetic operators in Smalltalk are addition +, subtraction -, multiplication *, division /, and modulo
. Each operator is treated as a message sent to a number object.

To illustrate, consider the following expressions and their evaluations in Smalltalk:

```
3 + 2 "Results in 5"
5 - 1 "Results in 4"
4 * 3 "Results in 12"
12 / 4 "Results in 3"
10 \\ 3 "Results in 1 (remainder)"
```

The + operator adds two numbers together:

```
| result |
result := 3 + 2. "5"
```

The - operator subtracts the second number from the first:

```
| result |
result := 5 - 1. "4"
```

The * operator multiplies two numbers:

```
| result |
result := 4 * 3. "12"
```

The / operator divides the first number by the second:

```
| result |
result := 12 / 4. "3"
```

The
operator calculates the remainder of the division of the first number by the second:

```
| result |
result := 10 \\ 3. "1"
```

Smalltalk handles arithmetic operations following standard operator precedence, and expressions are evaluated from left to right. To enforce specific precedence, parentheses can be used similar to mathematical notation. For instance:

```
| result |
result := (3 + 2) * (5 - 1). "20"
```

In the above example, $(3 + 2)$ is evaluated first, giving 5, and $(5 - 1)$ is evaluated next, resulting in 4. The final multiplication yields 20.

Smalltalk also supports compound and nested arithmetic expressions. For example:

```
| result |
result := (3 * 2) + (4 / 2) - (1 + 1). "7"
```

In this expression, $(3 * 2)$ evaluates to 6, $(4 / 2)$ evaluates to 2, and $(1 + 1)$ evaluates to 2. The overall result is calculated as $6 + 2 - 2$, which equals 6.

Errors in arithmetic operations, such as division by zero, will result in exceptions in Smalltalk. For example:

```
| result |
result := 12 / 0.
```

Executing the above snippet will raise a ZeroDivide exception. Proper handling of such exceptions is crucial for ensuring robust programs.

Arithmetic operations can also be performed on floating-point numbers. Consider the following:

```
| result |
result := 2.5 + 3.1. "5.6"
result := 5.0 - 2.2. "2.8"
result := 3.3 * 2.0. "6.6"
result := 7.2 / 3.6. "2.0"
```

The operations follow the same principles as with integers. Smalltalk provides consistent and predictable results across different number types.

Furthermore, Smalltalk supports arithmetic with large numbers, such as instances of LargeInteger or Fraction. This is particularly useful for applications requiring high-precision calculations. For instance:

```
| result |
result := 12345678901234567890 + 98765432109876543210. "111111111011111111100"
result := 2 / 3. "a Fraction instance representing 2/3"
```

Floating-point arithmetic might introduce precision errors due to the inherent limitations of representing decimal numbers in binary format. When absolute precision is necessary, using Fraction is advisable.

By understanding and correctly utilizing arithmetic operations in Smalltalk, you can effectively manipulate numerical data to fit the needs of your application.

3.6 Strings and Characters

In Smalltalk, strings are an essential data type used for representing and manipulating text. A string in Smalltalk is a sequence of characters enclosed within single quotes. For instance, 'Hello, World!' is a string. Similarly, characters are represented by prefixing the character with a dollar sign ($), such as $H for the character 'H'.

A string can contain any character, including special characters and whitespace. To include a single quote within a string, use a pair of single quotes. For example, the string 'It''s a good day' includes the word "It's" correctly.

```
'Hello, World!'
'Smalltalk is fun!'
'It''s a good day'
```

In Smalltalk, strings are instances of the String class, whereas individual characters are instances of the Character class. Strings and characters both offer a variety of methods for manipulation, comparison, and conversion.

String Creation and Concatenation The most straightforward way to create a string is to enclose text within single quotes as shown earlier. To concatenate two strings, you can use the comma operator (,).

```
'Hello, ' , 'World!' "Results in 'Hello, World!'"
```

Additionally, the String class provides methods such as concat: which serves the same purpose.

```
'Hello, ' concat: 'World!' "Results in 'Hello, World!'"
```

Accessing Characters in a String Each character in a string can be accessed using the at: method, where the index is one-based.

```
| str firstChar |
str := 'abcdef'.
firstChar := str at: 1. "Character a"
```

Similarly, at:put: can be used to modify a character at a given position.

```
| str |
str := 'abcdef'.
str at: 3 put: \$z. "Resulting in 'abzdef'"
```

String Comparison String comparison can be done using the equality operator (=), which checks if two strings have the same characters in the same sequence.

```
'hello' = 'hello' "Results in true"
'hello' = 'Hello' "Results in false"
```

For case-insensitive comparison, use compareCaseInsensitive:.

```
'hello' compareCaseInsensitive: 'Hello' "Results in true"
```

String Interpolation String interpolation is the process of embedding variables within a string. In Smalltalk, this is accomplished using the format: method.

```
| name age result |
name := 'Alice'.
age := 30.
result := 'Name: {1}, Age: {2}' format: { name. age }. "Results in 'Name: Alice, Age:
    30'"
```

String Substrings Extracting substrings can be performed using the copyFrom:to: method, which takes two arguments: the start index and the end index.

```
| fullString subString |
fullString := 'Smalltalk programming'.
subString := fullString copyFrom: 1 to: 9. "Results in 'Smalltalk'"
```

Character Methods The Character class includes methods to determine the type of character or to convert between cases. For instance, isDigit checks if the character is a digit:

```
\$5 isDigit "Results in true"
\$a isDigit "Results in false"
```

To convert a character to its uppercase or lowercase form, use asUppercase or asLowercase respectively:

```
\$a asUppercase "Results in \$A"
\$A asLowercase "Results in \$a"
```

Encoding and Decoding Smalltalk strings support various encodings. When dealing with different encodings, methods such as asString and asByteArray are useful. These methods help in converting between strings and byte arrays.

```
| byteArray string |
byteArray := #('72 '101 '108 '108 '111) asByteArray.
string := byteArray asString. "Results in 'Hello'"
```

These foundational operations with strings and characters equip you to handle textual information efficiently in Smalltalk, setting the stage for more complex manipulations and transformations in later chapters.

3.7 Basic Input and Output

In Smalltalk, handling basic input and output operations is fundamental for interactive applications. In this section, we explore methods to read input from the user and output data to the screen.

Smalltalk employs message passing to interact with the environment. Therefore, performing input and output operations involves sending messages to objects that handle streams. For output operations, Transcript is commonly used. To read input from the user, Smalltalk uses StandardFileStream or other stream classes.

Output Operations

To print messages to the console or a log, Smalltalk provides the Transcript stream. The Transcript is a global object that allows us to write text. Here's an example of writing a simple string to the Transcript:

```
Transcript show: 'Hello, Smalltalk!'; cr.
```

The show: message sends a string to the Transcript, and cr is used to add a newline character after the string. Using Transcript enables the display of formatted information essential for debugging and user interaction.

Combining Strings

Often, it's necessary to combine multiple pieces of information before printing. This can be achieved using the comma operator (,), which concatenates strings:

```
name := 'Alice'.
age := 30.
Transcript show: 'Name: ', name, '; Age: ', age printString; cr.
```

Note the use of printString to convert age, an integer, into its string representation. Concatenation ensures that all parts are seamlessly combined into a single output statement.

Input Operations

Reading input requires interaction with standard streams or files. For typical console input, Smalltalk may use StandardFileStream designed for reading and writing to files or the terminal.

To read a line of input from the user, use the following example:

```
| input |
Transcript show: 'Enter your name: '.
input := StandardFileStream stdin nextLine.
Transcript show: 'Hello, ', input, '!'; cr.
```

Here, StandardFileStream stdin nextLine captures the user's input until they press Enter. The input is then echoed back with a greeting.

Detailed Example: User Interaction

Combining both input and output operations, let's create a basic interactive application that asks for the user's name and age, then prints a personalized message:

```
| name age |
Transcript show: 'Enter your name: '.
name := StandardFileStream stdin nextLine.

Transcript show: 'Enter your age: '.
age := (StandardFileStream stdin nextLine) asInteger.
Transcript show: 'Hello, ', name, '. You are ', age printString, ' years old.'; cr.
```

This code snippet demonstrates multiple input and output operations. Note the conversion of the user's age input from a string to an integer using asInteger.

Handling Errors

Error handling is crucial. If the input is not a valid number, asInteger would raise an error. To prevent this, additional checks should be performed:

```
| name age |
Transcript show: 'Enter your name: '.
name := StandardFileStream stdin nextLine.

Transcript show: 'Enter your age: '.
[
  age := (StandardFileStream stdin nextLine) asInteger.
] on: Error do: [
  Transcript show: 'Invalid age! Please enter a number.'; cr.
  age := -1.
].
```

```
Transcript show: 'Hello, ', name, '. You are ', age printString, ' years old.'; cr.
```

Using on:do:, this snippet captures conversion errors, providing user-friendly error messages while maintaining program stability.

Understanding these basic input and output operations is essential for interacting with users and debugging programs. Practicing these methods will enhance your proficiency in building interactive Smalltalk applications.

3.8 Understanding Code Blocks

In Smalltalk, code blocks constitute an essential construct that greatly enhances the language's expressiveness and flexibility. A code block, also known simply as a block, is essentially an anonymous piece of code that can be stored as a value and executed on demand. Blocks can be stored in variables, passed as arguments to methods, and executed within the context of other code. They are similar to lambdas or closures in other programming languages.

Creation and Basic Syntax

A code block in Smalltalk is denoted by the use of square brackets [ ]. The code enclosed within these brackets is the block. Here is an example of a simple block:

```
[:x | x + 1 ]
```

In this example, [:x | x + 1] is a block that takes one parameter x and returns x + 1. The colon (:) before the parameter name x indicates that it is a block argument.

When there are no arguments, a block might look like this:

```
[ Transcript show: 'Hello, Smalltalk!'; cr ]
```

This block, when executed, will display the string "Hello, Smalltalk!" on the Transcript.

Executing Code Blocks

Code blocks can be executed using the value method. If a block takes arguments, value: or value:value: methods are used depending on the number of arguments.

Here is an example of executing a block without arguments:

```
| noArgBlock |
noArgBlock := [ Transcript show: 'No arguments block'; cr ].
noArgBlock value.
```

Output:

```
No arguments block
```

For a block that takes one argument:

```
| oneArgBlock |
oneArgBlock := [ :x | x squared ].
Transcript show: (oneArgBlock value: 4) printString; cr.
```

Output:

```
16
```

Nesting and Returning from Blocks

Blocks can be nested within other blocks and methods. Here is an example demonstrating a block nested within a method:

```
MyClass>>methodWithNestedBlock
  | outerBlock |
  outerBlock := [ | innerBlock |
    innerBlock := [ :y | y * 2 ].
    Transcript show: (innerBlock value: 10) printString; cr ].
  outerBlock value.
```

Output:

```
20
```

It is important to note the use of return in blocks. A return statement inside a block will return from the method in which the block is defined, not just from the block itself.

```
MyClass>>methodWithReturn
  | blockWithReturn |
  blockWithReturn := [ ^ 'Returning from method' ].
  blockWithReturn value.
  Transcript show: 'This will not be printed'; cr.
```

Output:

```
Returning from method
```

Block Properties and Closures

Blocks in Smalltalk are true closures, meaning they capture the lexical environment in which they are defined. This means that a block can reference variables that were in scope when the block was created, even if the block is later executed in a different scope.

```
| outerVar block |
outerVar := 5.
block := [ outerVar + 10 ].
outerVar := 20.
Transcript show: (block value) printString; cr.
```

Output:

```
15
```

In this example, the block captures the value of outerVar as it was when the block was defined, thus returning 15 even though we later change outerVar to 20.

By understanding code blocks in Smalltalk, we gain a powerful tool to write concise and expressive code. Blocks allow us to encapsulate behavior, pass code as arguments, and create closures, all of which contribute to the incredible flexibility and elegance of the Smalltalk programming language.

3.9 Introduction to Messaging in Smalltalk

In Smalltalk, the fundamental construct that drives the execution flow is the message. Unlike many other programming languages where functions or procedures are paramount, Smalltalk is based on the concept of objects communicating by sending and receiving messages. This section delves into the conceptual and practical aspects of messaging in Smalltalk, ensuring a robust understanding that is critical for effective programming in this language.

Message sending in Smalltalk can be categorized into three main types:

- Unary Messages
- Binary Messages
- Keyword Messages

Understanding each of these message types is key to mastering the syntax and semantics of Smalltalk.

Unary Messages

Unary messages are the simplest form of messages in Smalltalk. They do not take any arguments and are composed of a single identifier.

When an object receives a unary message, it responds by executing a method associated with that message.

Example:

```
anArray size.
```

In the example above, the message size is sent to anArray. The object anArray processes this message and responds with the result.

Binary Messages

Binary messages in Smalltalk consist of operators that typically perform simple arithmetic or relational operations. These messages involve two objects: the receiver and one argument.

Example:

```
3 + 4.
```

Here, the $+$ message is sent to the number 3 with 4 as its argument. Binary messages are an excellent example of how conventional arithmetic expressions integrate smoothly into Smalltalk's messaging system.

Keyword Messages

Keyword messages are the most flexible and commonly used form of messages in Smalltalk. They can take one or more arguments and are composed of keywords followed by colons and method parameters.

Example:

```
anArray at: 1 put: 42.
```

In this example, at:put: is a keyword message sent to anArray. The parameters 1 and 42 are supplied as arguments to the message, enabling the program to specify the exact elements and operations dynamically.

Message Cascading

Smalltalk provides a mechanism known as message cascading, which allows multiple messages to be sent to the same receiver in a concise manner. This is achieved using the semicolon (;) operator.

Example:

```
anArray
    add: 'first element';
    add: 'second element';
    add: 'third element'.
```

In this cascaded messaging, anArray receives three add: messages sequentially. This approach not only reduces code verbosity but also enhances readability by explicitly grouping operations performed on the same object.

Message Precedence

When multiple types of messages appear in the same expression, Smalltalk follows a specific precedence order to ensure consistent evaluation:

- Unary messages have the highest precedence.
- Binary messages have intermediate precedence.
- Keyword messages have the lowest precedence.

Example:

```
anObject size + 1 at: 2 put: 'value'.
```

This expression is evaluated as follows:

- size unary message is sent to anObject.
- 1 is added to the result of anObject size using the + binary message.
- The resulting value is then used as the index for the at:put: keyword message.

Understanding the Messaging Cycle

At its core, the messaging cycle in Smalltalk involves the following steps:

1. A message is sent to an object (receiver).
2. The receiver looks up its method dictionary to find a method corresponding to the message.
3. If found, the method is executed. If not, the receiver may respond with a default action, often an error message or by delegating the message.

Example:

```
anObject perform: #messageName.
```

In this example, anObject receives the perform: message with #messageName as its argument. This dynamic message handling is powerful in creating flexible and reusable code structures.

Dispatcher

Smalltalk uses a dynamic message dispatcher, which means the decision about which method to execute is made at runtime. This dynamic nature allows for high modularity and adaptability, where behaviors can be altered at runtime without changing the underlying object structures.

Algorithm 2: Basic Dynamic Messaging Cycle

Data: Message m to an object o
Result: Method corresponding to message m is executed

```
begin
    methodName ← lookUpMethod(o, m);
    if methodName exists then
        execute method(methodName);
    else
        handle error("Message not understood");
```

In this algorithm, the function lookUpMethod searches for the relevant method in the object's class hierarchy, ensuring robust message handling mechanisms are in place.

Mastering messaging in Smalltalk involves not only understanding the different types of messages but also recognizing how to leverage the dynamic messaging system to build efficient and flexible programs. By practicing and involving these messaging paradigms in various coding scenarios, one can become proficient in Smalltalk.

3.10 Writing and Executing Simple Methods

In Smalltalk, methods encapsulate a sequence of statements designed to perform a specific task. Methods are fundamental units within Smalltalk classes and hold a pivotal role in our capability to create modular, reusable, and organized code. This section delves into the syntax and structure involved in writing and executing simple methods, followed by examples that illustrate these concepts in practice.

Methods in Smalltalk are defined within classes. Each method belongs to either the instance or the class itself. Instance methods operate on individual instances of a class, whereas class methods relate to the class as a whole. The definition begins with the method's selector followed by a series of statements organized into a method body.

Below is a simple example to illustrate the structure of a method in Smalltalk. The following method calculates the factorial of a given number:

```
factorial
    "Calculates the factorial of the receiver"

    self = 0 ifTrue: [^1].
    ^self * (self - 1) factorial.
```

Several key points in the structure and syntax can be highlighted here:

- The factorial method is an instance method of a numerical class.
- The ifTrue: message is used to provide a conditional check.
- The method internally calls itself recursively with (self - 1) factorial.
- The caret symbol (^) is used to return a value from the method.

To comprehend some further aspects of method writing, let's create another method that sums the elements of a collection. Here, we will define a method within the Collection class.

```
sum
    "Calculates the sum of elements in the collection"

    | sum |
    sum := 0.
    self do: [:each | sum := sum + each].
    ^sum.
```

This code introduces new elements to our understanding:

- The variable sum is declared and initialized within the method body using the vertical bars (|).
- The do: method is utilized to iterate over each element in the collection.

- A block closure [:each | sum := sum + each] is employed within the iteration.

To invoke the methods defined, we send a message to the receiver object that corresponds to the method selector. For instance:

```
result := 5 factorial.
sumResult := #(1 2 3 4 5) sum.
```

In practical applications, error handling and edge cases are also crucial. Consider the following example that includes error checks:

```
factorialWithCheck

    "Calculates the factorial with input validation"

    self < 0 ifTrue: [^'Error: Negative numbers do not have factorials'].
    self = 0 ifTrue: [^1].
    ^self * (self - 1) factorialWithCheck.
```

The addition of the error check:

- Ensures that the input is not negative, returning an error message if it is.
- Continues to use recursive calls similar to the initial factorial method.

To execute the above methods in a Smalltalk environment, various Smalltalk development environments provide workspace or transcript areas where code can be run.

```
(Transcript show: (5 factorialWithCheck) asString).
(Transcript show: (#(1 2 3 4 5) sum) asString).
```

Properly understanding method creation and execution in Smalltalk involves both writing the method correctly and knowing how to invoke it. By progressing with increasingly complex methods, error checking, and practical examples, one can delve into the essence of Smalltalk's capability for object-oriented design and modular programming principles.

Further exploration will build upon these foundations, aiming at more compounded forms of method interactions and enhanced application scope.

3.11 Comments and Documentation

Comments and documentation are indispensable for maintaining code readability and facilitating collaboration among programmers. In Smalltalk, there are several mechanisms for adding comments within your code, as well as dedicated tools for generating extensive documentation. This section elucidates the various types of comments available in Smalltalk and offers best practices for documenting your code effectively.

Single-Line Comments

Single-line comments are the most basic form of commenting in Smalltalk. They are initiated using double quotation marks. Anything following the quotation marks on the same line is considered a comment and is ignored by the Smalltalk interpreter.

```
"Initialize the variable x with a value of 10."
x := 10.
```

In this example, the text "Initialize the variable x with a value of 10." is a comment.

Multi-Line Comments

Multi-line comments are also enclosed in double quotation marks but span multiple lines. Every line within the quotation marks is part of the comment.

```
"
Initialize variables for the calculation.
This multi-line comment provides detailed information
on the initialization process.
"
a := 5.
b := 10.
```

Multi-line comments are useful for providing more detailed explanations or notes within your code.

Inline Comments

Inline comments are comments placed on the same line as the code they describe. Similar to single-line comments, they start with double quotation marks.

```
x := 10. "Set initial value for x"
y := x + 20. "Add 20 to x and assign it to y"
```

Inline comments help clarify specific operations or logic without breaking the flow of the code.

Pseudo-Comments

Pseudo-comments, which start with the caret symbol (^), are less common and generally used for specific directives to the Smalltalk environment, such as pragmas. Examples include specifying method categories or instructing the compiler.

```
^initialize "Initialize the state of the object"
```

Documenting Methods

Effective documentation of methods is crucial for both individual and team-based projects. Smalltalk allows you to add comments directly within methods, usually at the beginning, to explain their purpose and usage.

```
MyClass >> calculateSum: aNumber
    "Calculate the sum of instance variable x and aNumber.
    Return the result."

    | sum |
    sum := x + aNumber.
    ^sum
```

In the calculateSum: method, the comment provides a concise explanation of what the method does and what it returns.

Class-Level Documentation

Documenting classes involves adding comments either at the class declaration or as class comments. These comments provide an overview of the class's purpose, its key methods, and usage examples.

```
Object subclass: MyClass [
    "MyClass represents a simple example class
    with basic arithmetic methods."

    | x |

    MyClass class >> newWithInitialValue: anInteger
        "Return a new instance of MyClass initialized with anInteger."
        ^self new initialize: anInteger.

    MyClass >> initialize: anInteger
        "Initialize the x variable with anInteger."
        x := anInteger.
]
```

Class comments are essential for understanding the overall design and intentions behind the class.

Using Documentation Tools

Smalltalk environments such as Squeak and Pharo offer built-in tools for generating comprehensive documentation. For instance, the "Help System" in Pharo allows you to create browsable documentation, complete with examples and explanations. Integrating documentation tools into your development workflow aids in maintaining up-to-date and accessible codebases.

When documenting, it is advisable to:

- Use clear, concise language.
- Keep comments relevant to the associated code.
- Regularly update comments to match code changes.
- Avoid over-commenting, which can clutter the code and reduce readability.

Comments and documentation enhance code understandability and maintainability. Consistently documenting your code facilitates easier debugging and smoother transitions for future developers engaging with your projects.

Chapter 4

Object-Oriented Principles in Smalltalk

This chapter delves into the core object-oriented concepts within Smalltalk, including objects and messages, classes and instances, and the principles of inheritance, polymorphism, and encapsulation. Readers will explore method definition and usage, the significance of the 'self' keyword, and the structure of metaclasses. Additionally, the chapter covers class hierarchies, relationships, object lifecycle management, and introduces common design patterns relevant to Smalltalk programming.

4.1 Introduction to Object-Oriented Programming

Object-oriented programming (OOP) is a paradigm in computer science that structures programs by defining data as objects and the interactions between these objects. The concept originated from the need to manage and model the complexities of systems and real-world entities more effectively. Smalltalk, created in the 1970s, epitomizes OOP, emphasizing objects as the central component of software design. This section elucidates the fundamental concepts underpinning OOP within the context of Smalltalk.

An object in Smalltalk encapsulates both state and behavior. The state is represented by variables known as instance variables, while the behavior is expressed through methods. Each object is an instance of a particular class, which defines the blueprint for the objects. Classes include the structure of the instance variables and the implementations of the methods.

Classes and instances form a symbiotic relationship. A class acts as a template for creating objects (instances), while an instance is a concrete realization of the class. For example, considering a class Car, different instances of Car can represent individual cars with unique attributes such as color, make, and model.

Object-oriented programming relies heavily on the concept of messages. An object communicates with another object by sending messages. In Smalltalk, every operation performed on an object is the result of a message sent to it. For example, if a message drive is sent to an instance of Car, the corresponding drive method in the Car class is invoked to execute the action.

Consider the following Smalltalk code which defines a simple Car class:

```
Object subclass: Car [
    | color model |

    Car class >> new [
        ^super new
    ]

    Car >> initialize [
        color := 'Unspecified'.
        model := 'Unspecified'.
    ]

    Car >> setColor: aColor [
        color := aColor
    ]

    Car >> setModel: aModel [
        model := aModel
    ]

    Car >> drive [
        Transcript show: 'The ', color, ' ', model, ' is driving.'; cr.
    ]
]
```

In this example, Car is a subclass of Object. The pipe symbols '|' define the instance variables color and model. The class method new creates a new instance of Car, and the initialize method sets default values for color and model. The methods setColor: and setModel: allow for setting the values of these attributes, and the drive method demonstrates using 'Transcript' to output a message indicating the car's action.

When an instance of Car receives the drive message, the text representing the action is printed:

```
The Unspecified Unspecified is driving.
```

The above output results from an instance of Car with default uninitialized attributes. If we set the color and model before invoking the drive method, the output changes accordingly.

Smalltalk's object-oriented model introduces essential principles such as inheritance, polymorphism, and encapsulation. Inheritance allows a class to inherit properties and methods from another class, facilitating code reuse and the creation of hierarchical relationships. Polymorphism gives the ability for different classes to be treated as instances of the same class through a common interface. Encapsulation ensures that an object's internal state is protected from unauthorized access and modification, providing a controlled mechanism for interaction.

Consider a SportsCar subclass inheriting from Car:

```
Car subclass: SportsCar [
    SportsCar >> drive [
        Transcript show: 'The sports car is driving fast!'; cr.
    ]
]
```

Here, SportsCar inherits the attributes and methods of Car but overrides the drive method to customize its behavior:

```
The sports car is driving fast!
```

Polymorphism allows instances of both Car and SportsCar to be treated uniformly yet respond differently to the drive message, underscoring the flexibility and power of OOP.

Lastly, encapsulation in Smalltalk is managed by controlling access to instance variables through methods. Direct access is typically restricted, emphasizing the use of accessor methods like setColor: and setModel: shown earlier, which properly manage how data is manipulated.

Armed with these foundational principles, we can approach more advanced topics within Smalltalk, such as method definition, metaclasses, and design patterns, with a solid understanding of the underlying object-oriented concepts. Here is the corrected LaTeX version of the section with all errors fixed:

"'latex

4.2 Objects and Messages

The foundational concept of Smalltalk lies in its treatment of everything as an object. Objects interact with each other through the exchange of messages. This is a core tenet of object-oriented programming (OOP) in Smalltalk, facilitating a high degree of modularity, flexibility, and reuse.

To grasp the interaction between objects and messages, it is important to clarify the fundamental structure and behavior of Smalltalk objects. Each object encompasses state and behavior, encapsulated respectively as instance variables and methods. The communication between objects happens exclusively through message passing.

Consider a simple example: creating an instance of a class and sending a message to it.

```
"Defining a simple class named 'Person'"
Object subclass: Person [
  | name age |

  Person class >> new [
    ^super new initialize
  ]

  Person >> initialize [
    name := ''.
    age := 0.
  ]

  Person >> name: aName [
    name := aName
  ]

  Person >> age: anAge [
    age := anAge
  ]

  Person >> displayInfo [
    ^'Name: ', name, ' Age: ', age printString
  ]
]
```

In this example, Person is a subclass of Object, which defines two instance variables: name and age. Upon instantiation, the object initializes these variables using the initialize method.

To create an instance of the class and send messages to it:

```
"Creating an instance of 'Person' and sending messages"
| personInstance |
personInstance := Person new.
personInstance name: 'Alice'.
personInstance age: 30.
```

```
Transcript show: personInstance displayInfo. "Outputs: Name: Alice Age: 30"
```

The interactions here involve sending the new message to Person to create an instance (personInstance), followed by sending name:, age:, and displayInfo messages to the personInstance object. This exemplifies how objects communicate and manipulate their data through messages.

It is crucial to differentiate between messages and methods:

- **Message:** A request for an action or information, sent to an object.
- **Method:** A sequence of instructions contained within a class that is executed when an object of that class receives the corresponding message.

This distinction is vital in understanding message dispatch and method lookup mechanisms in Smalltalk.

When an object receives a message, Smalltalk's message dispatch mechanism searches for the method associated with that message in the class of the object. If not found, the lookup proceeds up the inheritance hierarchy. Consider this flow outlined in Algorithm 3:

Algorithm 3: Message Dispatch Mechanism

Input : Object obj, Message msg
Output : Method Execution Result

```
begin
    class ← obj.class;
    while class ≠ Null do
        if class has method for msg then
            return Execute method of class for msg;
        class ← class.superclass;
    return MessageNotUnderstoodException;
```

Understanding message dispatch enables an appreciation of polymorphism—a principle allowing objects of different classes to respond to the same message, crucial for designing extensible software systems.

```
"Example demonstrating polymorphism"
Object subclass: Animal [
  Animal >> speak [
```

```
    ^'Each animal speaks differently.'
  ]
]

Animal subclass: Dog [
  Dog >> speak [
    ^'Woof!'
  ]
]

Animal subclass: Cat [
  Cat >> speak [
    ^'Meow!'
  ]
]

"Creating animal objects and sending the 'speak' message"
| animals |
animals := { Dog new. Cat new. }.
animals do: [ :animal | Transcript show: animal speak; cr ].
```

In this code snippet, both Dog and Cat classes inherit from Animal and override the speak method. Sending the speak message to an instance of Dog results in 'Woof!', while sending it to a Cat returns 'Meow!'. Through polymorphism, different class instances can be treated uniformly based on shared behavior.

Appropriately designing each class ensures that objects communicate via well-defined messages, achieving robust encapsulation and information hiding. This message-driven interaction encourages modular, comprehensible, and maintainable codebase, fostering a highly productive programming environment in Smalltalk.

4.3 Classes and Instances

In Smalltalk, the concepts of classes and instances are foundational to object-oriented programming. Understanding the relationship between these entities is essential for mastering Smalltalk.

A *class* is a blueprint for creating objects, defining the attributes (instance variables) and behaviors (methods) that the objects created from the class will have. An *instance* is an individual object created from a class, encapsulating its own state and responding to messages defined by its class's methods.

To define a class in Smalltalk, we use the Object class as the superclass unless otherwise specified. The following example demonstrates how to define a simple class named Car:

```
Object subclass: #Car
  instanceVariableNames: 'make model year'
  classVariableNames: ''
  poolDictionaries: ''
  category: 'Vehicles'
```

The above code defines a class Car with three instance variables: make, model, and year. These instance variables will store data specific to each instance of the Car class.

To create an instance of the Car class, we use the new method, which is a standard method inherited from Object. This method allocates memory for the new instance and initializes it. Consider the following code that creates an instance of Car and assigns values to its instance variables.

```
| myCar |
myCar := Car new.
myCar make: 'Tesla'.
myCar model: 'Model S'.
myCar year: 2023.
```

Here, myCar is an instance of Car, and we use message sends to set the values for make, model, and year attributes.

To define methods in the Car class, we extend the class's functionality in the instance side. For example, to define methods to set and get the make of the car, we write:

```
Car>>make: aString
  make := aString.

Car>>make
  ^make.
```

The make: method is a mutator for setting the value of the make instance variable, whereas the make method is an accessor for retrieving the value.

A custom constructor can be added to the class to simplify instance creation, as seen below:

```
Car class>>make: aMake model: aModel year: aYear
  ^self new
    make: aMake;
    model: aModel;
    year: aYear;
    yourself.
```

This class method simplifies creating a new Car instance by allowing the values for make, model, and year to be set in a single message send.

```
| myCar |
myCar := Car make: 'Tesla' model: 'Model S' year: 2023.
```

In this case, myCar is immediately assigned a new instance of Car with the specified attributes.

Classes can also have class variables, which are shared among all instances. To declare a class variable, use the corresponding slot in the subclass:instanceVariableNames:classVariableNames:poolDictionaries:category: method. However, management of this shared state must be done cautiously to avoid unintended side effects.

The interplay between classes and instances is central to leveraging polymorphism and inheritance in Smalltalk. For example, consider a subclass ElectricCar inheriting from Car:

```
Car subclass: #ElectricCar
  instanceVariableNames: 'batteryCapacity'
  classVariableNames: ''
  poolDictionaries: ''
  category: 'Vehicles'
```

In this code, ElectricCar inherits all attributes and behaviors of Car but adds a new instance variable, batteryCapacity.

To initialize this new class with additional parameters, we extend the ElectricCar class with its own constructor method:

```
ElectricCar class>>make: aMake model: aModel year: aYear batteryCapacity:
      aCapacity
  ^self new
    make: aMake;
    model: aModel;
    year: aYear;
    batteryCapacity: aCapacity;
    yourself.
```

An instance of ElectricCar can now be created with all required attributes, showcasing the enhanced functionality and specifics of subclassing:

```
| myElectricCar |
myElectricCar := ElectricCar make: 'Tesla' model: 'Model S' year: 2023
      batteryCapacity: 100.
```

The above sequence enforces the principle of inheritance, enriching new subclasses with specialized behaviors and characteristics while sharing common functionality with their superclass. This nuanced relationship between classes and instances forms the crux of object-oriented programming, providing a robust framework for designing, implementing, and maintaining flexible software systems in Smalltalk.

4.4 Inheritance and Polymorphism

Inheritance and polymorphism are fundamental concepts in object-oriented programming (OOP), and Smalltalk leverages these principles to facilitate code reuse and extensibility. In this section, we will thoroughly examine these concepts within the Smalltalk programming environment, providing detailed explanations and illustrative code examples.

Inheritance allows a class to inherit the properties and behavior of another class, referred to as the superclass. This mechanism is central to promoting code reuse and establishing a hierarchical relationship between classes. In Smalltalk, a class is defined using the subclass: message sent to an existing class. Consider the following example:

```
Object subclass: #Animal
instanceVariableNames: 'species'
classVariableNames: ''
poolDictionaries: ''
category: 'MyCategory'.
```

Here, Animal is a subclass of Object, inheriting all instance variables and methods from Object. This subclass will have its instance variable species defined as part of its own structure.

Polymorphism, on the other hand, refers to the ability of different classes to respond to the same message (method call) in different ways. This concept is a cornerstone of flexible and extensible systems. In Smalltalk, polymorphism is achieved through dynamic method dispatch, where the method to be executed is determined at runtime based on the object's class.

To illustrate inheritance and polymorphism, consider expanding the Animal class with specific animal subclasses:

```
Animal subclass: #Dog
instanceVariableNames: 'breed'
classVariableNames: ''
poolDictionaries: ''
category: 'MyCategory'.

Dog subclass: #Bulldog
instanceVariableNames: ''
classVariableNames: ''
```

```
poolDictionaries: ''
category: 'MyCategory'.
```

Here, Dog is introduced as a subclass of Animal, and Bulldog as a subclass of Dog. Each subclass inherits properties and behavior from its respective superclass.

Next, let's define methods in these classes to demonstrate polymorphic behavior. We will start by adding a speak method:

```
Animal>>speak
    ^'Some sound'.

Dog>>speak
    ^'Bark'.

Bulldog>>speak
    ^'Woof Woof'.
```

When the speak message is sent to an instance of Animal, Dog, or Bulldog, the method corresponding to the object's class is executed:

```
| genericAnimal dog bulldog |
genericAnimal := Animal new.
dog := Dog new.
bulldog := Bulldog new.

Transcript show: genericAnimal speak; cr. "Outputs: Some sound"
Transcript show: dog speak; cr. "Outputs: Bark"
Transcript show: bulldog speak; cr. "Outputs: Woof Woof"
```

The ability of genericAnimal, dog, and bulldog to respond differently to the speak message illustrates polymorphism.

To further explore these concepts, consider method overriding, which allows a subclass to provide a specific implementation for a method already defined in its superclass. Method overriding is a key aspect of achieving polymorphism. When a method in a subclass has the same name as one in its superclass, the subclass's method overrides the superclass's method. Here is an example:

```
Animal>>description
    ^'This is an animal'.

Dog>>description
    ^'This is a dog'.

Bulldog>>description
    ^'This is a bulldog'.
```

When the description message is sent to an instance, the method defined in the specific subclass is executed:

```
Transcript show: genericAnimal description; cr. "Outputs: This is an animal"
Transcript show: dog description; cr. "Outputs: This is a dog"
Transcript show: bulldog description; cr. "Outputs: This is a bulldog"
```

Finally, consider the implementation of inheritance in method dispatch. When a message is sent to an object, Smalltalk's method lookup process begins with the class of the object. If the class does not define the method, the lookup proceeds to the superclass, continuing up the inheritance chain until the method is found or the root class (Object) is reached.

Let's illustrate method inheritance:

```
Animal>>sleep
    ^'Sleeping'.

Transcript show: dog sleep; cr. "Outputs: Sleeping"
Transcript show: bulldog sleep; cr. "Outputs: Sleeping"
```

Neither Dog nor Bulldog defines the sleep method, so the method inherited from Animal is executed.

These examples illustrate the powerful object-oriented features provided by inheritance and polymorphism in Smalltalk. Understanding and effectively utilizing these principles enables the creation of modular, maintainable, and scalable software.

4.5 Encapsulation and Information Hiding

Encapsulation is a fundamental principle in object-oriented programming (OOP) that binds together the data and methods that manipulate the data, while keeping both safe from outside interference and misuse. The confines of an object protect its data from direct manipulation by external entities. This concept is often implemented through mechanisms such as information hiding, which restricts access to the inner workings of an object and exposes only necessary interfaces.

In Smalltalk, encapsulation is inherently robust due to the language's strict adherence to object-oriented principles. Every value and behavior in Smalltalk is an object, and interactions between objects occur solely through message passing. Here, we will explore encapsulation by examining how to define and utilize private and public methods and variables.

```
Object subclass: #Person
    instanceVariableNames: 'name age'
```

```
    classVariableNames: ''
    poolDictionaries: ''
    category: 'EncapsulationExample'.

Person>>initialize
    name := ''.
    age := 0.

Person>>setName: aName
    name := aName.

Person>>setAge: anAge
    age := anAge.

Person>>getName
    ^name.

Person>>getAge
    ^age.
```

In the code snippet above, a class Person is defined with two instance variables, name and age. The encapsulation principle is exhibited through the use of methods to get and set these variables. The initial values of these instance variables are set in the initialize method, ensuring that each Person object starts from a defined state.

The methods setName: and setAge: serve as 'mutators' or 'setters', allowing controlled modification of the instance variables. Conversely, getName and getAge are 'accessors' or 'getters', providing read access to these variables. This controlled access ensures that the properties of Person objects cannot be altered directly, maintaining the integrity of the object's state.

The visibility of these methods and variables is managed using terminology such as private, protected, and public, although Smalltalk encapsulates this using method protocols more than explicit declarations. Access to instance variables is inherently restricted to the object itself and its methods, embodying the principle of information hiding.

Example: Encapsulating Behavior

The following example demonstrates a more complex scenario where behavior is encapsulated within methods to hide the internal workings of an object:

```
Object subclass: #BankAccount
    instanceVariableNames: 'balance'
    classVariableNames: ''
    poolDictionaries: ''
    category: 'EncapsulationExample'.
```

```
BankAccount>>initialize
    balance := 0.

BankAccount>>deposit: anAmount
    balance := balance + anAmount.

BankAccount>>withdraw: anAmount
    (balance >= anAmount)
        ifTrue: [balance := balance - anAmount]
        ifFalse: [self error: 'Insufficient funds'].

BankAccount>>getBalance
    ^balance.
```

In this BankAccount class, the balance is an internal state not exposed for direct manipulation. Instead, interactions with the balance are tightly controlled through methods deposit: and withdraw:, which alter the balance while maintaining the integrity of the account. This practice ensures that the balance cannot be set to a negative value directly, encapsulating the logic necessary for maintaining a consistent state.

```
| account |
account := BankAccount new.
account deposit: 100.
account withdraw: 25.
account getBalance. "Output: 75"
account withdraw: 150. "Error: Insufficient funds"
```

In the example execution above, interactions with the BankAccount are shown. Deposits and withdrawals are performed, and the balance is queried through the getBalance method. Attempting to withdraw more than the available balance results in an error, showcasing the encapsulation of the rules governing balance management within the methods.

Employing encapsulation and information hiding, Smalltalk ensures that objects manage their state independently, preserving an abstraction barrier and reducing the risk of unintended interference. This principle makes the code easier to maintain, less prone to bugs, and more flexible to future changes or extensions.

4.6 Defining and Using Methods

In Smalltalk, methods are fundamental constructs that define the behavior of objects. A method in Smalltalk encapsulates a sequence of statements or expressions that perform a specific task, which can be invoked by sending a message to an object. This section delves into the syntax, structure, and application of methods in Smalltalk, reinforcing the object-oriented principles discussed earlier in the chapter.

The process of defining a method in Smalltalk involves specifying the method within the context of a class. Below is the basic syntax for defining a method:

```
ClassName>>methodName: parameter
    "The method body goes here"
    | localVariable |
    localVariable := parameter + 1.
    ^localVariable
```

Several key elements in this syntax include:

- ClassName»methodName:: Indicates that the method named methodName: belongs to ClassName and takes a single parameter.
- "The method body goes here": Comments in Smalltalk are enclosed in double quotes.
- | localVariable |: Declares local variables used within the method.
- localVariable := parameter + 1.: Illustrates an assignment operation, where the result of parameter + 1 is assigned to localVariable.
- localVariable: The caret character^ denotes the return value of the method.

Methods in Smalltalk can be categorized into two primary types: unary methods and keyword methods. Unary methods do not take any parameters, whereas keyword methods can take one or more parameters. Below, we explore both types with examples.

```
Object subclass: MyObject.

MyObject>>initialize
    "Unary method that initializes an object"
    value := 0.

MyObject>>incrementBy: amount
    "Keyword method that increments the value by a specified amount"
    value := value + amount.
    ^value
```

In the example above, MyObject defines two methods:

- initialize: A unary method that initializes the instance variable value to 0.

- incrementBy:: A keyword method that takes a parameter amount and increments the instance variable value by that amount, returning the new value.

To invoke these methods, we send messages to instances of MyObject. Below is an example of creating an instance of MyObject and using the defined methods:

```
| myInstance result |

myInstance := MyObject new.
myInstance initialize.
result := myInstance incrementBy: 5.
```

The sequence above performs the following actions:

- Creates a new instance of MyObject and assigns it to myInstance.
- Calls the initialize method to set up the instance.
- Sends the incrementBy: 5 message to the myInstance, storing the result in the result variable.

Method Overloading is not supported in Smalltalk. However, methods with different names or different numbers of parameters can coexist within the same class. Smalltalk identifies methods based on their name and parameter syntax.

```
MyObject>>increment: amount by: step
    "Method with two parameters"
    value := value + amount * step.
    ^value
```

In this example, MyObject now has an additional method increment: by: which takes two parameters. This method increments value by amount * step.

The self keyword in Smalltalk plays a crucial role within methods. It is used to refer to the receiver of the current message, akin to this in many other object-oriented languages. By using self, we can send messages to the object itself or access its properties. Here is an example of using self:

```
MyObject>>resetIfExceeded: limit
    "Resets value to 0 if it exceeds the specified limit"
    value > limit ifTrue: [ self resetValue ].

MyObject>>resetValue
    "Resets the value to 0"
    value := 0.
```

In the resetIfExceeded: method, self resetValue sends the resetValue message to the receiver object, resetting value to 0 if it exceeds the specified limit.

Method chaining is a notable advantage in Smalltalk, allowing the execution of multiple methods in a single expression by chaining method calls on self. This technique makes the code concise and expressive:

```
MyObject>>incrementAndPrint: amount
    "Increments the value and prints it"
    self incrementBy: amount.
    Transcript show: value; cr
```

This method, incrementAndPrint:, increments value and then prints it to the Transcript. Note that the semicolon (;) used after Transcript show: value sends the cr message to Transcript.

Understanding method definition and usage in Smalltalk is indispensable for proficient Smalltalk programming. Methods not only define the behavior of objects but also facilitate interaction between different objects, promoting modularity and code reuse. As methods are integral to the object-oriented paradigm, mastering their definition, invocation, and chaining will significantly enhance your ability to develop comprehensive Smalltalk applications.

4.7 The Concept of Self

The self keyword is fundamental in Smalltalk and other object-oriented programming languages. It serves as a reference to the current instance of the class in which the code is executing. This concept is pivotal for method invocation within an object and plays a crucial role in maintaining the coherence and integrity of object interactions. Understanding self is essential for mastering object-oriented principles in Smalltalk.

When a message is sent to self, it is dispatched to the current receiver, allowing the object to send messages to itself. This behavior is demonstrated in the definition of methods where self is used to access other instance methods or variables within the same object.

Let us consider the following example to observe the role and significance of self:

```
Object subclass: Person [
    | name age |
```

```
    Person class >> newName: aName age: anAge [
        ^ self new initializeName: aName age: anAge
    ]

    initializeName: aName age: anAge [
        name := aName.
        age := anAge.
        ^ self
    ]

    greet [
        ^ 'Hello, ', name, '. You are ', age printString, ' years old.'
    ]
]
```

In this example, the class Person is defined with instance variables name and age. The newName:age: class method initializes a new instance of Person with given name and age. This method calls initializeName:age: via self to assign the values.

The use of self in this context is critical: 1. self new creates a new instance. 2. self initializeName: aName age: anAge initializes the instance variables for the new instance.

In the initializeName:age: method, self is used to return the initialized object, ensuring the fluent interface style used in Smalltalk.

Methods often require interaction with other methods or variables within the same object. Using self ensures these interactions remain encapsulated within the object's boundary, preserving encapsulation and information hiding principles. This internal communication defines the behavior of the object consistently and predictably.

Message sends to self support polymorphic behavior, allowing method overriding in subclasses to modify or extend functionalities. When a message is sent to self, the method lookup starts from the receiver's class, enabling dynamic method dispatch.

Consider subclassing Person with Student:

```
Person subclass: Student [
    | major |

    Student class >> newName: aName age: anAge major: aMajor [
        ^ self new initializeName: aName age: anAge; major: aMajor
    ]

    major: aMajor [
        major := aMajor.
        ^ self
    ]

    greet [
        ^ super greet, ' Your major is ', major, '.'
```

```
    ]
]
```

In this subclass Student, the newName:age:major: method extends the Person initialization by adding major. The greet method in Student calls super greet, demonstrating polymorphism. self plays a vital role in chaining method calls and ensuring overridden methods are correctly called.

One should also be mindful of potential pitfalls when using self. Recursive calls or improper assumptions about the state of self can introduce bugs. It is often prudent to design methods mindful of their impact on the instance state and the overall object lifecycle.

Understanding and effectively utilizing self leads to robust and maintainable object-oriented designs in Smalltalk. It is a tool that empowers encapsulation, promotes polymorphism, and ensures the integrity of method interactions within objects.

4.8 Intro to Metaclasses

In Smalltalk, metaclasses are a fundamental part of the language's architecture, supporting its highly dynamic nature. Each class in Smalltalk is itself an instance of a metaclass. This means that metaclasses provide classes with the capability to define behavior that can be shared across instances of a class. To gain a thorough understanding of metaclasses in Smalltalk, it is crucial to comprehend the structure and relationship between classes, metaclasses, and their instances.

Classes in Smalltalk are instances of metaclasses, which in turn are instances of the special class called Metaclass. Metaclasses have class methods that define class-level behavior, as opposed to instance methods, which define behavior for instances of the class.

```
Object subclass: #Car
    instanceVariableNames: 'make model year'
    classVariableNames: ''
    poolDictionaries: ''
    category: 'Vehicles'.

Car class>>newMake: aMake model: aModel year: aYear[
    ^self new
        make: aMake;
        model: aModel;
        year: aYear;
        yourself.
]
```

In this example, the Car class is created with instance variables make, model, and year. The metaclass of Car has a method newMake:model:year: defined at the class level. This method is used to initialize new instances of the Car class.

Metaclasses provide a means to organize and manage class-specific behaviors, making Smalltalk's object model profoundly flexible. Understanding how metaclasses interact with classes helps in designing more robust and maintainable code, as it allows developers to encapsulate and reuse class-level behavior efficiently.

```
"Creating an instance of Car using the class method"
aCar := Car newMake: 'Toyota' model: 'Corolla' year: 2020.
```

The above code snippet demonstrates the creation of a Car instance using the class method defined in the metaclass. Notice how the method is invoked on the Car class itself rather than on an instance of Car.

Delving deeper, consider the following relationship diagram that illustrates the connections between an instance, class, and metaclass:

```
+-------------------+          +-------------------+
|      aCar         | Instance of  |      Car          |
|   (Object)        +---------------> |    (Class)        |
+-------------------+          +-------------------+
                                ^
                                |
                                |
                                v
                        +-------------------+
                        |    Car class      |
                        |   (Metaclass)     |
                        +-------------------+
```

In this diagram, aCar is an instance of the Car class. The Car class itself is an instance of the Car class metaclass. The metaclass defines the class-side behavior for Car, such as the newMake:model:year: method.

The hierarchy of metaclasses continues upwards to the Metaclass superclass, and eventually to Object, forming a continuous chain. This ensures that everything in Smalltalk, including classes, can benefit from the uniformity and power of the object model.

In practical terms, metaclasses allow for the definition of class-specific behaviors and traits. For instance:

```
Car class>>findModel: aModel[
    ^self allInstances select: [:car | car model = aModel].
]
```

This example introduces a class method findModel:, which searches for instances of Car with a specific model. Notice that this is again a method of the Car class's metaclass and operates on the class itself rather than on instances of Car.

Metaclasses facilitate dynamic and reflective programming techniques in Smalltalk, allowing developers to query and modify class behaviors at runtime. Leveraging this feature can lead to highly adaptable and powerful code constructs.

Understanding and utilizing metaclasses in Smalltalk enhances the developer's ability to craft sophisticated and flexible software architectures. This comprehension lies at the heart of mastering Smalltalk's object-oriented paradigm.

4.9 Class Hierarchies and Relationships

Class hierarchies in Smalltalk serve as the backbone of object-oriented programming within this language, allowing for an organized and structured approach to software development. Understanding class hierarchies and their relationships is essential for creating modular, reusable, and maintainable code. This section will explore the structure of class hierarchies, the significance of superclass and subclass relationships, and how inheritance facilitates code reuse and polymorphism.

The class hierarchy in Smalltalk is fundamentally a tree. At the root of this tree is the Object class, which is the parent of all classes. Every class in Smalltalk, unless explicitly stated otherwise, inherits from Object. This root class provides a set of default methods that are inherited by all other classes, ensuring a common interface and behavior.

Superclass and Subclass Relationships

In Smalltalk, a superclass is a class from which one or more subclasses inherit methods and properties. A subclass extends its superclass by adding new methods, overriding existing methods, or both. The creation of a subclass is achieved through the subclass: message, which defines the subclass and specifies its superclass.

```
Object subclass: #Person
    instanceVariableNames: 'name age'
    classVariableNames: ''
    poolDictionaries: ''
    category: 'MyApplication-Models'.
```

In this example, Person is a subclass of Object. The Person class will inherit methods from the Object class. Additionally, it introduces its own instance variables, name and age. This hierarchical structure allows the

Person class to reuse the functionalities of the Object class while also extending its behavior to suit specific needs.

Inheritance

Inheritance in Smalltalk is a mechanism that allows a subclass to inherit the properties and methods of its superclass. This inheritance is transitive, meaning that a subclass inherits not only from its direct superclass but also from all its ancestor classes up the hierarchy. The inherited methods can be directly utilized or overridden to cater to more specific behavior.

Consider the following subclass, Employee, which inherits from Person:

```
Person subclass: #Employee
    instanceVariableNames: 'employeeID department'
    classVariableNames: ''
    poolDictionaries: ''
    category: 'MyApplication-Models'.

Employee >> initialize
    super initialize.
    employeeID := ''.
    department := ''.
```

Here, the Employee class inherits from Person, which means it will have access to Person's methods and instance variables, in addition to its own instance variables employeeID and department. The initialize method in Employee calls super initialize to ensure that the initialization of Person is executed before the new instance variables are set.

Polymorphism

Polymorphism in Smalltalk allows different classes to respond to the same message (method call) in different ways. It is a critical feature that supports the dynamic behavior of objects in Smalltalk. Through polymorphism, method calls to an object can invoke methods defined in its superclass, subclass, or even overridden methods in its own class.

Consider a polymorphic scenario where both Person and Employee respond to a description message:

```
Person >> description
    ^'Name: ', name, ', Age: ', age printString.

Employee >> description
    ^super description, ', Employee ID: ', employeeID, ', Department: ', department.
```

When a Person object receives the description message, it will return its name and age. However, when an Employee object receives the same message, it will return the description from Person augmented with its employeeID and department details. This polymorphic behavior ensures that subclasses can enrich or change the superclass functionality.

Encapsulation and Information Hiding

Encapsulation ensures that an object's internal state is protected from unauthorized access and modification. This is achieved by using access control mechanisms such as instance variable visibility and providing public methods to interact with instance variables. Encapsulation supports maintaining the integrity of an object's state, promoting modularity, and reducing system complexity.

```
Person >> setName: aName
    name := aName.

Person >> age
    ^age.
```

In this example, setName: provides a controlled way to set the name instance variable, while age returns the age instance variable. Direct access to the instance variables name and age is not allowed, adhering to the encapsulation principle.

Relationships between Classes

Besides hierarchical relationships, classes in Smalltalk can establish associations based on composition and aggregation. Composition implies a strong ownership between objects where the lifespan of the contained object is controlled by the container object. Aggregation, on the other hand, is a weaker association where the contained object can exist independently of the container object.

```
Person subclass: #Company
    instanceVariableNames: 'employees'
    classVariableNames: ''
    poolDictionaries: ''
    category: 'MyApplication-Models'.

Company >> initialize
    employees := OrderedCollection new.
```

In this example, Company has an aggregation relationship with Person objects, stored in the employees collection. The Company class manages a collection of Employee objects, showing an aggregation relationship where employees can exist independently of Company.

This diligent examination of class hierarchies and relationships in Smalltalk serves to deepen the understanding of object-oriented design principles and enhance the capabilities of effective software design.

4.10 Object Lifecycle and Memory Management

Managing the lifecycle of objects in Smalltalk involves understanding the creation, utilization, and eventual destruction of these objects. Effective memory management ensures that the system efficiently handles resources, preventing memory leaks and optimizing performance. This section explores these critical processes in detail.

Object Creation

In Smalltalk, objects are instantiated from classes using the new method. This process involves allocating memory for the object's instance variables and setting up the initial state required by the object. Here is an example of creating an instance of a class:

```
Object subclass: MyExampleClass [
    "Class definition"
]

| myObject |
myObject := MyExampleClass new.
```

myObject is an instance of MyExampleClass. During the instantiation process, Smalltalk's memory management system allocates the necessary space and initializes the object.

Initialization

After the space for the object is allocated via the new method, it is often necessary to perform additional setup operations. This setup is typically done in the initialize method. The following code demonstrates how to define a class with an initialize method and subsequently instantiate it:

```
Object subclass: MyExampleClass [
    MyExampleClass >> initialize [
        "Initialization code goes here"
        super initialize.
        "Additional initial setup"
    ]
]

| myObject |
myObject := MyExampleClass new initialize.
```

Calling initialize ensures that the object is properly set up before use. It is common practice to call super initialize to ensure any inherited initialization logic is also performed.

Object Utilization

Objects in Smalltalk perform their operations by receiving messages. During their active lifecycle, these objects interact with other objects through message passing. The use of objects involves invoking methods that define the behaviors and responsibilities of the object.

```
MyExampleClass >> performTask [
    "Perform some task"
]

| myObject |
myObject := MyExampleClass new initialize.
myObject performTask.
```

Garbage Collection

Smalltalk employs an automatic garbage collection mechanism to manage memory. When objects are no longer needed and have no references, the garbage collector reclaims their memory, freeing up resources for other uses. Garbage collection in Smalltalk typically involves several strategies, such as:

- Mark-and-Sweep
- Generational Garbage Collection
- Reference Counting

The *Mark-and-Sweep* algorithm works by first marking objects that are reachable from the root set (usually global variables, stack variables, and registers), and then sweeping away unmarked objects.

Example of Mark-and-Sweep Algorithm

Memory Management Best Practices

Effective memory management involves ensuring that objects do not outlive their usefulness. Some best practices include:

- Nullifying references to objects that are no longer needed by setting variables to `nil`.
- Using weak references when objects should not prevent garbage collection.
- Regularly reviewing and profiling code to identify and optimize memory usage.

```
Data: Root set of objects
Result: Memory reclaimed by removing unreachable objects
Function markAndSweep(rootSet): ;
    markAll(rootSet) ;
    sweep() ;
Function markAll(rootSet): ;
    foreach object in rootSet do
        if object is not marked then
            object.mark() ;
            markAll(object.references) ;
Function sweep(): ;
    foreach object in allObjects do
        if object is not marked then
            free(object) ;
        else
            object.unmark() ;
```

The following code demonstrates nullifying a reference:

```
| myObject |
myObject := MyExampleClass new initialize.
myObject performTask.

"Nullify reference to allow garbage collection"
myObject := nil.
```

Ensuring that references to unused objects are properly released allows the garbage collector to reclaim memory efficiently, preventing memory leaks and promoting optimal application performance.

4.11 Design Patterns in Smalltalk

Design patterns represent best practices that help in solving common problems in software design. In Smalltalk, these patterns leverage the language's rich object-oriented nature to enhance code reuse, modularity, and maintainability. This section will explore several key design patterns, including the Singleton, Observer, and Factory patterns, demonstrating their implementation in Smalltalk.

Singleton Pattern

The Singleton pattern ensures a class has only one instance and provides a global point of access to it. In Smalltalk, this is typically achieved using class variables and class-side methods. Below is an example of a Singleton implementation:

```
Object subclass: Singleton [
    | classInstance |

    Singleton class [
        instance [
            classInstance ifNil: [ classInstance := Singleton new ].
            ^classInstance
        ]

        reset [
            classInstance := nil
        ]
    ]

    initialize [
        super initialize.
        "Additional initialization code here"
    ]
]
```

In this pattern, classInstance is a class variable that holds the single instance of Singleton. The instance method checks if classInstance is nil and creates a new instance if necessary. The reset method is used to set classInstance back to nil, though this should be used cautiously as it breaks the singleton guarantee.

Observer Pattern

The Observer pattern allows an object, known as the subject, to maintain a list of its dependents, called observers, and notify them automatically of any state changes. The pattern promotes loose coupling and is useful in implementing event-driven systems.

```
Object subclass: Subject [
    | observers |

    Subject class [
        new [
            ^super new initialize
        ]
    ]

    initialize [
        observers := OrderedCollection new.
    ]

    addObserver: anObserver [
        observers add: anObserver.
    ]
```

```
    removeObserver: anObserver [
        observers remove: anObserver.
    ]

    notifyObservers [
        observers do: [ :observer | observer update: self ].
    ]

    "Example state change method"
    changeState [
        "State changing code here"
        self notifyObservers
    ]
]
```

An observer typically implements an update: method. Below is an example of an observer class:

```
Object subclass: Observer [
    update: aSubject [
        "Handle the update from subject"
        Transcript show: 'Subject state changed to: ', aSubject state; cr.
    ]
]
```

The subject keeps track of its observers in an OrderedCollection and notifies them of changes by calling their update: method.

Factory Pattern

The Factory pattern deals with creating objects without specifying the exact class of object that will be created. It uses factory methods to create and return objects of various types based on some input.

```
Object subclass: ShapeFactory [
    ShapeFactory class [
        createShape: shapeType [
            shapeType = 'Circle' ifTrue: [ ^Circle new ].
            shapeType = 'Square' ifTrue: [ ^Square new ].
            "Additional shapes can be added here"
            ^nil "Return nil if no matching shape found"
        ]
    ]
]
```

In this pattern, the createShape: method is a class-side method in ShapeFactory that takes a shapeType string as an argument and returns an instance of the corresponding shape class.

```
Object subclass: Circle [
    "Circle specific implementations"
]

Object subclass: Square [
    "Square specific implementations"
```

```
]
```

When a client needs a shape, it calls the createShape: method of ShapeFactory:

```
| shape |
shape := ShapeFactory createShape: 'Circle'.
shape draw.
```

Benefits and Drawbacks of Design Patterns

Design patterns offer numerous benefits, including code reuse, improved readability, and easier maintenance. They provide a proven solution to common problems, facilitating communication among developers through a shared vocabulary of pattern names.

However, improper use of design patterns can lead to over-engineering and unnecessary complexity. It's crucial to apply patterns judiciously, ensuring they genuinely add value and simplify the design rather than complicating it.

Understanding and implementing design patterns effectively will significantly enhance your Smalltalk programming skills, enabling you to build robust, flexible, and maintainable software systems.

Chapter 5

Classes and Methods

This chapter provides an in-depth examination of classes and methods in Smalltalk. It covers defining classes, handling instance and class variables, and distinguishing between class methods and instance methods. Readers will learn about method definition syntax, method overriding, method categories, and organizational practices. The chapter also explores selectors, message passing, use of superclass methods, and the concept of metaclasses to deepen understanding of Smalltalk's class and method structure.

5.1 Defining a Class

In Smalltalk, defining a class is a fundamental operation that lays the groundwork for object-oriented programming. Class definitions specify the blueprint for objects, encapsulating data and behavior. Classes in Smalltalk are typically defined using the class creation message, subclass:, which adheres to the syntax conventions of the language. This section will elucidate the syntax and semantics of class definitions, including how to use instance variables and class variables.

To illustrate, consider the following example that defines a simple class Person:

```
Object subclass: #Person
    instanceVariableNames: 'name age'
    classVariableNames: ''
    poolDictionaries: ''
```

```
category: 'MyApplication'
```

Here, Person is a subclass of Object, the root class of most classes in Smalltalk. This definition specifies several elements:

- subclass: is the message sent to the class Object, indicating the creation of a new subclass.
- #Person is the symbol that names the new class.
- instanceVariableNames: 'name age' declares two instance variables: name and age.
- classVariableNames: '' indicates that no class variables are defined.
- poolDictionaries: '' is for shared variable pools, which are not used in this example.
- category: 'MyApplication' specifies the category in which the class resides, useful for organization within the development environment.

Let's analyze each component in detail:

subclass: is a method defined in the Class class that specifies the relationship of inheritance. The new class (in this case, Person) inherits all the methods and behaviors of its superclass, Object, but can also have additional methods and properties.

The argument #Person is a symbol that uniquely identifies the new class within the Smalltalk environment. Symbols in Smalltalk are unique and commonly used for identifiers.

The instanceVariableNames: keyword is followed by a space-separated string, listing the names of instance variables. In our example, Person objects will have name and age as instance variables. These variables store the state data specific to each instance of the class.

The optional classVariableNames: argument is used to list any variables that should be shared among all instances of the class. These are not used in our current example but can be essential for maintaining state or data that is universal to all instances.

poolDictionaries: is another optional argument used to specify shared pools of variables across different classes, primarily for performance optimization or managing namespace issues. In this example, it is left empty.

Finally, category: is a string that categorizes the class within the system browser. This allows developers to organize classes in a modular way, making the codebase easier to navigate.

Consider a scenario where you need to initialize the instance variables. You might define an initialize method as follows:

```
Person >> initialize
    name := ''.
    age := 0.
```

This code snippet illustrates a method definition for initialize, which sets default values for name and age. The syntax Person » initialize indicates that the method initialize is being added to the Person class.

To instantiate a Person object and invoke the initialize method, you would use:

```
john := Person new.
john initialize.
```

When creating classes, developers often write accessor methods to interact with instance variables. Here are examples of getter and setter methods for name and age:

```
Person >> name
    ^name.

Person >> name: aString
    name := aString.

Person >> age
    ^age.

Person >> age: aNumber
    age := aNumber.
```

Accessing and modifying the values of name and age is now streamlined using the defined getter and setter methods. For instance:

```
john name: 'John Doe'.
john age: 30.
```

This assigns the name 'John Doe' and age 30 to the john object. Calling the getter methods retrieves these values:

```
john name. "Returns: 'John Doe'"
john age. "Returns: 30"
```

```
'John Doe'
30
```

Defining classes, managing instance variables, and implementing accessor methods form the foundational aspects of class design in Smalltalk, fostering modular and reusable code structures.

5.2 Instance Variables and Accessors

Instance variables in Smalltalk are essential elements that store the state of an object. Each object maintains its instance variables independently, and these variables are accessible only within the object they belong to. In Smalltalk, instance variables are defined within a class, and when an object is instantiated from the class, it includes space for its own copies of the instance variables.

An instance variable is used to hold an object's attributes or properties, and typically, it should not be directly accessed from outside the object. Instead, accessors - getter and setter methods - are commonly used to read from or write to instance variables. This encapsulation practice is a cornerstone of object-oriented design, ensuring that the internal representation of the object can be changed without affecting the code that uses them.

To declare instance variables in Smalltalk, you include them in the class definition. Here is how a typical class definition with instance variables looks:

```
Object subclass: #Person
    instanceVariableNames: 'name age'
    classVariableNames: ''
    poolDictionaries: ''
    category: 'MyCategory'
```

In this example, Person class has two instance variables: name and age.

The next step is to create accessor methods for these instance variables. Accessor methods typically follow a naming convention: the getter method is named after the instance variable, and the setter method begins with the keyword set followed by the instance variable name with an initial capital letter. Below is an example of getter and setter methods for the instance variable name:

```
Person>>name
    ^name
```

```
Person>>setName: aString
    name := aString
```

The getter method name simply returns the value of the instance variable name, and the setter method setName: assigns a new value to name. The^ symbol in the getter method denotes a return value in Smalltalk.

It is good practice to always use these accessor methods instead of directly manipulating instance variables, even within the class itself. This allows you to add validation or additional processing in the accessor methods later without changing the rest of the codebase. For instance, you may want to ensure that name is not assigned an empty string:

```
Person>>setName: aString
    aString isEmpty ifTrue: [^self error: 'Name cannot be empty'].
    name := aString
```

Similarly, accessors for the age instance variable could be defined as follows:

```
Person>>age
    ^age

Person>>setAge: anInteger
    (anInteger < 0 or: [anInteger > 150])
        ifTrue: [^self error: 'Age must be between 0 and 150'].
    age := anInteger
```

In this setter method for age, additional logic ensures that the age is within a valid range. This encapsulates validation within the setter, ensuring invalid values cannot be assigned to the instance variable.

Using accessor methods promotes more maintainable and flexible code. If the representation of the data changes - for example, storing full names as a single string instead of separate first and last names - only the accessor methods need to be updated, and the rest of the code remains unchanged.

For completeness, below is a demonstration of how to instantiate the Person class and use the accessor methods:

```
| person |
person := Person new.
person setName: 'John Doe'.
person setAge: 30.

Transcript show: person name; cr.
Transcript show: person age; cr.
```

The outputs in the transcript would display:

John Doe
30

Through these examples, the importance of instance variables and accessors becomes apparent. They ensure that the object's state is well-managed, validated, and encapsulated, providing a robust foundation for object-oriented programming in Smalltalk.

5.3 Class Variables and Shared Data

Class variables in Smalltalk provide a means to share data among all instances of a class as well as the class itself. Unlike instance variables, which hold data unique to each instance, class variables maintain a single shared state. This shared state can be particularly useful when there is a need for constants, configuration settings, or counters that should be consistent across all instances of a class.

To define class variables in Smalltalk, one typically includes the class variable names within the classVariableNames part of the class definition template. The class definition syntax in Smalltalk supports specifying class variables seamlessly.

```
Object subclass: #BankAccount
    instanceVariableNames: 'balance'
    classVariableNames: 'InterestRate'
    poolDictionaries: ''
    category: 'Financial'
```

Here, the InterestRate is a class variable that will be shared among all instances of the BankAccount class. Notably, class variables are prefixed with a capital letter by convention to differentiate them from instance variables.

Accessing and modifying class variables can be accomplished using class methods. Class methods are defined within the class method protocol associated with the class. For example, to set and get the value of the InterestRate class variable, one would write:

```
BankAccount class>>setInterestRate: aRate
    InterestRate := aRate.

BankAccount class>>interestRate
    ^InterestRate.
```

In this code snippet, setInterestRate: is a class method used to set the value of InterestRate, while interestRate returns its current value.

Note the use of BankAccount class to denote that these methods are class methods, thus operating at the level of the class rather than its instances.

To ensure data integrity and encapsulation, it is a recommended practice to provide accessor methods (such as the aforementioned setters and getters) for class variables instead of accessing them directly. Direct access might lead to unintended side effects, especially in large and complex systems.

The shared nature of class variables positions them as convenient storage for data that should be consistent across all instances. Consider a scenario where the InterestRate is applied uniformly across all bank accounts. Changing the interest rate for one instance inadvertently affects all instances, demonstrating the utility and risk inherent to shared data.

To see the usage of class variables, consider the following example:

```
| account1 account2 |

"Setting the interest rate using a class method"
BankAccount setInterestRate: 0.05.

"Creating instances of BankAccount"
account1 := BankAccount new.
account2 := BankAccount new.

"Retrieving the shared interest rate from instances"
Transcript show: (BankAccount interestRate); cr. "Outputs 0.05"
```

```
0.05
```

In this example:

- The class method setInterestRate: initializes the InterestRate class variable.
- Two instances of BankAccount, account1 and account2, are created.
- The shared interest rate is retrieved using BankAccount interestRate.

This signifies the shared nature of class variables, as both instances reflect the same interest rate.

A pivotal point in utilizing class variables is ensuring they do not inadvertently introduce complexity or unexpected dependencies. Overuse of class variables can make code harder to understand and maintain.

Therefore, it's essential to employ class variables judiciously and prefer instance variables for instance-specific data.

Next, we will demonstrate a more complex use of class variables in tandem with instance methods and variables to maintain consistent behavior across instances while enabling individualized modifications. Consider an enhancement to the BankAccount class, introducing a concept of a minimum balance threshold shared among all accounts:

```
Object subclass: #BankAccount
    instanceVariableNames: 'balance'
    classVariableNames: 'InterestRate MinBalance'
    poolDictionaries: ''
    category: 'Financial'

BankAccount class>>setMinBalance: aMinBalance
    MinBalance := aMinBalance.

BankAccount class>>minBalance
    ^MinBalance.

BankAccount>>withdraw: anAmount
    (balance - anAmount < BankAccount minBalance)
        ifTrue: [^self error: 'Withdrawal would bring balance below minimum.']
        ifFalse: [balance := balance - anAmount].
```

This extension introduces a MinBalance class variable to enforce a minimum balance policy across all bank accounts:

```
| account |

"Setting shared class data"
BankAccount setInterestRate: 0.05.
BankAccount setMinBalance: 100.00.

"Creating a bank account instance and attempting a withdrawal"
account := BankAccount new.
account deposit: 200.00.
account withdraw: 150.00. "Triggers error due to MinBalance policy."
```

```
Error: Withdrawal would bring balance below minimum.
```

This example underscores the effective application of class variables for shared policies while leveraging instance methods to ensure compliance at the individual instance level, thereby integrating shared data and individual operations cohesively.

5.4 Class Methods vs. Instance Methods

Understanding the distinction between class methods and instance methods is essential for mastering Smalltalk. Both types of methods play crucial roles in object-oriented programming, but their applications and behaviors are distinct. In practice, discerning when to use each type ensures proper execution of Smalltalk programs and adherence to object-oriented principles.

In Smalltalk, every object is an instance of a class. Methods that operate on instances of a class are known as instance methods. Conversely, methods that operate at the class level, rather than on individual instances, are known as class methods. The differentiation between these two is symbolized within Smalltalk's browser by the placement of methods in corresponding categories.

Instance methods are defined to operate on instance variables specific to an object. These methods manipulate the state of an object and access the data encapsulated by it. An example of an instance method is provided below, performing a basic operation on an integer with given instance variables:

```
Integer>>add: anInteger
    ^self + anInteger
```

Here, Integer»add: is an instance method that takes another integer as an argument and returns the sum. The self keyword refers to the instance of the class Integer, allowing the method to operate on the specific data of that instance.

Class methods, on the other hand, perform operations related to the class itself, rather than any particular object instantiated from the class. Class methods can be used to create instances or initialize class-level variables. Below is an example of a class method from the Array class, which is responsible for creating new arrays:

```
Array class>>with: anObject
    ^Array new add: anObject; yourself
```

In this example, Array class»with: is a class method that creates a new array starting with a given object. Here, Array class indicates that the method is associated with the array class itself, not with any particular instance of Array.

To illustrate their differences further, consider the following examples. First, an instance method:

```
Point>>setX: xValue setY: yValue
    x := xValue.
    y := yValue.
```

The method setX:setY: on the Point class sets the coordinates x and y for a specific instance of Point. The instance variables x and y are directly modified, showcasing typical instance method behavior.

Alternatively, a class method to create a new instance might look like this:

```
Point class>>newX: xValue newY: yValue
    | newPoint |
    newPoint := self new.
    newPoint setX: xValue setY: yValue.
    ^newPoint
```

The Point class»newX:newY: method, creates a new instance of Point and sets its coordinates. Notice how self here refers to the class Point rather than an instance, and the instance method setX:setY: is called on the newly created instance.

To formalize the design and implementation, the following creates a new standard instance using an algorithm:

Algorithm 4: Creating a New Point Instance

Input: $xValue$, $yValue$

Output: New Point Instance

1 newPoint ← self new;
2 newPoint setX: $xValue$ setY: $yValue$;
3 **return** *newPoint*

The immediate differentiation of using instance methods over class methods is also evident in method binding. When invoking a method on an instance object, Smalltalk first searches the instance methods defined in the class, then in the class hierarchy. Conversely, invoking a class method invokes it directly on the class object. This can be visualized through the following example:

```
| point |
point := Point newX: 3 newY: 4.
point displayString.
```

In the above code, newX:newY: is a class method called directly on the class Point. Once an instance, point, is created, the instance method displayString is called on it.

Class methods can often serve as factories for instance creation, utilities specific to the class, or operations aggregating instances of the class. Emphasizing proper use of these construction methods aligns the design with software engineering principles, such as encapsulation and cohesion.

Careful classification of methods ensures structured, maintainable, and comprehensible codebases, crucial for advanced Smalltalk programming proficiency. Thus, understanding and differentiating between both method types solidifies foundational knowledge in object-oriented paradigms, especially within Smalltalk's uniquely reflective environment.

5.5 Method Definition Syntax

In Smalltalk, the definition of methods is crucial for encapsulating behavior within objects. Methods are blocks of code associated with a class that define how objects of the class should respond to messages. Each method is defined with a clear structure which ensures consistency and readability.

Basic Method Definition: The syntax for defining a method in Smalltalk is minimalistic and straightforward. A method definition consists of a method signature followed by the method body. Here is an example of defining a simple method that increments a value by one:

```
increment
    "Increase the value by 1"
    value := value + 1.
```

In this example, increment is the selector, and the body of the method is responsible for performing the action. The comment in double quotes provides a brief description of what the method does.

Method Signature: The first line of the method definition is the method signature, which can include the method name and any parameters.

- Unary messages (no parameters):

```
increment
    "Some code here"
```

- Binary messages (one parameter, usually used for operations like +, -, etc.):

```
add: aNumber
    "Adds a number to the value"
    value := value + aNumber.
```

- Keyword messages (one or more named parameters):

```
setX: xCoordinate andY: yCoordinate
    "Sets the coordinates"
    x := xCoordinate.
    y := yCoordinate.
```

Method Body: After the method signature comes the method body, which contains the executable code. Statements within the method body are separated by periods. Each statement usually consists of an assignment or a message send.

For example, the statement:

```
value := value + aNumber.
```

assigns the result of value + aNumber back to value.

Return Values: By default, Smalltalk methods return the value of the last expression evaluated. If an explicit return is required, the caret symbol (̂) is used:

```
getValue
    "Return the value"
    ^value.
```

In this case, v̂alue ensures that the method returns the value of the value variable.

Temporary Variables: Temporary variables can be declared at the beginning of the method body within vertical bars. These variables hold data temporarily for the duration of the method execution.

```
calculateAverage: a b: b c: c
    | sum |
    sum := a + b + c.
    ^sum / 3.
```

Here, sum is a temporary variable used to store the sum of the arguments.

Control Structures: Smalltalk provides various control structures to handle conditional execution and looping.

- Conditional execution using ifTrue:ifFalse::

```
isPositive: aNumber
    "Check if a number is positive"
    ^aNumber > 0 ifTrue: [true] ifFalse: [false].
```

- Looping using timesRepeat::

```
repeatTenTimes
    "Repeat an action ten times"
    10 timesRepeat: [self doSomething].
```

Method Context and Self: Within a method, self refers to the receiver of the message, allowing access to the receiver's instance variables and methods.

```
increaseValueBy: aNumber
    "Increase value by a specified number"
    self setValue: (self getValue + aNumber).
```

In the above method, self is used to invoke other methods of the same object.

Method Protocols: Organizing methods into categories or protocols is essential for maintaining readable and manageable code. This organization does not affect the method execution but helps developers understand and navigate the codebase.

For instance, methods related to accessing variables might be grouped under a protocol named accessing, while methods related to calculations might fall under a calculating protocol.

Every method should be crafted with clarity and maintainability in mind, adhering to the conventions and semantics established within the class and its hierarchy.

5.6 Method Overriding and Polymorphism

Method Overriding is a cornerstone of object-oriented programming in Smalltalk, allowing a subclass to provide a specific implementation of a method that is already defined in its superclass. This capability is essential for dynamic polymorphism, where the actual method that gets executed is determined at runtime based on the object's class.

To override a method, one simply defines a method in the subclass with the same selector (name and signature) as the method in the superclass. When an instance of the subclass receives a message corresponding to the overridden method, the subclass's version of the method is executed.

Consider the following code example where we have a superclass Animal with a method makeSound:

```
Object subclass: Animal [

    Animal class >> new [
        ^super new initialize.
    ]

    Animal >> initialize [
        "Initialization code goes here"
        ^self.
    ]

    Animal >> makeSound [
        ^'Some generic animal sound'.
    ]
]
```

In this example, Animal has a method makeSound that returns the string 'Some generic animal sound'. Now, let's define a subclass Dog that overrides the makeSound method:

```
Animal subclass: Dog [

    Dog class >> new [
        ^super new initialize.
    ]

    Dog >> initialize [
        "Initialization code specific to Dog"
        ^self.
    ]

    Dog >> makeSound [
        ^'Bark'.
    ]
]
```

In the Dog class, the makeSound method is overridden to return 'Bark'. When we create an instance of Dog and send it the makeSound message, the Dog class's version of the method is executed:

```
| myDog |
myDog := Dog new.
Transcript show: (myDog makeSound).
```

The output of the code above will be:

```
Bark
```

This demonstrates that the method in the subclass has successfully overridden the method in the superclass.

Polymorphism allows objects of different classes to respond to the same message in different ways. This is a key concept in object-oriented programming that enhances flexibility and maintainability. In Smalltalk, polymorphism is achieved using method overriding. When different classes implement methods with the same selector, instances of these classes can be treated uniformly based on their behavior rather than their specific class.

Consider a further example where we introduce another subclass Cat:

```
Animal subclass: Cat [

    Cat class >> new [
        ^super new initialize.
    ]

    Cat >> initialize [
        "Initialization code specific to Cat"
        ^self.
    ]

    Cat >> makeSound [
        ^'Meow'.
    ]
]
```

In the Cat class, the makeSound method is overridden to return 'Meow'. Now we can demonstrate polymorphism by iterating through a collection of different Animal objects and calling the makeSound method on each:

```
| animals |
animals := {Dog new. Cat new.}.
animals do: [:each | Transcript show: (each makeSound); cr].
```

The output will be:

```
Bark
Meow
```

Each object in the collection responds to the same makeSound message according to its class-specific implementation. This is the essence of polymorphism.

Moreover, method overriding can call the superclass method using super. This invocation can augment or partially modify the inherited behavior rather than completely replace it. Consider refining the Dog class to prepend its sound to the generic animal sound:

```
Dog >> makeSound [
    ^'Bark, ' , (super makeSound).
]
```

In this refined version of Dog, the makeSound method first produces

'Bark' and then calls the superclass's makeSound method, concatenating the two results. When executed:

```
| myDog |
myDog := Dog new.
Transcript show: (myDog makeSound).
```

The output will be:

```
Bark, Some generic animal sound
```

This demonstrates the ability of subclasses to extend or modify the behavior of inherited methods while retaining a degree of the original functionality through the use of super.

Understanding and effectively using method overriding and polymorphism in Smalltalk promotes code reuse and flexibility. These principles support the development of robust and scalable object-oriented software systems.

5.7 Method Categories and Organization

Smalltalk employs method categories to systematically organize methods within a class. This practice improves readability and maintainability of code by clustering related methods into coherent groups. Method categories are essentially named groupings of methods that facilitate the structuring of a class's functionality into discernible sections.

To define or assign a method to a category in Smalltalk, utilize the browser tool provided by most Smalltalk development environments. This tool typically contains panels for listing classes, methods, and categories, enabling a visual and interactive means to manage your code.

For example, consider a class Person that includes various methods for handling personal information and behaviors. You might have categories such as accessing, initialization, printing, and comparisons.

```
Object subclass: Person [
    "Category: initialization"
    Person class >> initialize [
        "Class-level initialization code"
    ]

    initialize [
        "Instance-level initialization code"
    ]

    "Category: accessing"
    name [
```

```
        ^ name
    ]

    name: aString [
        name := aString
    ]

    "Category: printing"
    printOn: aStream [
        aStream nextPutAll: 'Person: '; nextPutAll: name.
    ]

    "Category: comparisons"
    = aPerson [
        ^ (self name) = (aPerson name)
    ]
]
```

In this example, initialize methods are grouped under the initialization category, accessor methods name and name: under the accessing category, printOn: under printing, and the equality method = under comparisons.

Categories aid significantly when working in collaborative environments or when returning to code after some time. By glancing at the categories, a developer can quickly understand the structure and locate methods related to a particular functionality.

To further illustrate, during the development process, if you need to add a new method for setting a person's age, you might decide this logically belongs in a new category called modifying. You would create this category and place the new method within it.

```
Object subclass: Person [
    "Category: initialization"
    ...

    "Category: initializing"
    ...

    "Category: accessing"
    ...
    age [
        ^ age
    ]

    "Category: modifying"
    age: anInteger [
        age := anInteger
    ]

    "Category: printing"
    ...

    "Category: comparisons"
    ...
]
```

In this revised Person class, we added a new category modifying, and placed the new method age: within it. This clear categorization enables straightforward identification of method roles.

While adding methods to categories is a primary aspect of organization, method interception can also occur. This involves method redefinition or method overriding, and the intent should be clearly documented within respective categories to avoid ambiguity.

For more complex scenarios involving method extension in subclasses, categories are extended similarly. In subclassing, previously defined categories can aid in understanding what functionalities can be augmented or overridden:

```
Person subclass: Student [
    "Category: accessing"
    enrollmentNumber [
        ^ enrollmentNumber
    ]

    enrollmentNumber: anInteger [
        enrollmentNumber := anInteger
    ]

    "Category: printing"
    printOn: aStream [
        aStream nextPutAll: 'Student: '; nextPutAll: name;
        nextPutAll: ' (Enrollment: ';
        nextPutAll: enrollmentNumber printString;
        nextPutAll: ')'
    ]
]
```

In the Student subclass, categories such as accessing and printing are used similarly. The method printOn: is overridden to include additional student-specific details.

Efficient method organization requires nurtured conventions within development teams, ensuring all developers adhere to a consistent approach. This leads to a coherent and navigable codebase that bolsters collaboration and eases code maintenance. For example, using standard category names such as accessing, initialization, printing, and so forth across multiple classes helps in establishing a uniform method organization policy.

In practice, utilizing method categories and ensuring their proper use is a pivotal part of Smalltalk programming. The labelling of methods into these intuitive groups paves the way for advanced navigation, code reusability, and a deeper comprehension of class functionalities, thereby fostering an environment conducive to both individual and collaborative development.

5.8 Selectors and Message Passing

Understanding selectors and message passing is critical for mastering Smalltalk programming. In Smalltalk, computation is achieved by sending messages to objects. The selector plays a central role in determining which method will handle the message.

A selector in Smalltalk is essentially the name of a method. When a message is sent to an object, the object's class hierarchy is searched for a method with a matching selector. If found, the corresponding method is executed.

Message passing in Smalltalk can be detailed as follows:

1. **Unary Messages:** Unary messages are the simplest form of messages and take no arguments. They are composed of just the selector.

```
anObject selector
```

Here, selector is the method name, and anObject is the receiver. The resulting action is the execution of the method named selector on anObject. For example:

```
5 factorial
```

This message sends the factorial selector to the integer 5, resulting in the computation of 5!.

2. **Binary Messages:** Binary messages use selectors that are typically special characters and take a single argument. An example:

```
3 + 4
```

Here, + is the selector, while 3 and 4 are the receiver and the argument respectively. The + method defined in the Number class will be executed.

3. **Keyword Messages:** Keyword messages can be identified by their colons and are used when multiple arguments need to be passed.

```
anObject drawFrom: 10 to: 50 color: Color red
```

In this example, drawFrom:to:color: is the selector, with arguments 10, 50, and Color red. The receiver anObject will execute the method named drawFrom:to:color: with the provided arguments.

Message passing follows a simple but powerful model. When a message is sent to an object, the Smalltalk runtime will:

1. Look up the method dictionary of the receiver's class for a method corresponding to the selector.

2. If not found, the lookup continues in the superclass, recursively until the Object class is reached.

3. If the method is still not found, the doesNotUnderstand: message is sent to the receiver.

Below is an algorithm to describe message passing in Smalltalk, written using the algorithm2e package for clarity:

Data: Receiver object, Message selector, Arguments
Result: Execution of method corresponding to the selector

```
while currentClass is not nil do
    if selector exists in currentClass's method dictionary then
        execute the method with arguments on the receiver
        return
    currentClass ← superclass of currentClass
if selector not found then
    send doesNotUnderstand: selector message to receiver
```

Message chaining, a powerful feature in Smalltalk, allows for a series of messages to be sent in a single expression. For instance:

```
(10 + 5) factorial
```

This expression sends the + message to 10 and, subsequently, sends the factorial message to the result of 10 + 5. Proper parenthesis handling ensures that messages are evaluated in the correct order.

Furthermore, Smalltalk's message passing model supports dynamic method invocation, enhancing its flexibility. Methods can be invoked at runtime using the perform: method, as shown below:

```
anObject perform: #selector
```

The perform: message sends the message specified by selector to anObject. If arguments are needed, perform:with:, perform:with:with:, and so on, can be used.

In scenario where selective behavior is required based on method presence, the respondsTo: can be employed:

```
anObject respondsTo: #selector
```

This returns a boolean indicating whether anObject can respond to the message named selector.

Selectors and message passing provide the backbone of Smalltalk's object-oriented paradigm, facilitating communication between objects in a manner that is both flexible and robust. As methods can be cynamically attached to objects, the power and modularity offered are valuable for complex system design.

5.9 Arguments and Return Values

Arguments and return values form the backbone of method interactions in Smalltalk, enabling methods to communicate and operate on varying data. This section dives deep into the conventions and syntactical structure involved in passing arguments to methods and handling return values.

To pass arguments to a method in Smalltalk, the method name itself can be designed to reflect the expected arguments. For instance, consider a method that adds two numbers:

```
addNumber: a toNumber: b
  ^ a + b
```

Here, addNumber:toNumber: is the method selector, and a and b are the arguments. The^ symbol indicates the return value of the method, which in this case is the sum of a and b.

In the definition addNumber: a toNumber: b, each part of the method name is followed by a colon and a local variable to which the argument will be assigned. This makes message sends in Smalltalk very readable. To invoke this method, you use:

```
result := myObject addNumber: 3 toNumber: 5.
```

This sends the addNumber:toNumber: message to myObject with 3 and 5 as arguments. The result is assigned to result.

Methods in Smalltalk can accept multiple arguments, as demonstrated. Additionally, they can easily return complex objects. Consider this example where we define a method to create a point:

```
createPointWithX: xValue andY: yValue
```

```
  ^ Point x: xValue y: yValue
```

In this case, createPointWithX:andY: takes two arguments, xValue and yValue, and returns a new Point object constructed with these values.

Smalltalk methods can also return conditional values. Suppose we have a method that checks if a number is even or odd:

```
isEven: number
  ^ (number \\ 2) = 0
```

Here, the modulo operation is used to check if the number is even. The method returns true if the number is even and false otherwise. The ^ symbol is essential as it specifies the value returned from the method.

In certain complex scenarios, a method might need to return more than one value or a collection of values. This can be handled using arrays or other collection types. For example, consider a method that returns an array of the quotients when two numbers divide each other:

```
quotientsOf: a and: b
  ^ Array with: (a // b) with: (b // a)
```

This method returns an array containing the quotient of a divided by b and b divided by a.

Additionally, it is critical to handle method arguments and return values properly in Smalltalk, not only for maintaining code clarity but also for ensuring robust and error-free applications. Arguments in Smalltalk are passed by reference, meaning changes to the object referenced by an argument within a method will reflect outside the method. To avoid unintended side effects, one may clone objects if the method needs to modify the argument's value.

Consider the method for summing elements of an array:

```
sumElements: anArray
  | sum |
  sum := 0.
  anArray do: [ :element | sum := sum + element ].
  ^ sum
```

In this method, anArray is iterated over and its elements are summed. The local variable sum is initialized to zero and accumulates the total. The final sum is returned.

Handling return values carefully is equally important. The Smalltalk convention of using the caret symbol for return values ensures that once the caret statement is executed, the method immediately exits and returns the specified value. This follows the best practice of making return statements explicit, improving readability and reducing bugs.

5.10 Using Superclass Methods

When working with classes in Smalltalk, leveraging superclass methods is a fundamental practice that promotes code reuse and ensures efficient programming. In Smalltalk, a superclass is a class from which other classes inherit properties and behaviors. By inheriting from a superclass, a subclass can access and utilize the methods defined in its superclass, thereby enabling method reuse and reducing redundancy. Understanding how to properly use superclass methods enhances your ability to write concise, maintainable, and flexible code.

Inheritance in Smalltalk is a pivotal concept where a subclass can inherit methods and properties from its superclass. This inheritance mechanism allows subclasses to utilize and, if necessary, override methods defined in the superclass. To invoke a method from the superclass within a subclass method, the 'super' keyword is utilized. This section will elucidate the importance of the 'super' keyword, demonstrate its usage with detailed examples, and discuss its impact on method resolution.

Consider a superclass named Vehicle that defines a method move. The Vehicle class provides a general implementation of movement which can be utilized or extended by subclasses.

```
Object subclass: Vehicle [
  | speed |

  Vehicle class >> new [
    ^super new initialize
  ]

  Vehicle >> initialize [
    speed := 0.
  ]

  Vehicle >> move [
    Transcript show: 'Vehicle moving at speed ', speed printString; cr.
  ]

  Vehicle >> setSpeed: aSpeed [
    speed := aSpeed.
  ]
]
```

In the example, the Vehicle class has an instance variable speed and methods for initializing (initialize), setting the speed (setSpeed:), and moving (move). A subclass Car can inherit from Vehicle and use or extend these methods.

```
Vehicle subclass: Car [
  | wheels |

  Car class >> new [
    ^super new initialize
  ]

  Car >> initialize [
    super initialize.
    wheels := 4.
  ]

  Car >> move [
    super move.
    Transcript show: 'Car with ', wheels printString, ' wheels moving.'; cr.
  ]
]
```

In the Car class, the initialize method first calls super initialize to perform the initialization defined in the Vehicle superclass before executing its initialization code for wheels. This ensures that the initial setup from the superclass is included in the subclass's initialization.

The move method in the Car class calls super move to execute the move method from the Vehicle superclass and then adds additional behavior specific to Car. This allows Car to reuse the move functionality defined in Vehicle while extending it with its unique behavior.

Executing the code to observe the output:

```
| myCar |
myCar := Car new.
myCar setSpeed: 60.
myCar move.
```

The output when invoking myCar move would be:

```
Vehicle moving at speed 60.
Car with 4 wheels moving.
```

This demonstrates the sequential execution of the move methods in both the superclass and subclass. By using the super keyword in the subclass's method, Smalltalk ensures that the superclass method is executed, allowing the subclass to benefit from the superclass's implementation.

The use of super in Smalltalk is not confined to basic method extension but can also be strategically employed to refine and augment existing methods in more complex inheritance hierarchies. This practice maintains the fundamental structure and behavior of the superclass, fostering a hierarchical and organized codebase.

It is critical to understand the nuances of method resolution and the inheritance chain. When a message is sent to an object, Smalltalk first looks for a corresponding method in the immediate class. If not found, it proceeds to the superclass, continuing this process up the inheritance chain until it either finds the method or reaches the topmost class, often Object, which acts as the root class.

Utilizing superclass methods judiciously is key to achieving polymorphism, an essential object-oriented programming principle. Polymorphism allows objects of different classes to be treated as objects of a common superclass. Proper use of the 'super' keyword ensures that the method implementations in the superclass are honored, providing a consistent and reliable extension mechanism that is vital for designing robust and scalable systems in Smalltalk.

5.11 Metaclasses and Class Methods

In Smalltalk, the concepts of metaclasses and class methods provide a powerful framework for reflective abilities, allowing classes themselves to be treated as first-class objects. This section delves into the role of metaclasses and the implementation and usage of class methods in Smalltalk.

The metaclass in Smalltalk is an implicit class associated with every class. It is responsible for handling class methods. When you define a class method in Smalltalk, it is stored in the metaclass. Every class in Smalltalk is an instance of a metaclass, and every metaclass is a subclass of the Behavior class, which encapsulates the essential behavior for all classes.

Defining Class Methods: Class methods are defined in a similar manner to instance methods, but they are placed within the context of the metaclass. To define a class method, select the class in the browser and switch to the class side, where you can add methods that pertain to the class itself rather than any instance of the class.

```
Object subclass: MyClass [

  MyClass class >> myClassMethod [
    "This is a class method"
    ^ 'Class Method Called'
  ]
```

```
    MyClass >> myInstanceMethod [
       "This is an instance method"
       ^ 'Instance Method Called'
    ]
]
```

In this example, myClassMethod is a class method, whereas myInstanceMethod is an instance method.

Invocation of Class Methods: Class methods can be invoked directly on the class, whereas instance methods require an instance of the class. The following code demonstrates the invocation of both.

```
| instance resultFromClassMethod resultFromInstanceMethod |
"Invocation of a class method"
resultFromClassMethod := MyClass myClassMethod.
"Creating an instance of MyClass"
instance := MyClass new.

"Invocation of an instance method"
resultFromInstanceMethod := instance myInstanceMethod.
```

```
Result from class method: 'Class Method Called'
Result from instance method: 'Instance Method Called'
```

Role of Metaclasses: As mentioned, each class in Smalltalk has an associated metaclass that holds its class methods. This relationship creates a powerful and flexible system of behavior modeling. The metaclass hierarchy mirrors the class hierarchy, but at a meta level. For example, the metaclass of MyClass is a subclass of the metaclass of Object.

```
"MyClass's metaclass"
MyClass class.

"Superclass of MyClass's metaclass"
MyClass class superclass.
```

```
MyClass class -> MyClass class (Metaclass instance)
MyClass class superclass -> Object class (Metaclass instance)
```

Behavior of Metaclasses: Metaclasses define behavior that applies to classes themselves. This is particularly useful for implementing design patterns that rely on class-level responsibilities, such as singletons.

```
Object subclass: SingletonClass [

   SingletonClass class >> instance [
      "Ensures only one instance of the class exists"
      | uniqueInstance |
      uniqueInstance isNil ifTrue: [ uniqueInstance := self new ].
      ^ uniqueInstance
```

```
    ]
]
```

In this code, SingletonClass ensures that only one instance is created by checking if uniqueInstance is nil and then creating a new instance if it is.

Reflective Capabilities of Metaclasses: The reflective capabilities of metaclasses allow for advanced metaprogramming techniques. By accessing the metaclass, one can dynamically inquire and modify class behavior. This can be particularly useful for scenarios that require runtime class modifications or plugin systems.

```
"MyClass's metaclass"
MyClass class compile: 'newClassMethod [
    ^ ''Newly added method''
]'.
```

Invocation of newly added method: 'Newly added method'

This code dynamically adds a new method newClassMethod to MyClass at runtime, demonstrating the flexibility and power of Smalltalk's metaclass system.

Understanding metaclasses and class methods in Smalltalk is critical for leveraging the full capabilities of the language, allowing developers to create more modular, reusable, and dynamically adaptable code.

Chapter 6

Control Structures and Collections

This chapter explores the use of control structures and collections in Smalltalk. It covers conditional statements, loops, and iteration mechanisms, as well as the handling and manipulation of various collection types such as arrays, dictionaries, and sets. Readers will learn about common collection methods, block closures in control structures, and advanced techniques like using 'select', 'collect', and manipulating nested collections and multidimensional arrays.

6.1 Introduction to Control Structures

In Smalltalk, control structures are fundamental to directing the flow of program execution. These structures, including conditional statements, loops, and iteration mechanisms, allow for the construction of dynamic and flexible code. Understanding how to effectively use control structures is key to mastering Smalltalk programming.

Control structures in Smalltalk are different from those in languages like C or Java. Instead of built-in keywords, Smalltalk uses message passing, wherein control structures are implemented by sending messages to objects.

One of the key concepts in Smalltalk is the block closure. A block is a section of code enclosed within square brackets [ ]. Blocks can contain expressions or statements that are executed when the block is evaluated. Here is how a simple block is defined and evaluated:

```
| simpleBlock |
simpleBlock := [Transcript show: 'Hello, Smalltalk!'].
simpleBlock value.
```

In this code, simpleBlock is assigned a block that sends the message show: 'Hello, Smalltalk!' to the Transcript. When the value message is sent to simpleBlock, the code inside the block is executed, resulting in the following output:

```
Hello, Smalltalk!
```

Blocks play a crucial role in implementing control structures. For example, conditional execution is achieved through the use of blocks in combination with messages like ifTrue: and ifFalse:. Similarly, loops utilize blocks to repeatedly execute a section of code.

The flexibility of blocks allows for defining very concise and readable control structures. This can be illustrated with the ifTrue: message used for conditional execution:

```
| x |
x := 10.
(x > 5) ifTrue: [Transcript show: 'x is greater than 5'].
```

In this example, the conditional expression $x > 5$ is evaluated. If the result is true, the block following the ifTrue: message is executed. This would produce the output:

```
x is greater than 5
```

Loops in Smalltalk are implemented using messages such as whileTrue: and timesRepeat:. For instance, to repeat an action a fixed number of times, the timesRepeat: message can be used:

```
5 timesRepeat: [Transcript show: 'Hello, Smalltalk! '; cr].
```

This code will output the string "Hello, Smalltalk!" five times, each followed by a newline:

```
Hello, Smalltalk!
Hello, Smalltalk!
Hello, Smalltalk!
Hello, Smalltalk!
Hello, Smalltalk!
```

For more complex iterations, such as looping with a condition, one can employ the whileTrue: message:

```
| count |
count := 1.
[count <= 5] whileTrue: [
  Transcript show: 'Count: ', count printString; cr.
  count := count + 1.
].
```

In the provided code, the block [count <= 5] is the condition for the loop. As long as this condition evaluates to true, the block following the whileTrue: message is repeatedly executed. The output will be:

```
Count: 1
Count: 2
Count: 3
Count: 4
Count: 5
```

This demonstrates the power and flexibility of Smalltalk's control structures, allowing complex logic to be expressed in a concise and readable manner. The subsequent sections will delve deeper into each type of control structure, providing additional detail and practical examples to enhance your proficiency in Smalltalk programming.

6.2 Conditional Statements: ifTrue:ifFalse:

In Smalltalk, conditional statements determine the execution flow based on boolean expressions. The fundamental conditional construct in Smalltalk is the ifTrue:ifFalse: message sent to boolean objects. It allows the program to evaluate a condition and execute one of the two code blocks based on the truth value of the condition.

The syntax for ifTrue:ifFalse: is straightforward:

```
aBoolean ifTrue: [trueBlock] ifFalse: [falseBlock]
```

aBoolean is the boolean expression to evaluate, trueBlock is the block of code executed if aBoolean evaluates to true, and falseBlock is the block of code executed if aBoolean evaluates to false.

Here is an example illustrating how it works:

```
| isEven number |
number := 10.
isEven := number % 2 = 0.
isEven ifTrue: [Transcript show: 'Number is even.']
        ifFalse: [Transcript show: 'Number is odd.'].
```

In this example:

- number is assigned the value 10.
- isEven is a boolean object resulting from the expression number % 2 = 0, which checks if the number is divisible by 2.
- The conditional statement prints 'Number is even.' to the Transcript if isEven is true, otherwise, it prints 'Number is odd.'.

The blocks are enclosed in square brackets [], and they can contain one or more statements. The code inside trueBlock executes only if the condition evaluates to true; otherwise, the code in falseBlock executes.

For situations where the false case does not require any action, the ifTrue: message can be used alone:

```
| isPositive number |
number := -5.
isPositive := number > 0.
isPositive ifTrue: [Transcript show: 'Number is positive.'].
```

Here, the message ifTrue: checks if number is greater than 0. If isPositive is true, it prints 'Number is positive.'.

Conversely, if only the false case matters, the ifFalse: message can be employed:

```
| isNegative number |
number := -5.
isNegative := number < 0.
isNegative ifFalse: [Transcript show: 'Number is zero or positive.'].
```

The boolean result of the expression number < 0 is stored in isNegative. If isNegative is false, it prints 'Number is zero or positive.'.

An advanced use case of conditionals merges boolean logic with assignments:

```
| number result |
number := 5.
result := (number > 0)
   ifTrue: ['Positive']
   ifFalse: ['Non-positive'].
```

Here, the result variable is assigned the string 'Positive' if number is greater than 0; otherwise, it gets 'Non-positive'.

Boolean operations can also be nested inside the condition to enhance the decision-making logic:

```
| x y result |
x := 10.
y := 5.
```

```
result := (x > y)
    ifTrue: [
        (x > 0) ifTrue: ['x is greater than y and positive']
                ifFalse: ['x is greater than y and non-positive']]
    ifFalse: [
        (y > 0) ifTrue: ['y is greater than x and positive']
                ifFalse: ['y is greater than x and non-positive']].
```

In this nested example, result is assigned a more specific string depending on the relational and positivity comparison between x and y.

Employing ifTrue:ifFalse: is fundamental in Smalltalk, enabling flexible control flow structures within the code. It is crucial to utilize boolean expressions adequately to implement conditional logic precisely as per the requirements.

6.3 Loops and Iteration: whileTrue: and repeat

In *Smalltalk*, looping constructs enable the repeated execution of code blocks while certain conditions remain true or until certain conditions are met. Two fundamental looping constructs are whileTrue: and repeat. Mastering these constructs is pivotal for efficient and effective Smalltalk programming. This section delves deeply into both constructs, providing syntax, practical examples, and common use cases.

The whileTrue: loop repeatedly executes a block of code as long as the condition specified in the receiver block evaluates to true. The basic syntax is as follows:

```
[ condition ] whileTrue: [ codeBlock ]
```

Here, condition is a block that represents a boolean expression, and codeBlock is the block of code that will be executed repeatedly as long as the condition is true.

To illustrate the whileTrue: loop, consider a simple example where we print numbers from 1 to 10:

```
| i |
i := 1.
[ i <= 10 ] whileTrue: [
    Transcript show: i printString; cr.
    i := i + 1.
].
```

In this example, the variable i is initialized to 1. The loop condition [i

<= 10] is checked before each iteration, and as long as it remains true, the codeBlock is executed. Within the codeBlock, the current value of i is printed to the Transcript, then i is incremented by 1.

It's critical to ensure that the loop condition will eventually become false to avoid infinite loops, which can halt program execution and consume resources indefinitely.

```
1
2
3
4
5
6
7
8
9
10
```

Now, let's examine the repeat loop. In *Smalltalk*, the repeat message causes the enclosed codeBlock to execute indefinitely. Typically, repeat is combined with an exit condition within the block to break out of the loop. The basic syntax is:

```
[ codeBlock ] repeat
```

To illustrate, consider an example where we again print numbers from 1 to 10, but this time using repeat:

```
| i |
i := 1.
[
    i <= 10 ifTrue: [
        Transcript show: i printString; cr.
        i := i + 1.
    ] ifFalse: [
        ^ self.
    ].
] repeat.
```

In this example, the variable i is initialized to 1. The loop continues indefinitely due to repeat. The ifTrue:ifFalse: control structure checks the value of i; if i is less than or equal to 10, the current value of i is printed, and i is incremented. Otherwise, ŝelf is used to exit the loop.

Using both whileTrue: and repeat effectively can significantly improve code readability and efficiency, particularly in scenarios involving repeated actions or checks. Key considerations include ensuring loop conditions will eventually terminate and maintaining clear, understandable block structures.

Let's further explore a practical use case by implementing a loop to find the first element in a collection that matches a specific condition. Suppose we have an array of integers and we want to find the first element greater than 10:

```
| collection result i |
collection := #(3 7 5 12 14 2).
i := 1.
result := nil.
[
    i <= collection size and: [ result isNil ]
] whileTrue: [
    collection at: i > 10 ifTrue: [
        result := collection at: i.
    ].
    i := i + 1.
].
Transcript show: 'First element greater than 10: ', result printString; cr.
```

In this code, the collection is an array of integers. We use both i and result to iterate through the array and store the first element greater than 10. The loop continues while i is within the bounds of the array and result has not been assigned a value. Within the whileTrue: block, if an element greater than 10 is found, it is assigned to result, and the loop is terminated by ensuring result is no longer nil.

```
First element greater than 10: 12
```

Understanding and correctly implementing whileTrue: and repeat can lead to more efficient and robust Smalltalk programs, especially when dealing with iterative processes and repetitive tasks.

6.4 Handling Collections in Smalltalk

Collections are a fundamental aspect of programming in Smalltalk, enabling the handling and organization of groups of objects efficiently. Smalltalk provides a rich set of collection classes, each designed for specific types of operations and use cases. Understanding how to work with these collections is crucial for leveraging the full power of Smalltalk.

Smalltalk collections are divided into several categories: sequences, sets, dictionaries, and intervals. The most common collections are Array, OrderedCollection, Set, and Dictionary. Each of these collection types offers unique properties and methods, supporting the manipulation of their contained elements in a way that is both performant and intuitive.

Array: The Array class represents a fixed-size, indexed collection of objects. Each element in the array can be accessed directly via its index:

```
| myArray |
myArray := #(3 1 4 1 5 9).
myArray at: 1. "Returns the first element, 3"
myArray at: 3 put: 2. "Sets the third element to 2"
```

Arrays are useful when the number of elements is known beforehand and remains constant.

OrderedCollection: Unlike arrays, OrderedCollection is a dynamic, indexed collection that can grow or shrink as elements are added or removed:

```
| myOrderedCollection |
myOrderedCollection := OrderedCollection new.
myOrderedCollection add: 3.
myOrderedCollection add: 1.
myOrderedCollection add: 4. "Adds elements to the collection"
myOrderedCollection remove: 1. "Removes the element 1 from the collection"
```

This collection type is ideal for situations where the number of elements is subject to change.

Set: The Set class represents an unordered collection of unique elements. It automatically handles the uniqueness of elements:

```
| mySet |
mySet := Set new.
mySet add: 1.
mySet add: 2.
mySet add: 1. "Duplicate element 1, won't be added"
mySet includes: 2. "Returns true if element 2 is in the set"
```

Sets are particularly useful for maintaining collections where element duplication is not allowed.

Dictionary: The Dictionary class stores associations of key-value pairs, providing efficient key-based access to values:

```
| myDictionary |
myDictionary := Dictionary new.
myDictionary at: 'a' put: 1.
myDictionary at: 'b' put: 2.
myDictionary at: 'a'. "Returns the value associated with the key 'a', which is 1"
myDictionary removeKey: 'b'. "Removes the key-value pair for key 'b'"
```

Dictionaries are valuable for scenarios where quick access to elements via a unique key is required.

The add: and remove: Methods: Elements are added to a collection using the add: method and removed using the remove: method. Note that removal operations can potentially raise errors if the element is not found:

```
| orderedCollection |
orderedCollection := OrderedCollection with: 'first' with: 'second'.
orderedCollection add: 'third'.
orderedCollection remove: 'second'.
orderedCollection remove: 'fourth'. "Raises an error as 'fourth' is not found"
```

In order to remove an element safely, it's often useful to check its existence first:

```
| anOrderedCollection |
anOrderedCollection := OrderedCollection with: 'item1' with: 'item2' with: 'item3'.
(anOrderedCollection includes: 'item2')
    ifTrue: [anOrderedCollection remove: 'item2'].
(anOrderedCollection includes: 'item4')
    ifTrue: [anOrderedCollection remove: 'item4'].
```

Iteration over Collections: Smalltalk provides powerful iteration mechanisms like do: and collect: to traverse and manipulate collections. Using the do: method, every element in the collection can be processed:

```
| myArray |
myArray := #(2 3 5 7 11).
myArray do: [:each | Transcript show: each printString; cr].
```

For a collect: example which transforms every element according to the block provided:

```
| numbers squares |
numbers := #(1 2 3 4 5).
squares := numbers collect: [:each | each * each].
"squares now contains #(1 4 9 16 25)"
```

The collect: method returns a new collection containing the results of applying the block to each element.

Collections can be further manipulated using methods like select:, reject:, and detect:, providing more finely-grained control over operations based on specific conditions. By understanding and effectively utilizing Smalltalk's collection handling capabilities, developers can create robust, efficient programs that leverage the flexibility and power of this dynamic language.

6.5 Arrays and OrderedCollections

Arrays and OrderedCollections are fundamental collection structures in Smalltalk programming, providing essential mechanisms for managing ordered data. Understanding their differences, functionalities, and appropriate usage scenarios is crucial for efficient and effective Smalltalk programming.

An Array in Smalltalk is a fixed-size, indexed collection that allows fast access to its elements. The size of an Array is determined at the time of its creation and cannot be changed thereafter. Arrays are particularly useful for situations where the number of elements is known in advance and does not vary.

Here is an example of creating and manipulating an array in Smalltalk:

```
"Creating an array with specified elements"
| myArray |
myArray := #(10 20 30 40 50).

"Accessing elements by index"
Transcript show: (myArray at: 1). "Prints 10"

"Modifying array elements"
myArray at: 3 put: 100. "Replaces 30 with 100"

"Iterating over array elements"
myArray do: [:each |
    Transcript show: each; show: ' '.
].
```

The OrderedCollection, in contrast, is a mutable, dynamic collection that grows and shrinks as needed. This flexibility makes OrderedCollections particularly suitable for scenarios where the number of elements can change during the runtime of the program.

Here's an example of using an OrderedCollection:

```
"Creating an OrderedCollection"
| myOrderedCollection |
myOrderedCollection := OrderedCollection new.

"Adding elements"
myOrderedCollection add: 10.
myOrderedCollection add: 20.
myOrderedCollection add: 30.

"Accessing and modifying elements"
Transcript show: (myOrderedCollection at: 2). "Prints 20"
myOrderedCollection at: 2 put: 100. "Replaces 20 with 100"

"Removing elements"
myOrderedCollection remove: 10. "Removes the element 10"
```

```
"Iterating over OrderedCollection elements"
myOrderedCollection do: [:each |
    Transcript show: each; show: ' '.
].
```

An essential distinction between Array and OrderedCollection lies in their performance characteristics and use cases. Accessing elements by index is constant time, $O(1)$ in arrays, making them ideal for performance-critical applications with static datasets. Conversely, OrderedCollection operations such as adding, removing, or inserting elements generally operate in linear time, $O(n)$, due to potential reallocations or shifts of underlying data, which is a trade-off for their flexibility.

In practical applications, considerations for choosing between Array and OrderedCollection rely on factors such as:

- **Size Variability:** If the collection size is fixed and known beforehand, Array is more suitable. If the collection size needs to adjust dynamically, OrderedCollection is recommended.
- **Performance:** For situations demanding fast, constant-time access to elements, Array is preferable. On the other hand, for operations heavily involving additions or deletions, OrderedCollection's flexibility is beneficial.
- **Element Manipulation:** When frequent modifications of element positions are required, OrderedCollection offers more straightforward methods for adding or removing elements.

Considering the order-preservation attributes shared by both Array and OrderedCollection, they guarantee that the sequence of elements remains consistent as per their insertion order. However, this property should not be confounded with uniqueness constraints, which are absent in both collections. Thus, duplicate elements are permissible unless explicitly handled by the programmer.

To further understand the utility and integration of these collections within larger Smalltalk applications, consider a scenario where data is read from an external source, processed, and stored. The choice of collection type impacts the implementation efficiency and clarity:

```
| dataSource records processedData |

"Assume dataSource is an operation that reads data and returns an array"
dataSource := #(34 67 23 45 89 12 97 54).

"Processing data"
records := OrderedCollection new.
```

```
dataSource do: [:each |
    (each > 50) ifTrue: [records add: each].
].

"processedData now holds values greater than 50"
processedData := records asArray.

"Print processed data"
processedData do: [:each |
    Transcript show: each; show: ' '.
].
```

In this example, an OrderedCollection is used for intermediate storage, leveraging its dynamic nature during the data processing phase. Once the processing is complete, the resulting collection is converted to an Array for fixed-size efficient access subsequently.

Deciding between Array and OrderedCollection thus requires an understanding of the specific requirements and constraints of the application at hand, ensuring optimal performance and code maintainability.

6.6 Dictionaries and Sets

In Smalltalk, dictionaries and sets are fundamental collection types that enable efficient data retrieval and unique element storage. A Dictionary is a collection of associations between keys and values, allowing for fast lookups based on unique keys. A Set, on the other hand, is a collection that stores unique elements, ensuring no duplicates.

Dictionaries

A Dictionary in Smalltalk is an associative collection that maps unique keys to values. The keys within a dictionary must be unique, while values can be repeated. Dictionaries are ideal for use cases where key-based lookup is required, providing efficient and fast access to stored values.

To create a dictionary, use the Dictionary class. The example below illustrates how to instantiate a dictionary and perform basic operations such as adding, accessing, and removing key-value pairs.

```
| dict |
dict := Dictionary new.

"Adding key-value pairs"
dict at: #name put: 'John'.
dict at: #age put: 25.
dict at: #city put: 'New York'.
```

```
"Accessing values by keys"
dict at: #name. "Returns 'John'"
dict at: #age. "Returns 25"

"Removing a key-value pair"
dict removeKey: #city.

"Checking presence of a key"
dict includesKey: #name. "Returns true"
dict includesKey: #city. "Returns false"
```

In the code above, the Dictionary instance is created using Dictionary new. Key-value pairs are added using the at:put: method. To access values, the at: method is employed. Removal of key-value pairs is facilitated by the removeKey: method, and key presence is checked using the includesKey: method.

Dictionaries can also be created from a pre-existing collection of associations:

```
| assocDict |
assocDict := Dictionary newFrom: {#name -> 'Alice'. #age -> 30. #city -> 'San
    Francisco'}.
```

Here, the dictionary assocDict is created using the newFrom: method, taking an array of associations as input.

Sets

A Set in Smalltalk is a collection that ensures all elements are unique, without any duplicated values. Sets are useful when the uniqueness of elements is a required property. The Set class provides methods to add, remove, and check membership of elements.

To create a set and perform basic operations, use the following example:

```
| mySet |
mySet := Set new.

"Adding elements"
mySet add: 'apple'.
mySet add: 'banana'.
mySet add: 'apple'. "Duplicate, won't be added again"

"Removing an element"
mySet remove: 'banana'.

"Checking membership"
mySet includes: 'apple'. "Returns true"
mySet includes: 'banana'. "Returns false"
```

In this example, a Set instance is created with Set new. Elements are added to the set using the add: method. Duplicate elements are ignored, ensuring all elements remain unique. To remove an element, the remove: method is used. Membership checking is done via the includes: method.

Sets can also be created from a pre-existing collection:

```
| uniqueSet |
uniqueSet := Set withAll: #(10 20 30 10 40).
```

The resulting uniqueSet contains the elements 10, 20, 30, and 40, with the duplicate 10 retained only once.

Common Operations on Dictionaries and Sets

Both dictionaries and sets support various common operations, such as enumeration, size retrieval, and element conversion to arrays.

Enumeration over dictionaries can be performed using do:, keysDo:, and valuesDo: methods:

```
"Enumerating over keys and values in a dictionary"

dict keysAndValuesDo: [:key :value |
    Transcript show: key printString; show: ' -> '; show: value; cr].
```

For sets, enumeration is straightforward:

```
"Enumerating over elements in a set"
mySet do: [:element |
    Transcript show: element; cr].
```

The size method returns the number of elements in dictionaries and sets:

```
dict size. "Returns the number of key-value pairs"
mySet size. "Returns the number of unique elements"
```

To convert a dictionary or set to an array, the asArray method is used:

```
| dictArray setArray |
dictArray := dict asArray.
setArray := mySet asArray.
```

In practice, dictionaries and sets provide robust solutions for problem domains requiring unique element storage and fast key-based retrieval, enhancing flexibility and efficiency in Smalltalk programming.

6.7 Enumerating Collections

Enumerating collections in Smalltalk is a fundamental aspect of handling data structures effectively. Enumeration methods provide a means to traverse elements in a collection, perform operations on those elements, and sometimes accumulate results based on conditions. This section delves into the commonly used enumeration methods in Smalltalk, detailing their usage, syntax, and potential applications.

do:

The do: method is one of the most straightforward enumeration methods. It applies a block of code to each element in the collection.

```
| collection |
collection := #(1 2 3 4 5).
collection do: [:each | Transcript show: each printString; cr].
```

In this example, the block [:each | Transcript show: each printString; cr] is executed for each element in the array collection. This results in each number being printed to the Transcript, one per line.

collect:

The collect: method is used to apply a block to each element in a collection and collect the results into a new collection of the same type.

```
| collection result |
collection := #(1 2 3 4 5).
result := collection collect: [:each | each * 2].
Transcript show: result printString.
```

Here, each element in the original array collection is multiplied by 2, and the results are placed into the new array result. The output to the Transcript is:

```
#(2 4 6 8 10)
```

select: and reject:

The select: method filters elements based on a condition specified in the block. It returns a new collection with elements that match the condition. In contrast, reject: works oppositely, returning elements that do not match the condition.

```
| collection evenNumbers oddNumbers |
collection := #(1 2 3 4 5 6 7 8 9 10).
evenNumbers := collection select: [:each | each even].
oddNumbers := collection reject: [:each | each even].
```

```
Transcript show: 'Even: ', evenNumbers printString; cr.
Transcript show: 'Odd: ', oddNumbers printString; cr.
```

The select: method creates a new array evenNumbers containing the even numbers, while reject: creates oddNumbers with the odd numbers. The output to the Transcript is:

```
Even: #(2 4 6 8 10)
Odd: #(1 3 5 7 9)
```

detect: and detect:ifNone:

The detect: method returns the first element in a collection that matches a condition. If no elements meet the condition, detect:ifNone: can be used to specify an alternative action.

```
| collection match |
collection := #(1 2 3 4 5).
match := collection detect: [:each | each > 3].
Transcript show: 'Match: ', match printString; cr.
```

In this instance, detect: finds the first element in the array collection that is greater than 3. The output to the Transcript is:

```
Match: 4
```

If no matching element is found, detect:ifNone: can be used:

```
| collection match |
collection := #(1 2 3).
match := collection detect: [:each | each > 3] ifNone: [0].
Transcript show: 'Match: ', match printString; cr.
```

In this case, no element is greater than 3, so ifNone: returns 0. The output is:

```
Match: 0
```

inject:into:

The inject:into: method is used for accumulating a result by applying a block that takes two arguments; one for the current accumulation and one for the current element of the collection.

```
| collection sum |
collection := #(1 2 3 4 5).
sum := collection inject: 0 into: [:acc :each | acc + each].
Transcript show: 'Sum: ', sum printString; cr.
```

Here, inject: 0 into: [:acc :each | acc + each] starts the accumulation at 0 and adds each element from the collection to acc. The output to the Transcript is:

Sum: 15

Each of these enumeration methods provides a way to process collections concisely and expressively. They facilitate operations ranging from simple iterations to complex queries and transformations, enabling a functional programming approach that complements Smalltalk's object-oriented paradigm.

6.8 Common Collection Methods

In Smalltalk, collections are fundamental structures used to group objects. A variety of methods are available for interacting with these collections, enabling programmers to perform numerous operations such as adding, removing, iterating, and transforming elements.

Basic Collection Operations

The most basic operations on collections involve adding and accessing elements. Collections such as OrderedCollection and Array have specific methods for these operations.

To add elements to an OrderedCollection, use the add: method:

```
| orderedColl |
orderedColl := OrderedCollection new.
orderedColl add: 'element1'.
orderedColl add: 'element2'.
```

Accessing elements in a collection is typically done by their index with the at: method:

```
| array element |
array := #(1 2 3 4).
element := array at: 2.
"element now contains 2"
```

Indexes in Smalltalk collections are 1-based, meaning the first element's index is 1.

Conditional Filtering with select:

The select: method is used to filter collections based on a condition. This method iterates over the collection, applying a block closure to each element and collecting those elements for which the block returns true. For example:

```
| numbers evens |
numbers := #(1 2 3 4 5 6).
evens := numbers select: [:each | each even].
```

The evens collection will contain #(2 4 6).

Transforming Collections with collect:

collect: is used to transform each element in a collection, returning a new collection with the transformed elements. For example:

```
| numbers squares |
numbers := #(1 2 3 4).
squares := numbers collect: [:each | each squared].
```

Here, the squares collection will contain #(1 4 9 16).

Aggregating Elements with inject:into:

The inject:into: method is employed for aggregating elements of a collection into a single value. This method takes two arguments: an initial value and a binary block. The block takes two parameters at a time and accumulates the result. For instance, summing the elements of a collection can be done as follows:

```
| numbers total |
numbers := #(1 2 3 4).
total := numbers inject: 0 into: [:sum :each | sum + each].
```

The total will be 10.

Determining Collection Contents with includes:

To check if a collection contains a specific element, use includes::

```
| numbers containsFive |
numbers := #(1 2 3 4 5).
containsFive := numbers includes: 5.
```

containsFive will be true.

Removing Elements with remove:

To remove a specific element from a collection, use remove::

```
| numbers |
numbers := OrderedCollection with: 1 with: 2 with: 3.
numbers remove: 2.
```

The numbers collection will now contain #(1 3).

Additional Useful Methods

- detect:: Finds the first element matching a specified condition:

```
| numbers firstEven |
```

```
numbers := #(1 3 5 6 8).
firstEven := numbers detect: [:each | each even] ifNone: [nil].
```

- reject:: Selects elements not matching the condition

```
| numbers odds |
numbers := #(1 2 3 4 5).
odds := numbers reject: [:each | each even].
```

- do:: Performs an operation on each element

```
| numbers |
numbers := #(1 2 3 4).
numbers do: [:each | Transcript show: each; cr].
```

Understanding and mastering these methods allows for efficient manipulation of collections, thereby enhancing overall programming effectiveness in Smalltalk.

6.9 Block Closures in Control Structures

Block closures in Smalltalk are a powerful feature that allows for the encapsulation of code within blocks. These blocks can be passed as arguments, stored in variables, and utilized in various control structures, offering significant flexibility. They are akin to anonymous functions or lambdas in other programming languages.

Block closures are defined using square brackets [ ]. Inside the brackets, you write the sequence of statements that compose the block. A block can take arguments, which are declared using a colon followed by the pipe symbol :|. The scope of the block is limited to its context, providing a means to create concise and reusable chunks of code.

```
[ :arg1 :arg2 | arg1 + arg2 ] value: 3 value: 5.
```

This code snippet defines a block that takes two arguments arg1 and arg2, then returns their sum. The value: messages apply the block to the arguments 3 and 5, evaluating the block and returning 8.

In Smalltalk, block closures are extensively used in control structures, such as conditionals and loops. A notable example is the ifTrue:ifFalse: message, which can evaluate a block based on a Boolean condition.

```
(3 > 2) ifTrue: [ 'True block executed' ] ifFalse: [ 'False block executed' ].
```

The ifTrue:ifFalse: message sends the appropriate block based on the

Boolean expression $3 > 2$. Since the expression evaluates to true, the block ['True block executed'] is executed, and the output is as follows:

```
'True block executed'
```

Blocks also play a crucial role in loops and iterations. Consider the following example with whileTrue:.

```
| counter |
counter := 1.
[counter <= 10] whileTrue: [
    Transcript show: counter printString; cr.
    counter := counter + 1
].
```

In this code, the block [counter <= 10] provides the condition for the whileTrue: loop. The loop will continue executing the associated block until the condition is no longer true. The counter is incremented in each iteration, and its value is printed to the Transcript.

Using blocks with collections is another example where their power shines through. The do: method on collections accepts a block to execute for each element.

```
#(1 2 3 4 5) do: [ :each | Transcript show: (each * 2) printString; cr ].
```

Here, each element in the array #(1 2 3 4 5) is passed to the block as the variable each. The block multiplies each element by 2 and prints the result.

Furthermore, blocks can exhibit sophisticated behavior when employed in methods like collect: and select:. The collect: method transforms a collection by applying a block to each element, returning a new collection of the results.

```
| doubledArray |
doubledArray := #(1 2 3 4 5) collect: [ :each | each * 2 ].
Transcript show: doubledArray printString; cr.
```

In this instance, the collect: message produces a new array doubledArray containing the elements #(2 4 6 8 10), which is then printed.

Consider the usage of select:, which filters elements based on a condition.

```
| evenNumbers |
evenNumbers := #(1 2 3 4 5 6) select: [ :each | each even ].
Transcript show: evenNumbers printString; cr.
```

The block [:each | each even] filters the array, collecting only the even numbers. This results in the array #(2 4 6), which is subsequently displayed.

Blocks in control structures enable elegant and potent coding patterns in Smalltalk, making code more expressive and concise. Their flexible nature allows for nested blocks, higher-order functions, and custom control structures. When used judiciously, they enhance readability and maintainability, key facets in proficient Smalltalk programming.

6.10 Using Select, Collect, and Other Collection Methods

In Smalltalk, collections provide powerful and flexible ways to store, manipulate, and traverse data. The language provides several methods to perform operations on collections concisely and efficiently. In this section, we will delve into some of the most commonly used collection methods, particularly select:, collect:, and other useful methods that facilitate complex data manipulation tasks.

Select: and collect: are commonly used methods in Smalltalk which operate on collections using blocks. A block is a chunk of code that can be passed around and executed. This capability enriches Smalltalk with functional programming constructs that allow for expressive and powerful operations on collections.

```
exampleCollection := #(1 2 3 4 5 6 7 8 9 10).
```

To illustrate the usage of select:, let's assume we want to filter exampleCollection to include only even numbers. The select: method accepts a block that returns true for elements to be included in the resulting collection and false otherwise.

```
evenNumbers := exampleCollection select: [ :each | each \\ 2 = 0 ].
```

Executing the above code will result in the following collection:

anArray(2 4 6 8 10)

Here, the block [:each | each
2 = 0] evaluates whether each element in exampleCollection is even, thus filtering out the odd numbers.

The collect: method, on the other hand, transforms each element of the collection using the provided block. This method is useful for mapping operations where each element in the collection is modified in some way.

```
squaredNumbers := exampleCollection collect: [ :each | each * each ].
```

The resulting collection after execution will be:

```
anArray(1 4 9 16 25 36 49 64 81 100)
```

In this example, each number in exampleCollection is squared, and the new values are collected into squaredNumbers.

Moreover, Smalltalk collections offer a multitude of other methods such as detect:, reject:, do:, and collect: which allow for further operations:

- detect: finds the first element that satisfies the condition in the block.
- reject: performs the opposite of select:, excluding elements that meet the block's condition.
- do: executes the block for each element in the collection, useful for operations where the result is not accumulated into a collection.
- sort: sorts the collection based on the criteria defined in the block.

For instance:

```
firstEvenNumber := exampleCollection detect: [ :each | each \\ 2 = 0 ].
numbersNotSquared := exampleCollection reject: [ :each | each * each < 20 ].
exampleCollection do: [ :each | Transcript show: each printString; cr ].
sortedCollection := exampleCollection sort: [ :a :b | a < b ].
```

Executing these will yield the following results:

```
firstEvenNumber: 2
numbersNotSquared: anArray(1 2 3 4 5)
```

In the do: block, each element of exampleCollection is printed to the Transcript. The sort: method rearranges exampleCollection in ascending order since the block [:a :b | a < b] defines the sorting criteria.

Smalltalk's collection methods leverage blocks to provide a succinct and powerful way to perform complex data manipulations with minimal code. These methods not only make the code more readable but also enhance maintainability and expressiveness. Understanding their applications and utilizing them effectively are crucial for mastering Smalltalk programming.

6.11 Nested Collections and Multidimensional Arrays

Nested collections and multidimensional arrays are powerful tools in Smalltalk that provide developers with the flexibility to handle complex data structures. Understanding these concepts enables the efficient management of data that naturally fits into a hierarchical or multi-level format. This section delves into how nested collections and multidimensional arrays are implemented and manipulated in Smalltalk.

Nested Collections: In Smalltalk, collections can contain other collections, leading to nested structures. This is particularly useful when dealing with data that can be categorized into sub-groups. For example, a collection of collections can represent a matrix or a table where each sub-collection corresponds to a row.

Creating nested collections is straightforward. The outer collection can be an OrderedCollection, Array, or any other collection type, with its elements being other collections. Here is an example of creating a nested collection:

```
outerCollection := OrderedCollection new.
innerCollection1 := OrderedCollection with: 1 with: 2 with: 3.
innerCollection2 := OrderedCollection with: 4 with: 5 with: 6.
outerCollection add: innerCollection1.
outerCollection add: innerCollection2.
```

This creates an outerCollection containing two inner collections, innerCollection1 and innerCollection2. Accessing elements in nested collections requires successive use of the at: method:

```
firstRow := outerCollection at: 1. "Returns innerCollection1"
firstElement := (outerCollection at: 1) at: 1. "Returns 1"
```

Manipulating Nested Collections: Operations on nested collections involve iterating through each sub-collection. Consider the task of summing all elements in a nested collection. This can be achieved using do: to iterate through each sub-collection and then through each element within the sub-collections:

```
sum := 0.
outerCollection do: [ :innerCollection |
    innerCollection do: [ :element |
        sum := sum + element.
    ].
].
```

Multidimensional Arrays: When dealing with grids, tables, or matrices, multidimensional arrays offer a structured approach. In Smalltalk, multidimensional arrays can be represented as arrays of arrays. Creating a 2D array (matrix) involves initializing an array with sub-arrays:

```
rows := 3.
columns := 4.
matrix := Array new: rows.
1 to: rows do: [ :i |
    matrix at: i put: (Array new: columns).
].
(matrix at: 1) at: 1 put: 1. "Setting the element at row 1, column 1"
(matrix at: 2) at: 3 put: 5. "Setting the element at row 2, column 3"
```

Accessing elements in a multidimensional array follows a similar pattern:

```
element := (matrix at: 2) at: 3. "Retrieving the element at row 2, column 3"
```

Manipulating Multidimensional Arrays: Operations on multidimensional arrays can be executed using nested loops. For instance, to print all elements of a 2D array:

```
1 to: rows do: [ :i |
    1 to: columns do: [ :j |
        Transcript show: ((matrix at: i) at: j); space.
    ].
    Transcript cr.
].
```

Using built-in methods like collect: and select:, we can perform sophisticated transformations and filters on nested collections and multidimensional arrays. For example, doubling all elements in a matrix:

```
matrix collect: [ :row |
    row collect: [ :element |
        element * 2
    ]
].
```

This example demonstrates the use of collect: to apply a block to every element across the entire matrix, making transformations intuitive and concise.

Nested collections and multidimensional arrays empower developers to elegantly handle complex data structures in Smalltalk. Understanding these concepts and their manipulation opens up numerous possibilities for efficient data organization and processing.

Chapter 7

Advanced Collections and Streams

This chapter delves into advanced collection types and the use of streams in Smalltalk. It addresses sorted collections, identity dictionaries, and weak collections, along with techniques for creating custom collections. Readers will gain knowledge on working with streams, including file streams for reading and writing files, binary streams, and byte arrays. The chapter also covers filtering and transforming streams, processing large data sets, stream combinators, and performance considerations for collections and streams.

7.1 Understanding Advanced Collection Types

Advanced collection types in Smalltalk provide powerful mechanisms for managing and manipulating data. These collections go beyond the basic arrays and dictionaries, introducing sophisticated features for sorting, identity management, and memory efficiency. In this section, we explore the intricacies of three such advanced collections: SortedCollection, IdentityDictionary, and WeakCollection.

A SortedCollection maintains its elements in a specific order, determined by a sort block provided at the time of initialization. This collection ensures that any modifications, such as additions or removals, adhere to the defined sorting criteria.

```
"Example of creating a SortedCollection"
sortedCollection := SortedCollection sortBlock: [:a :b | a < b].
sortedCollection add: 3; add: 1; add: 2.
sortedCollection. "Results in: a SortedCollection(1 2 3)"
```

In this example, the SortedCollection is initialized with a sort block that defines an ascending order. As items are added, they are positioned according to this sort order.

An IdentityDictionary differs from a standard Dictionary in that it uses the identity of its keys, rather than their value, for comparisons. This unique behavior is particularly useful when keys are objects whose identity is more significant than their data.

```
"Example of creating an IdentityDictionary"
key1 := 'a' copy.
key2 := 'a' copy.

dict := IdentityDictionary new.
dict at: key1 put: 1.
dict at: key2 put: 2.

"Although key1 and key2 contain the same value,
they are distinct objects with different identities."
(dict at: key1) = 1. "Results in: true"
(dict at: key2) = 2. "Results in: true"
```

This example emphasizes the behavior of IdentityDictionary, where key1 and key2 are treated as distinct keys despite having identical content.

Weak collections, such as WeakArray, WeakDictionary, and WeakSet, facilitate efficient memory management by allowing the garbage collector to reclaim objects that are no longer referenced strongly elsewhere in the program. The use of weak references is crucial in scenarios like caching or maintaining listeners, where objects should not be kept alive solely due to their presence in a collection.

```
"Example of using a WeakDictionary"
object1 := Object new.
object2 := Object new.

weakDict := WeakDictionary new.
weakDict at: object1 put: 'aValue'.
weakDict at: object2 put: 'bValue'.

object1 := nil. "Dereferencing object1"
Smalltalk garbageCollect.

weakDict at: object1 ifAbsent: ['Object1 is gone']. "Results in: 'Object1 is gone'"
weakDict at: object2. "Continued to be 'bValue'"
```

In this illustration, after dereferencing object1 and invoking the garbage collector, the WeakDictionary no longer retains the key-value pair for object1, demonstrating the effective use of weak references.

Understanding the internal behavior of these advanced collections enhances the ability to choose suitable data structures that cater to specific programming requirements. Users may leverage sorting mechanisms, identity management, and memory-efficient storage to develop robust and efficient Smalltalk applications.

7.2 SortedCollections and IdentityDictionaries

To effectively harness the power of Smalltalk's advanced collections, it is essential to have a firm understanding of SortedCollections and IdentityDictionaries. These special types of collections offer unique functionalities that can enhance program efficiency and organization.

SortedCollections maintain elements in a specific order according to a sorting block or the natural order of elements, while **IdentityDictionaries** use the identity of objects (rather than their content) to compare keys. Mastery of these collections facilitates better handling of data with certain sorted order requirements and when dealing with object identity.

SortedCollection is a collection that maintains its elements in a sorted sequence. When an element is added, it is inserted in the correct order, rather than appended to the end. Sorting criteria are specified by a comparison block which returns true if the first argument is less than or equal to the second argument.

```
"Creating a simple SortedCollection"
sortedCollection := SortedCollection new.
sortedCollection add: 4; add: 2; add: 3; add: 1.
```

When executed, the sortedCollection will contain the elements in sorted order:

```
a SortedCollection(1 2 3 4)
```

To customize sorting behavior, a sorting block can be assigned:

```
"Creating a SortedCollection with a custom sorting block"
sortedCollection := SortedCollection sortBlock: [:a :b | a > b].
sortedCollection addAll: #(4 2 5 1 3).
```

Here, elements will be sorted in descending order, resulting in:

```
a SortedCollection(5 4 3 2 1)
```

For more complex data types such as objects, the sorting block can evaluate specific attributes. Consider a collection of dictionaries where sorting by a particular key is required:

```
"Sorting dictionaries by a specific key"
dictionaries := SortedCollection sortBlock: [:a :b | (a at: 'age') < (b at: 'age')].
dictionaries add: (Dictionary newFrom: {'name' -> 'Alice'. 'age' -> 30}).
dictionaries add: (Dictionary newFrom: {'name' -> 'Bob'. 'age' -> 25}).
dictionaries add: (Dictionary newFrom: {'name' -> 'Charlie'. 'age' -> 35}).
```

The result will be a sorted collection of dictionaries:

```
a SortedCollection(an IdentityDictionary('name'->'Bob' 'age'->25)
                   an IdentityDictionary('name'->'Alice' 'age'->30)
                   an IdentityDictionary('name'->'Charlie' 'age'->35))
```

IdentityDictionary is a specialized Dictionary that uses the identity of objects for key comparison. This means that keys are compared using the identity (==) operator rather than the equality (=) operator. This is useful when maintaining collections where unique objects, rather than their values, are pivotal.

```
"Creating an IdentityDictionary"
identityDict := IdentityDictionary new.
key1 := Object new.
key2 := Object new.
identityDict at: key1 put: 'Object 1'.
identityDict at: key2 put: 'Object 2'.
```

Here, key1 and key2 are different objects, so their identity ensures uniqueness in the IdentityDictionary regardless of potential value similarities. Using identity comparison is particularly useful in scenarios where object references are critical.

To illustrate further:

```
"Comparing IdentityDictionary with Dictionary"
regularDict := Dictionary new.
regularDict at: 'key' put: 'value'.
anotherDict := Dictionary new.
anotherDict at: 'key' put: 'another value'.

"With regular Dictionary, 'key' entries would overwrite each other. With
    IdentityDictionary, they are stored distinctly."
identityDict := IdentityDictionary new.
identityDict at: regularDict put: 'First entry'.
identityDict at: anotherDict put: 'Second entry'.
```

Accessing values from identityDict will show that both keys are treated as unique entries due to their object identity:

```
(identityDict at: regularDict) "will output 'First entry'"
(identityDict at: anotherDict) "will output 'Second entry'"
```

Understanding the nuances between Dictionary and IdentityDictionary and the appropriate use of SortedCollection for managing ordered data is vital. These advanced collections enable more complex data manipulation and storage, improving both the performance and reliability of Smalltalk programs.

7.3 Using WeakCollections for Garbage Collection

WeakCollections in Smalltalk offer a sophisticated method for managing memory by participating in garbage collection (GC). WeakCollections hold objects in a manner that allows them to be reclaimed by the garbage collector if they are no longer strongly referenced elsewhere. This is critical for optimizing memory usage and maintaining efficient application performance. There are various kinds of WeakCollections, such as WeakArray, WeakDictionary, and WeakSet, each serving unique purposes.

To understand the utility of WeakCollections, it's essential to recognize that objects within these collections will not prevent automatic garbage collection. When the garbage collector identifies that an object is only referenced by WeakCollections and no other strong reference exists, it will reclaim the object, thereby freeing the associated memory.

WeakCollections are particularly useful in caching mechanisms, where you might store objects that are expensive to compute or retrieve, but do not want to retain them in memory indefinitely. By holding such objects weakly, they can be discarded when memory resources are constrained, yet recalculated or re-retrieved when needed again.

Let's explore the practical aspects of using WeakCollections in Smalltalk with examples.

```
"Creating a WeakDictionary example"
| weakDict key1 key2 value1 value2 |
key1 := 'key1'.
key2 := 'key2'.
value1 := 'value1'.
value2 := 'value2'.

weakDict := WeakDictionary new.
weakDict at: key1 put: value1.
weakDict at: key2 put: value2.
```

In this example, a WeakDictionary is created and populated with two key-value pairs. If the keys or values referenced by key1, key2, value1, and value2 lose their strong references elsewhere in the application, they become candidates for garbage collection. The keys or values may eventually be removed from the WeakDictionary when the GC cycle executes.

To observe the behavior of WeakCollections, one can force a garbage collection and inspect the current state of the collection.

```
"Inspecting the state of WeakDictionary after garbage collection"
key1 := nil.
key2 := nil.
Smalltalk garbageCollect.
weakDict inspect.
```

In this scenario, setting key1 and key2 to nil removes the strong references to the keys. After invoking Smalltalk garbageCollect, the garbage collector may reclaim the memory used by the now-unreferenced keys and their corresponding values. After garbage collection, inspecting the WeakDictionary may reveal that it no longer holds the original key-value pairs.

WeakSets function similarly by holding elements weakly. The following example demonstrates usage with a WeakSet.

```
"Creating a WeakSet example"
| weakSet anObject |
weakSet := WeakSet new.
anObject := 'expensiveObject'.
weakSet add: anObject.

"Strong reference removal"
anObject := nil.
Smalltalk garbageCollect.
weakSet inspect.
```

Initially, the WeakSet contains an element anObject. When the strong reference to anObject is removed and the garbage collector is invoked, the WeakSet is eligible to discard the "expensiveObject" if it is not referenced elsewhere. Inspecting the WeakSet after garbage collection can reveal whether the included object has been reclaimed by the GC.

WeakCollections prove essential in scenarios where retaining obsolete objects indefinitely would be wasteful. For example, event listener lists or dependency managers often employ WeakSet to avoid memory leaks, ensuring listeners that are no longer in use do not persist unnecessarily.

When implementing WeakCollections, consider the balance between retaining necessary objects and allowing garbage collection to naturally reclaim memory. Ensure that objects critical to application functionality maintain strong references during their required lifecycle.

WeakReferences and their management form the bedrock on which WeakCollections operate. Understanding their underpinning concepts—weak references, strong references, garbage collection triggers, and resource constraints—empowers developers to harness WeakCollections for optimal memory management.

Integrating WeakCollections into a system entails comprehending the nuances of reference management and lifecycle of objects. Allocating objects to WeakCollections necessitates maintaining additional vigilance over strong references, ensuring vital objects remain accessible while non-essential objects are efficiently handled.

7.4 Custom Collections

The ability to define custom collections is a crucial skill for Smalltalk programmers who need collections tailored to specific requirements. This section explores the creation of custom collections, extending existing collection classes, and implementing collection-specific behavior in Smalltalk.

Defining a New Collection Class

To define a custom collection, create a subclass of an appropriate existing collection class. The choice of the superclass depends on the desired default behavior. For instance, you might use OrderedCollection if you need a collection that maintains the order of elements.

```
Object subclass: #MyCustomCollection
  instanceVariableNames: 'elements'
  classVariableNames: ''
  poolDictionaries: ''
  category: 'MyCollections'.
```

In this example, MyCustomCollection is a subclass of Object, with an instance variable elements to store the collection's elements.

Initializing the Collection

We define the initialize method to set up the instance variable upon creating an instance of MyCustomCollection:

```
MyCustomCollection>>initialize
  elements := OrderedCollection new.
```

Adding Elements

Custom collections should provide methods for adding elements. Here is an example method add: for adding a single element:

```
MyCustomCollection>>add: anElement
  elements add: anElement.
```

Accessing Elements

A method to access elements is necessary for iteration and testing. In this example, the at: method retrieves an element by its index:

```
MyCustomCollection>>at: anIndex
  ^elements at: anIndex.
```

Size of the Collection

Implementing a size method provides the number of elements in the custom collection:

```
MyCustomCollection>>size
  ^elements size.
```

Enumerating Elements

To enumerate over elements, Smalltalk collections typically implement the do: method. Here, do: takes a block as an argument and applies it to each element:

```
MyCustomCollection>>do: aBlock
  elements do: aBlock.
```

Removing Elements

A custom collection should also offer methods to remove elements. The remove: method removes a specified element:

```
MyCustomCollection>>remove: anElement
  elements remove: anElement ifAbsent: [self error: 'Element not found'].
```

Customizing Behavior

Custom collections may introduce unique behaviors. For illustration, consider implementing a uniqueAdd: method, which adds elements only if they are not already present:

```
MyCustomCollection>>uniqueAdd: anElement
  (elements includes: anElement) ifFalse: [self add: anElement].
```

Subclassing Existing Collections

Subclasses of existing collection classes can inherit most behaviors while overriding specific methods for customization. For instance, creating a custom dictionary that monitors access patterns might involve subclassing Dictionary and overriding the at: and at:put: methods.

Defining the subclass:

```
Dictionary subclass: #AccessMonitoringDictionary
  instanceVariableNames: 'accessCount'
  classVariableNames: ''
  poolDictionaries: ''
  category: 'MyCollections'.
```

Overriding initialize to set up tracking:

```
AccessMonitoringDictionary>>initialize
  super initialize.
  accessCount := 0.
```

Overriding at: to include access counting:

```
AccessMonitoringDictionary>>at: aKey
  accessCount := accessCount + 1.
  ^super at: aKey.
```

Testing Custom Collections

Effective testing ensures custom collections function as intended. Unit testing frameworks such as SUnit facilitate writing test cases for all custom behaviors. Example tests for MyCustomCollection:

```
MyCustomCollectionTest>>testAdd
  | collection |
  collection := MyCustomCollection new.
  collection add: 1.
  self assert: (collection size = 1).
  self assert: (collection at: 1 = 1).
```

Handling Special Cases

Handling special cases, such as adding nil or ensuring thread safety in concurrent environments, requires additional methods and careful design. Custom collections should document such considerations clearly to guide users in employing the collections correctly.

This comprehensive approach to creating custom collections in Smalltalk demonstrates the flexibility and power of Smalltalk's object model. Properly designed custom collections can significantly enhance the functionality and maintainability of Smalltalk applications.

7.5 Streams in Smalltalk

Streams in Smalltalk offer a robust and flexible means of sequentially accessing and processing collections of data elements. The core concept revolves around streams being abstractions for ordered sequences, where elements can be read from an input stream or written to an output stream. For clarity and precision, this section provides an in-depth exploration of Smalltalk streams, starting with fundamental operations and advancing to more intricate usage patterns.

A stream can be thought of as a position marker within a collection, providing a window through which elements are accessed. The pointer's movement, either forward or backward, determines the element accessed next. The most common types of streams include ReadStream, WriteStream, and ReadWriteStream.

Creating and Using Streams

To create a stream from a collection, Smalltalk provides several convenient methods. For example, you can create a read stream, a write stream, or a read-write stream from an array, a string, or any other collection type:

```
| readStream writeStream readWriteStream |

readStream := ReadStream on: #(1 2 3 4 5).
writeStream := WriteStream on: (String new: 100).
readWriteStream := ReadWriteStream on: 'Smalltalk'.
```

In this snippet: - The readStream is created to sequentially read from an array. - The writeStream is initialized to write to a newly created string. - The readWriteStream allows both reading from and writing to the string 'Smalltalk'.

Reading from Streams

Reading from a stream involves advancing the stream's position to fetch consecutive elements. The next message is commonly used to retrieve the next element in the stream:

```
| readStream element |

readStream := ReadStream on: #(10 20 30 40 50).
element := readStream next. "element is 10"
element := readStream next. "element is 20"
```

It is also possible to read multiple elements at once using next: which takes the number of elements to read as an argument:

```
| readStream elements |

readStream := ReadStream on: #(a b c d e f).
elements := readStream next: 3. "elements is #(a b c)"
```

To check the end of a stream, the atEnd message returns a boolean indicating whether the stream has reached its end:

```
| readStream |

readStream := ReadStream on: #(1 2).
[ readStream atEnd ] whileFalse: [
  Transcript show: readStream next; cr.
].
```

This loop continues to read and display elements of the stream until it reaches the end.

Writing to Streams

Writing elements to a stream is fundamentally similar to reading, but it appends elements to the end of the stream's associated collection. Smalltalk's WriteStream supports messages like nextPut:, allowing single element writes:

```
| writeStream |

writeStream := WriteStream on: (String new: 50).
writeStream nextPut: $S.
writeStream nextPut: $m.
writeStream contents. "returns 'Sm'"
```

To write multiple elements at once, the nextPutAll: message is used:

```
| writeStream |
writeStream := WriteStream on: (String new: 50).
writeStream nextPutAll: 'Stream'.
writeStream contents. "returns 'Stream'"
```

ReadWriteStream Operations

ReadWriteStream combines the functionalities of both reading and writing, allowing for more complex manipulations within the same stream instance. This duality is useful for scenarios requiring simultaneous read and write operations, such as modifying elements in-place:

```
| rwStream |

rwStream := ReadWriteStream on: (String new: 20).
rwStream nextPut: $A.
rwStream reset.
rwStream nextPutAll: 'BCD'.
rwStream contents. "returns 'BCD'"
```

The reset message repositions the stream at the beginning, enabling overwrite operations from the start of the collection.

Stream Positioning and Navigation

Stream positioning is crucial for efficient read/write operations. Smalltalk provides methods to handle stream navigation. The position message retrieves the current position, while position: sets it. The skip: message advances the position by a specified number of elements:

```
| rwStream |

rwStream := ReadWriteStream on: 'abcdefg'.
rwStream skip: 3.
rwStream next. "returns $d"
rwStream position: 1.
rwStream next. "returns $b"
```

Modifying the position dynamically allows for flexible stream manipulation and efficient element access.

Practical Stream Applications

Streams can process various data sources such as files, network connections, and user inputs. Streams facilitate the handling of large data sets and real-time data processing. Here's an example of reading data from a file stream:

```
| fileStream |

fileStream := FileStream readOnlyFileNamed: 'example.txt'.
[ fileStream atEnd ] whileFalse: [
  Transcript show: fileStream nextLine; cr.
].
fileStream close.
```

This code reads and displays each line from the file 'example.txt' until the end of the file is reached, finally closing the stream to release its resources.

Understanding streams in Smalltalk and applying them effectively requires a good grasp of their fundamental operations and available methods. Mastery of stream usage enables efficient manipulation and processing of sequential data elements, which is pivotal in numerous programming scenarios.

7.6 File Streams: Reading and Writing Files

The process of reading from and writing to files in Smalltalk is a pivotal part of many applications, particularly those involving data persistence or interaction with the operating system. File streams provide an interface for handling file input and output (I/O) operations efficiently. This section elucidates the mechanisms and best practices for utilizing file streams in Smalltalk.

FileStream is a class dedicated to handling file I/O. It inherits from PositionableStream, enabling bidirectional movement within a file, thus facilitating both sequential and random access.

Opening a File To begin reading from or writing to a file, we must first open a FileStream. A file stream can be opened in various modes: read, write, and read-write. Here's how to explicitly open a file for reading:

```
| fileStream |
fileStream := FileStream fileNamed: 'example.txt'.
fileStream isReadable ifTrue: [
  "File can be read"
] ifFalse: [
  "Handle the error"
].
```

Reading from a File Once opened, reading from a file is manageable via several methods tailored for different requirements: reading a single character, a specified number of characters, or the entire file content.

To read the entire content:

```
| fileStream content |
fileStream := FileStream fileNamed: 'example.txt'.
content := fileStream contents.
fileStream close.
```

For reading line-by-line to handle large files without loading the entire file into memory:

```
| fileStream line |
fileStream := FileStream fileNamed: 'example.txt'.
[fileStream atEnd] whileFalse: [
    line := fileStream nextLine.
    "Process each line"
].
fileStream close.
```

Writing to a File Writing to a file in Smalltalk entails opening a file stream in write mode. This can either create a new file or overwrite an existing one:

```
| fileStream |
fileStream := FileStream newFileNamed: 'output.txt'.
fileStream nextPutAll: 'This is a sample text'.
fileStream close.
```

To append to an existing file without overwriting, use FileStream newFileNamed:append::

```
| fileStream |
fileStream := FileStream newFileNamed: 'output.txt' append: true.
fileStream nextPutAll: 'Appending some more text'.
fileStream close.
```

Binary File Streams In scenarios requiring binary data handling, FileStream can be employed to read and write bytes directly instead of character data, which is essential when dealing with non-text files:

```
| fileStream buffer |
fileStream := FileStream fileNamed: 'image.bin'.
buffer := fileStream binary.
fileStream begining.
[fileStream atEnd] whileFalse: [
    buffer add: fileStream next.
].
fileStream close.
```

For writing binary data:

```
| fileStream buffer |
fileStream := FileStream newFileNamed: 'image_copy.bin'.
fileStream binary.
buffer := ByteArray with: 255 with: 0 with: 255.
fileStream nextPutAll: buffer.
fileStream close.
```

Error Handling Robust applications need to handle potential I/O errors (e.g., file not found, permission denied). Smalltalk supports exception handling constructs:

```
| fileStream |
[fileStream := FileStream fileNamed: 'nonexistent.txt'.
 fileStream contents.
```

```
fileStream close.] on: Error do: [:ex |
    Transcript show: 'An error occurred: ', ex messageText; cr.
].
```

Combining File Streams with Other Streams Sometimes, reading files directly into other kinds of streams is efficient. For example, transferring file content to a String stream:

```
| fileStream stringStream |
fileStream := FileStream fileNamed: 'example.txt'.
stringStream := String new writeStream.
fileStream contents do: [ :char |
    stringStream nextPut: char.
].
fileStream close.
```

Proficient manipulation of file streams in Smalltalk requires comprehension of both the underlying stream concepts and the specific methods available for FileStream operations. Employing these techniques ensures effective and efficient file handling in a variety of contexts.

7.7 Binary Streams and Byte Arrays

Binary streams and byte arrays play a crucial role in the efficient handling of raw binary data, enabling fine-grained manipulation and storage of byte-level information. This section will delve into their characteristics, usage, and best practices within the Smalltalk environment.

Binary Streams: Binary streams in Smalltalk are specialized streams designed to handle binary data. Unlike text streams that deal with character encoding and line endings, binary streams treat data as a continuous series of bytes. This distinction is essential when working with files or network protocols that require precise control over byte-level operations.

```
"Creating a binary read stream"
fileStream := FileStream fileNamed: 'example.dat' binary.
data := fileStream contents.
fileStream close.
```

In this example, FileStream is used to open 'example.dat' in binary mode. The contents message reads the entire file into memory as a byte array, and the close message ensures that the file is properly closed after reading.

Byte Arrays: Byte arrays (ByteArray) in Smalltalk are collections that store unsigned 8-bit bytes. They are particularly useful for low-level data manipulation. Byte arrays are efficient and provide a direct way to handle sequences of raw bytes, which is often required in binary data processing.

```
"Creating and initializing a ByteArray"
byteArray := ByteArray new: 10. "A ByteArray of length 10"
byteArray at: 1 put: 255. "Setting the first byte to 255"
```

Here, a new ByteArray of length 10 is created. The at:put: method is used to set the value of the first byte to 255. This operation is integral when encoding data into byte arrays for computational tasks or data transmission.

Reading and Writing Individual Bytes: One of the key operations with binary streams and byte arrays is the ability to read and write individual bytes. Both BinaryStream and ByteArray provide methods to facilitate this:

```
"Writing a byte to a binary stream"
fileStream := FileStream newFileNamed: 'output.dat' binary.
fileStream nextPut: 42. "Writing the byte 42"
fileStream close.

"Reading a byte from a binary stream"
fileStream := FileStream fileNamed: 'output.dat' binary.
byte := fileStream next. "Reading a single byte"
fileStream close.
```

The nextPut: method writes a single byte to the stream, while the next method retrieves a byte from the stream. Such byte-level control is crucial when dealing with protocol implementations or data encodings where exact byte values must be maintained.

Combining Byte Arrays and Binary Streams: Often, it is useful to combine the flexibility of byte arrays with the streaming capabilities of binary streams. This allows for efficient manipulation of binary data stored in memory before writing it to a file or transmitting it over a network.

```
"Writing a ByteArray to a binary stream"
byteArray := ByteArray withAll: #(65 66 67 68). "ByteArray containing ASCII values
    for 'ABCD'"
fileStream := FileStream newFileNamed: 'example.dat' binary.
fileStream nextPutAll: byteArray.
fileStream close.

"Reading data into a ByteArray from a binary stream"
fileStream := FileStream fileNamed: 'example.dat' binary.
byteArray := fileStream contents.
fileStream close.
```

Here, nextPutAll: writes the entire ByteArray to the binary file, while contents retrieves the data from the file into a ByteArray. These operations simplify the process of transferring data between memory and persistent storage.

Performance Considerations: Binary streams and byte arrays, due to their low-level nature, often provide performance advantages for specific operations. Use cases such as reading from or writing to large binary files, processing image data, and implementing communication protocols can benefit from their efficient handling of raw bytes.

When dealing with large data sets, it is efficient to read or write data in chunks rather than byte by byte:

```
"Efficiently reading a file in chunks"
fileStream := FileStream fileNamed: 'largefile.dat' binary.
[ fileStream atEnd ] whileFalse: [
    chunk := fileStream next: 1024. "Read next 1024 bytes"
    "Process the chunk"
].
fileStream close.
```

In this example, the file is read in chunks of 1024 bytes, thus minimizing the number of I/O operations and improving performance.

The meticulous handling of binary streams and byte arrays is essential in Smalltalk for tasks that require byte-level operations, such as file manipulation, data encoding, and network communication. Understanding and utilizing these constructs effectively can significantly enhance the performance and robustness of applications dealing with binary data.

7.8 Filtering and Transforming Streams

In Smalltalk, streams represent sequences of elements that can be traversed and possibly modified. The ability to filter and transform these streams is crucial for efficient data processing. This section covers the essential techniques for stream filtering and transformation, focusing on various methods available within Smalltalk to this end. The concepts taught here build upon the reader's understanding of basic stream operations discussed in previous sections.

Filtering streams involves selecting elements that match specific criteria. This typically results in a new stream containing only the elements that fulfill the provided condition. The select: method is used for filtering streams. This method takes a block that represents the filtering criterion, and the result is a new collection containing only the elements for which the block evaluates to true.

```
filteredStream := aStream select: [ :each | each > 0 ].
```

In this example, filteredStream will contain only the positive elements from aStream. The block [:each | each > 0] serves as the filtering criterion.

For cases where the elimination of certain elements from a stream is required, the reject: method performs the opposite operation of select:. It removes the elements that match the given condition.

```
rejectedStream := aStream reject: [ :each | each > 0 ].
```

Here, rejectedStream will contain only the non-positive elements of aStream.

Transformation, on the other hand, involves altering each element of a stream following a specific rule to produce a new stream. In Smalltalk, transformation is typically performed using the collect: method. This method applies a block to each element of the stream and collects the results into a new stream.

```
transformedStream := aStream collect: [ :each | each * 2 ].
```

In this case, transformedStream will contain elements that are twice the value of each corresponding element in aStream. The block [:each | each * 2] specifies the transformation rule.

Combining filtering and transformation operations on streams enables powerful data manipulation capabilities. For example, one might first filter a stream to select only certain elements and then transform those elements. Consider the following code snippet, which first filters for positive numbers and then doubles them.

```
filteredAndTransformedStream := (aStream select: [ :each | each > 0 ]) collect: [ :each |
    each * 2 ].
```

This operation leads to a new stream consisting of all positive elements from aStream, each multiplied by two.

Smalltalk supports more complex stream manipulations through the use of compositions of different transformations and filters. Filters and transformations are not limited to simple operations like those shown above. More sophisticated manipulations can achieve complex data-processing tasks. Consider a scenario where filtering is based on a composite condition:

```
filteredStream := aStream select: [ :each | (each > 0) & (each even) ].
```

This example filters aStream to retain only those elements that are both positive and even.

In certain situations, particularly when dealing with large data sets or streams, breaking down the filtering and transformation into smaller, manageable steps becomes important. One practical aspect is the use of stream combinators, which can chain multiple operations without creating intermediate collections unnecessarily. This reduces memory overhead and can improve performance.

To illustrate this, consider a stream transformation that first squares each element and then filters the results to include only those greater than a specific threshold:

```
squaredFilteredStream := aStream
    collect: [ :each | each * each ]
    thenSelect: [ :each | each > 100 ].
```

This pipeline approach ensures that operations are efficiently chained, optimizing both memory usage and execution speed.

Stream filtering, transformation, and combination operations play a vital role in Smalltalk programming, particularly when processing large or complex data sets. They enable developers to apply precise, systematic changes to data streams effectively and efficiently. Understanding and leveraging these techniques is crucial for mastering advanced data manipulation in Smalltalk.

7.9 Processing Large Data Sets with Streams

Processing large data sets efficiently is a fundamental requirement in modern computing. In Smalltalk, streams provide a powerful abstraction for handling large data sequences by enabling sequential processing. A stream allows reading from or writing to a data structure incrementally, which is especially useful for large data sets where loading the entire content into memory is impractical.

Streams in Smalltalk can be categorized into several types, such as ReadStream for input, WriteStream for output, and ReadWriteStream for both reading and writing. To illustrate, consider a file too large to load into memory. Using streams, we can process this file line-by-line or byte-by-byte without exceeding memory capacity.

To utilize streams effectively, understanding fundamental operations such as next, nextPut:, and atEnd is crucial. Below is a detailed example demonstrating how to open a file stream, read its contents line-by-line, process each line, and write output to another file using streams.

```
| inputStream outputStream inputFile outputFile line |
inputFile := 'largeInput.txt'.
outputFile := 'processedOutput.txt'.

"Open the input file for reading"
inputStream := FileStream readOnlyFileNamed: inputFile.
"Open the output file for writing"
outputStream := FileStream writeFileNamed: outputFile.

[inputStream atEnd] whileFalse: [
    "Read next line from input stream"
    line := inputStream nextLine.
    "Process the line (example: convert to uppercase)"
    line := line asUppercase.
    "Write the processed line to the output stream"
    outputStream nextPutAll: line; cr.
].

"Close the streams after processing"
inputStream close.
outputStream close.
```

In this example, the FileStream class is employed to handle both reading from and writing to files. The whileFalse: loop continues processing until the inputStream reaches the end of the file, indicated by atEnd. Each line read from the input file is converted to uppercase and then written to the output file.

Streams also enable complex data processing tasks such as filtering, transforming, and aggregating data. The combination of streams with collections can provide a powerful mechanism for handling large data sets. For instance, we can filter and transform elements on-the-fly during the reading process.

```
| inputStream outputStream inputFile outputFile line |
inputFile := 'largeInput.txt'.
outputFile := 'filteredOutput.txt'.

"Open the input file for reading"
inputStream := FileStream readOnlyFileNamed: inputFile.
"Open the output file for writing"
outputStream := FileStream writeFileNamed: outputFile.

[inputStream atEnd] whileFalse: [
    "Read next line from input stream"
    line := inputStream nextLine.
    "Filter lines that contain a specific word"
    (line includesSubString: 'Smalltalk') ifTrue: [
        "Write the filtered line to the output stream"
```

```
        outputStream nextPutAll: line; cr.
    ].
].

"Close the streams after processing"
inputStream close.
outputStream close.
```

Here, the program reads each line and filters those containing the substring *Smalltalk* before writing the filtered lines to the output file. This method efficiently processes potentially large input without consuming excessive memory.

To further illustrate the power of streams in processing extensive data, consider reading through a binary file and performing operations on binary data sequences. Smalltalk's BinaryStream enables this functionality:

```
| inputStream binaryData |
inputStream := FileStream oldFileNamed: 'largeBinaryInput.dat'.
inputStream binary.

"Process binary data in chunks"
[inputStream atEnd] whileFalse: [
    "Read next chunk of binary data"
    binaryData := inputStream next: 1024. "Read 1024 bytes"
    "Perform operations on binaryData"
    "Example: print size of data processed so far"
    Transcript show: 'Processed: ', binaryData size printString; cr.
].

"Close the binary input stream"
inputStream close.
```

In this example, binary data is read in chunks of 1024 bytes at a time, allowing operations to be performed on each data chunk sequentially. This is essential when dealing with very large binary files or streams, ensuring that memory usage remains manageable.

Leveraging streams for large data set processing is also about choosing the right type of stream and understanding their APIs. ReadStream and WriteStream help maintain the simplicity and efficiency of incremental data processing, making Smalltalk a robust choice for handling extensive datasets. By integrating streams with file operations, binary manipulations, and data filtering techniques, developers can create efficient and scalable systems capable of processing vast amounts of data.

Understanding and utilizing the full capabilities of streams are pivotal for effective large scale data management in Smalltalk. These techniques provide both theoretical insights and practical tools necessary for developing high-performance Smalltalk applications.

7.10 Stream Combinators and Operands

In the domain of Smalltalk programming, streams serve as powerful abstractions for handling sequences of data elements. Stream combinators significantly enhance the flexibility and functionality provided by streams. This section delves into the various combinators and operands available in Smalltalk for stream manipulation, ensuring that the reader comprehends their utility and implementation.

Stream combinators are higher-order functions that take one or more streams as input and yield a new stream. They enable complex operations on streams such as merging, splitting, or filtering in a concise and expressive manner. Understanding and utilizing these combinators can elevate the efficiency and readability of your code when working with streams.

Concatenation (#comma)

The concatenation operator #comma combines multiple streams into a single stream, processing elements sequentially from each input stream.

```
| stream1 stream2 concatenatedStream |
stream1 := #(1 2 3) readStream.
stream2 := #(4 5 6) readStream.
concatenatedStream := stream1 , stream2.
concatenatedStream contents. "Output: #(1 2 3 4 5 6)"
```

The #comma operator ensures that the elements from stream1 are followed by those from stream2, preserving the order of data.

Mapping over Streams

The collect: combinator applies a block to each element of the stream and produces a new stream of the transformed elements. This is analogous to the map function in many functional programming languages.

```
| stream mappedStream |
stream := #(1 2 3 4) readStream.
mappedStream := stream collect: [:each | each * 2].
mappedStream contents. "Output: #(2 4 6 8)"
```

The resultant mappedStream contains elements that are double the value of the original elements in stream.

Filtering Streams

The select: combinator filters elements of a stream based on a given condition. It constructs a new stream containing only those elements that satisfy the predicate.

```
| stream filteredStream |
stream := #(1 2 3 4 5 6) readStream.
filteredStream := stream select: [:each | each even].
filteredStream contents. "Output: #(2 4 6)"
```

The select: combinator has effectively filtered out all odd numbers, leaving only the even ones in filteredStream.

Reducing Streams

The inject:into: combinator reduces a stream to a single value by applying a binary block cumulatively to the elements of the stream, starting with an initial value.

```
| stream sum |
stream := #(1 2 3 4) readStream.
sum := stream inject: 0 into: [:acc :each | acc + each].
sum. "Output: 10"
```

The inject:into: combinator sums all elements within the stream, resulting in a sum of 10.

Zipping Streams

The with:collect: combinator merges two streams by applying a block to corresponding elements of both streams, creating a new stream from the results.

```
| stream1 stream2 zippedStream |
stream1 := #(1 2 3) readStream.
stream2 := #(4 5 6) readStream.
zippedStream := stream1 with: stream2 collect: [:a :b | a + b].
zippedStream contents. "Output: #(5 7 9)"
```

Here, the zippedStream contains elements which are the result of adding corresponding elements from stream1 and stream2.

Combining Streams with Conditionals

The inject:into:select:reject: combinator provides a mechanism to combine the suite of transformation, selection, and rejection in a single operation.

```
| stream transformedStream |
stream := #(1 2 3 4 5 6) readStream.
transformedStream := stream collect: [:each | each * 2] select: [:each | each < 10] reject:
      [:each | each = 4].
transformedStream contents. "Output: #(2 6 8)"
```

This example demonstrates constructing a transformedStream by first doubling the elements, then selecting elements less than 10, and finally rejecting those equal to 4.

Combining Multiple Streams

The zipWith: combinator is particularly powerful for combining multiple streams.

```
| stream1 stream2 zippedStream |
stream1 := #(1 2 3) readStream.
stream2 := #(4 5 6) readStream.
zippedStream := stream1 zipWith: stream2.
zippedStream contents. "Output: #((1 4) (2 5) (3 6))"
```

By leveraging zipWith:, each corresponding pair of elements from the input streams is zipped together into a tuple, resulting in zippedStream.

Effective use of these combinators and operands allows for concise and readable stream operations, enhancing the expressiveness and flexibility of stream manipulation within Smalltalk.

7.11 Collections and Streams Performance Considerations

Optimizing the performance of collections and streams in Smalltalk is crucial for ensuring efficient and responsive applications. Understanding the underlying mechanisms of how collections and streams operate can provide significant insights into potential bottlenecks and areas for performance improvement.

Collections Performance Analysis:

Collections such as OrderedCollection, Set, Dictionary, and their specialized counterparts (e.g., SortedCollection, IdentityDictionary) each have unique performance characteristics. The key metrics to evaluate are time complexity and memory usage for common operations like insertion, deletion, lookup, and iteration.

For instance:

- OrderedCollection: Efficient for ordered sequences with average-case time complexity of O(1) for appending elements at the end, but O(n) for inserting or deleting elements at arbitrary positions.
- Set: Optimized for membership testing with average-case time

complexity of O(1) for insertions, deletions, and lookups. However, its performance relies on effective hashing and minimal hash collisions.

- Dictionary: Similar to Set, but stores key-value pairs and provides average-case O(1) time complexity for insertions, deletions, and lookups.

- SortedCollection: Maintains elements in a sorted order with a guaranteed O(log n) time complexity for insertions and deletions due to the underlying binary search mechanism.

Understanding the typical usage patterns of your collections will help choose the most appropriate type. For example, use Set or Dictionary when membership testing is frequent, whereas OrderedCollection is more suitable for scenarios where element order is a priority and append operations are common.

Streams Performance Analysis:

Streams provide a powerful and flexible mechanism for handling sequences of data. File streams, binary streams, and byte arrays are some common types utilized in Smalltalk applications. Performance considerations for streams include I/O speed, buffering strategies, and handling large data volumes.

Key performance factors involve:

- Buffering: Utilizing buffers reduces the number of I/O operations by temporarily storing data in memory before writing to or reading from a file. Adjusting buffer sizes can significantly impact performance.

- Lazy Evaluation: Streams that lazily evaluate their data can defer computations until necessary, minimizing the overhead when accessing large datasets.

- Pipelining: Combining multiple streams operations into a pipeline can reduce overhead and optimize throughput. The use of Stream combinators enables efficient data transformations and filtering.

Consider an example using file streams to read a file:

```
| fileStream buffer |
fileStream := FileStream readOnlyFileNamed: 'largeFile.txt'.
```

```
buffer := ''.

[fileStream atEnd] whileFalse: [
    buffer := buffer, (fileStream next: 1000).
].
fileStream close.
```

In this example, reading data in chunks of 1000 characters optimizes performance by reducing the number of I/O operations. Closing the stream releases system resources promptly.

For binary streams:

```
| binaryStream buffer |
binaryStream := FileStream newFileNamed: 'output.bin'.
buffer := ByteArray new: 1024.

1 to: 1000 do: [:i |
    buffer at: i put: (Random new nextInt: 256).
].
binaryStream nextPutAll: buffer.
binaryStream close.
```

Efficiently handling byte arrays and ensuring the stream is closed after operations avoids unnecessary memory usage and potential memory leaks.

Handling Large Datasets:

Processing large datasets requires strategies to mitigate memory constraints and processing time. One effective approach is to use stream processing to handle data incrementally:

```
| inputStream outputStream buffer |
inputStream := FileStream readOnlyFileNamed: 'largeInput.txt'.
outputStream := FileStream newFileNamed: 'largeOutput.txt'.
buffer := ''.

[inputStream atEnd] whileFalse: [
    buffer := inputStream next: 1024.
    outputStream nextPutAll: buffer asUppercase.
].
inputStream close.
outputStream close.
```

In this example, reading and writing in chunks ensures that memory usage is kept within limits while transforming the data as it is processed.

Advanced Optimizations:

Advanced users can leverage profiling tools to identify performance bottlenecks in collection and stream operations. Tools such as MessageTally in Smalltalk help profile method execution times and can pinpoint areas where performance degrades:

```
MessageTally spyOn: [
    "Your code block here"
].
```

Analyzing the results and understanding the execution flow allows for targeted optimizations, such as replacing inefficient collection types or adjusting buffer sizes. Careful consideration of both algorithm complexity and resource usage will ultimately lead to more efficient Smalltalk programs.

Chapter 8

Graphics and User Interface Programming

This chapter provides an introduction to graphics and user interface programming in Smalltalk. It covers basic drawing operations, the use of graphics contexts, canvases, and drawing surfaces. Readers will learn about creating and handling windows, event handling, and user interaction. Additionally, the chapter explores building basic user interfaces with widgets and control elements, managing layouts, customizing UI components, and advanced graphics techniques like animation and transformations within various UI frameworks in Smalltalk.

8.1 Introduction to Graphics in Smalltalk

Graphics programming in Smalltalk involves creating visual elements that improve user interactions and interface intuitiveness. By utilizing Smalltalk's powerful graphics capabilities, developers can build sophisticated and highly interactive applications. This section explores the foundational concepts and tools available in Smalltalk for graphics programming, providing essential knowledge required for venturing into more complex graphical tasks.

Smalltalk's graphics system is built on a set of fundamental classes and methods, enabling developers to draw shapes, render text, and handle images with precision and ease. The core classes involve drawing operations, managing graphical contexts, and rendering onto various drawing surfaces.

To begin with, Smalltalk's graphics operations are typically conducted within a GraphicsContext. The GraphicsContext class is responsible for providing a common interface to perform all rendering operations. Here, we will introduce several key methods available in GraphicsContext and how these are used to execute basic drawing commands.

```
| gc |
gc := GraphicsContext new.
gc drawRectangle: (Rectangle origin: 10@10 extent: 50@50) fillColor: Color red.
```

The above code creates a new GraphicsContext instance, then draws a red rectangle positioned at coordinates (10, 10) with a width and height of 50 units each. This is a simple illustration of how graphical objects like rectangles can be drawn using Smalltalk.

Text rendering is another crucial aspect of graphics programming in Smalltalk. The GraphicsContext class provides robust support for text rendering with various fonts and styles.

```
| gc font |
gc := GraphicsContext new.
font := TextFont default.
gc drawString: 'Hello, Smalltalk!' at: 10@70 font: font color: Color blue.
```

This example demonstrates how to render text. By specifying the desired font and color, the drawString: method is used to display the text "Hello, Smalltalk!" at the coordinates (10, 70).

Images are integral to many graphical applications. Smalltalk's graphics system allows efficient handling and display of images. The Form class in Smalltalk is primarily used for image manipulation and rendering.

```
| gc image |
gc := GraphicsContext new.
image := Form fromFileNamed: 'example.png'.
gc drawImage: image at: 100@100.
```

In this code, an image is loaded from the filesystem and then drawn at coordinates (100, 100). The Form class makes it straightforward to incorporate images into your graphics context.

Understanding the GraphicsContext enables precise and efficient rendering tasks, forming the bedrock of graphics programming in Smalltalk. It also ensures a consistent approach to drawing and rendering, regardless of the specific graphical element being manipulated.

Graphics programming further extends into handling graphical surfaces or canvases. A canvas, represented by the Canvas class, provides an abstraction over the raw graphics context, allowing more structured and stateful drawing operations. For instance, a canvas can manage multiple layers or drawing buffers, making it easier to create complex graphical scenes.

```
| canvas |
canvas := Canvas new.
canvas setColor: Color green.
canvas drawEllipse: (Rectangle origin: 150@150 extent: 100@50).
```

Here, a new canvas instance is created, the color is set to green, and an ellipse is drawn within the specified rectangular bounds.

The architecture of Smalltalk's graphics system ensures that it is both flexible and powerful, accommodating a wide range of graphical needs from simple renderings to elaborate animations and visual effects. Advanced graphic operations build upon these core concepts, progressively introducing more sophisticated techniques as developers gain experience and skill. The interplay between different graphical objects, contexts, and surfaces forms the foundation for more elaborate graphical applications and user interfaces that will be explored in subsequent sections of this chapter.

Through understanding the basics of drawing operations, graphical contexts, and working with images, one can begin to harness the full potential of Smalltalk's graphics capabilities, setting the stage for creating dynamic and visually appealing applications.

8.2 Basic Drawing Operations

Basic drawing operations form the foundation of graphical applications in Smalltalk. These operations enable the creation of simple shapes, lines, and textual elements, which are integral to the development of more complex user interfaces and graphics. This section explores the core drawing functionalities available in the Smalltalk environment.

To perform drawing operations, one must interact with a GraphicsContext, which acts as an intermediary between the drawing commands and the actual rendering surface. The GraphicsContext provides a set of primitive operations for rendering lines, shapes, text, and images.

Drawing Lines

Lines are fundamental elements in computer graphics. To draw a line, you need to invoke the drawLineFrom:to: message on a GraphicsContext object.

```
| graphicsContext |
graphicsContext := Display getCanvas.
graphicsContext
    drawLineFrom: (0 at 0)
    to: (100 at 100).
```

In this example, graphicsContext represents the drawing context, and the drawLineFrom:to: method is employed to draw a line from coordinates (0,0) to (100,100).

Drawing Rectangles

Rectangles are another basic element used extensively in graphics and user interfaces. The GraphicsContext object has several methods for drawing rectangles, including fillRectangle: and drawRectangle:.

```
| graphicsContext |
graphicsContext := Display getCanvas.
graphicsContext
    fillRectangle: (0 at 0 extent: 50 at 50).
graphicsContext
    drawRectangle: (100 at 100 extent: 50 at 50).
```

Here, fillRectangle: is used to draw a filled-in rectangle with the upper-left corner at (0,0) and dimensions of 50 by 50 pixels. The drawRectangle: method outlines a rectangle without filling it.

Drawing Ellipses and Circles

Ellipses and circles can be drawn using the fillEllipse: and drawEllipse: methods on the GraphicsContext object. The method signatures are similar to those for rectangles.

```
| graphicsContext |
graphicsContext := Display getCanvas.
graphicsContext
    fillEllipse: (0 at 0 extent: 50 at 50).
graphicsContext
    drawEllipse: (100 at 100 extent: 50 at 50).
```

This code draws a filled ellipse at coordinates (0,0) with a width and height of 50 pixels, as well as an outlined ellipse at coordinates (100,100) with the same dimensions.

Drawing Text

Text rendering is crucial for displaying information within graphical interfaces. The GraphicsContext provides the drawString:at: method to draw text.

```
| graphicsContext |
graphicsContext := Display getCanvas.
graphicsContext
    drawString: 'Hello, Smalltalk!'
    at: (50 at 50).
```

In this example, the string 'Hello, Smalltalk!' is drawn at the coordinate (50,50).

Setting Colors

Colors enhance the visual appeal of drawings. One can set the pen and fill colors of the GraphicsContext before executing drawing commands. This is done via the penColor: and fillColor: messages.

```
| graphicsContext |
graphicsContext := Display getCanvas.
graphicsContext
    penColor: Color red.
graphicsContext
    fillColor: Color green.
graphicsContext
    fillRectangle: (10 at 10 extent: 80 at 40).
graphicsContext
    drawRectangle: (10 at 60 extent: 80 at 40).
```

In this snippet, the pen color is set to red and the fill color to green. A filled rectangle and an outlined rectangle are then drawn with these colors.

Combining Drawing Operations

Combining these operations can result in more complex graphics. By layering different shapes and text, intricate designs can be created.

```
| graphicsContext |
graphicsContext := Display getCanvas.
graphicsContext
```

```
    penColor: Color blue.
graphicsContext
    drawLineFrom: (20 at 20)
    to: (200 at 20).
graphicsContext
    fillColor: Color yellow.
graphicsContext
    fillRectangle: (50 at 50 extent: 100 at 100).
graphicsContext
    drawString: 'Complex graphic'
    at: (60 at 60).
graphicsContext
    penColor: Color purple.
graphicsContext
    drawEllipse: (150 at 150 extent: 80 at 80).
```

This code draws a blue line, a filled yellow rectangle, a text string, and a purple ellipse. By appropriately sequencing these commands, a composite graphic is produced.

Understanding and mastering these basic drawing operations is essential for anyone aiming to build graphical user interfaces and applications in Smalltalk. These primitives serve as the building blocks for more sophisticated graphical components and custom UI elements.

8.3 Understanding the Graphics Context

A fundamental concept in graphics and user interface programming is the GraphicsContext. This object encapsulates all the parameters that define how drawing operations should be performed. These parameters typically include color, line widths, font information, and transformations such as scaling and rotation. Understanding and manipulating the GraphicsContext is crucial for performing precise and efficient drawing operations within any graphics system, including Smalltalk.

In Smalltalk, a GraphicsContext manages the state information needed for drawing, which ensures that operations such as drawing shapes, text, and images are performed consistently. The GraphicsContext is often associated with a drawing surface or canvas, which provides the actual medium where the drawing occurs.

Properties of a Graphics Context

The GraphicsContext maintains several properties that influence the rendering of graphics primitives. These properties typically include:

- ForegroundColor - Defines the color used for drawing lines and text.

- BackgroundColor - Specifies the color used for filling shapes.
- LineWidth - Determines the thickness of drawn lines.
- Font - Provides the font information used when rendering text.
- Transform - Represents the current transformation matrix applied to all drawing operations.

By modifying these properties, developers can customize the appearance of their graphics output to achieve the desired visual effects.

Manipulating the Graphics Context

Consider an example where we change the ForegroundColor and LineWidth before drawing a line. The following Smalltalk code snippet demonstrates this modification:

```
| graphicsContext canvas |
canvas := Form extent: 100@100 depth: 32.
graphicsContext := canvas getCanvas.

"Set the foreground color to red"
graphicsContext foregroundColor: Color red.

"Set the line width to 5 pixels"
graphicsContext lineWidth: 5.

"Draw a line from point (10,10) to (90,90)"
graphicsContext displayLineFrom: 10@10 to: 90@90.
```

This example creates a new canvas with a size of 100 by 100 pixels and a color depth of 32 bits. It then obtains a GraphicsContext from the canvas. The ForegroundColor is set to red and the LineWidth to 5 pixels before drawing a diagonal line across the canvas.

The state contained within a GraphicsContext is cumulative, meaning that changes to the context remain in effect until they are explicitly modified again. This persistence allows for the easy implementation of complex drawing operations with consistent appearance settings.

Using Transformations

One of the powerful features of the GraphicsContext is the ability to apply transformations to all subsequent drawing operations. The transformation matrix can be manipulated to perform scaling, rotation, and translation operations, providing flexibility in rendering graphics.

For instance, to apply a rotation transformation before drawing a rectangle, one might use:

```
| graphicsContext canvas |
canvas := Form extent: 100@100 depth: 32.
graphicsContext := canvas getCanvas.

"Rotate the coordinate system by 45 degrees"
graphicsContext transformBy: (Matrix2x3 rotation: (Float pi / 4)).

"Draw a rectangle at the origin"
graphicsContext displayRectangle: (0@0 corner: 50@50).
```

In this example, the coordinate system of the GraphicsContext is rotated by 45 degrees (π/4 radians) before drawing a rectangle. As a result, the rectangle appears rotated in the output. This technique can be extended to include more complex transformations, such as scaling and skewing, providing extensive control over how graphics are rendered.

Clipping Regions

The GraphicsContext also supports the concept of clipping regions, which restricts drawing operations to a specified area. By setting a clipping region, you can ensure that all drawing is confined within a defined boundary, which is particularly useful for managing complex layouts and GUI elements.

To set a clipping region, the following code can be used:

```
| graphicsContext canvas clippingRegion |
canvas := Form extent: 100@100 depth: 32.
graphicsContext := canvas getCanvas.

"Define a rectangular clipping region"
clippingRegion := (Rectangle origin: 10@10 extent: 80@80).
graphicsContext clippingBox: clippingRegion.

"Draw a line that exceeds the clipping region"
graphicsContext displayLineFrom: 0@0 to: 100@100.
```

In this code snippet, a clipping region is defined as a rectangle starting at (10,10) and extending 80 pixels in both width and height. Any drawing operation outside this region will be clipped. Thus, when drawing a line that starts at (0,0) and extends to (100,100), only the portion within the clipping region is rendered.

By mastering the manipulation of the GraphicsContext, including adjustments to properties, application of transformations, and defining clipping regions, developers can greatly enhance their control over the visual representation of their graphical applications in Smalltalk.

8.4 Using Canvases and Drawing Surfaces

In Smalltalk, graphical operations are performed on canvases and drawing surfaces, critical components for rendering visual elements within user interfaces. A canvas serves as an abstraction for a drawing surface, providing a context on which various graphical entities can be drawn, such as lines, shapes, text, and images.

To effectively utilize canvases and drawing surfaces, one must understand how to create and manipulate these entities using Smalltalk's extensive graphical libraries. This section delves into creating canvases, managing their properties, and performing basic and advanced drawing operations on them.

Creating Canvases

Creating a canvas in Smalltalk typically involves obtaining a drawing context from a window or a component capable of rendering graphics. The code snippet below demonstrates how to create a canvas from a window:

```
| window canvas |
window := Window new.
window open.

canvas := window graphicsContext.
canvas fillColor: Color white.
canvas clear.
```

In this example, a new window is instantiated and opened, subsequently obtaining the graphicsContext from the window. The canvas is then set to a fill color of white, and the clear message is sent to clear any existing graphics, ensuring the canvas is ready for new drawing operations.

Drawing on Canvases

With the canvas prepared, various drawing operations can be performed. Drawing on a canvas generally involves specifying the color, style, and shape or text to be drawn. Below are fundamental operations for drawing lines, shapes, and text:

```
| canvas |
canvas := window graphicsContext.
canvas line: (10 @ 10) to: (100 @ 100).
```

```
canvas fillColor: Color red.
canvas fillRectangle: (20 @ 20) corner: (80 @ 80).

canvas textColor: Color blue.
canvas drawString: 'Hello, Smalltalk!' at: (30 @ 30).
```

In this code, the line:to: message draws a line from point (10,10) to point (100,100). To draw a filled rectangle, the fillColor and fillRectangle:corner: messages are used. Finally, drawing text involves setting the textColor and invoking the drawString:at: message with the desired text and position.

Advanced Drawing Techniques

Beyond basic drawing, Smalltalk provides more sophisticated operations, including transformations and layering. For instance, to perform rotation or scaling, one must manipulate the transformation matrix of the canvas:

```
| canvas |
canvas := window graphicsContext.
canvas translateBy: 50 @ 50.
canvas rotateByDegrees: 45.
canvas scaleBy: 2.
canvas fillRectangle: (0 @ 0) corner: (50 @ 50).
```

Here, translation, rotation, and scaling are applied sequentially to the canvas. The translateBy:, rotateByDegrees:, and scaleBy: messages adjust the canvas's transformation matrix. The drawn rectangle is thus translated, rotated, and scaled according to these transformations.

Handling Off-Screen Buffers

To optimize rendering and avoid flickering, off-screen buffers can be employed. An off-screen buffer is a secondary drawing surface where graphics are rendered before being transferred to the visible canvas. This technique allows complex rendering without directly affecting the display, enhancing performance and visual smoothness.

```
| buffer canvas window |
window := Window new.
window open.

buffer := window createOffScreenBuffer: window extent.
canvas := buffer graphicsContext.

canvas fillColor: Color white.
```

```
canvas clear.
canvas fillRectangle: (10 @ 10) corner: (100 @ 100).
window drawOn: canvas.
```

The createOffScreenBuffer: message creates an off-screen buffer of the same size as the window. Graphics operations are performed on the buffer's canvas, and the rendered content is then drawn onto the window using the drawOn: message.

By mastering canvases and drawing surfaces, one acquires the foundational skills for graphic and user interface programming in Smalltalk, enabling the creation of intricate and responsive visual designs within applications.

8.5 Creating and Handling Windows

Creating and handling windows in Smalltalk involves interfacing with the system's windowing capabilities to allow the user to interact with the graphical content. In this section, we will discuss the foundational steps required to create a window, manage its properties, and handle various window events.

To create and manage windows in Smalltalk, we utilize the framework provided by the system window manager. Typically, in most Smalltalk environments, this interoperation is facilitated using classes such as Window, Pane, and associated event handling mechanisms.

Creating a Basic Window

To create a basic window in Smalltalk, instantiate an object of the class Window. This requires setting initial properties like size, title, and position. Here is a simple example demonstrating how to create a window:

```
| myWindow |
myWindow := Window new.
myWindow extent: 600@400.
myWindow title: 'My First Window'.
myWindow open.
```

In the above code, we create a new window instance myWindow, set its size to 600x400 pixels using the extent: method, assign a title using the title: method, and finally, open the window with the open method.

Setting Window Properties

Beyond basic creation, a window's properties can be customized extensively. This includes adjusting its color, border, and other attributes.

```
myWindow backgroundColor: Color lightGray.
myWindow borderWidth: 2.
```

The above code snippet sets the background color of the window to light gray and the border width to 2 pixels.

Handling Window Events

Interactivity within windows is handled by managing events such as mouse clicks, key presses, and window resizing. These events are captured using event-handling methods.

```
myWindow when: #mouseClick do: [ :event |
  Transcript show: 'Mouse clicked at ', event position printString; cr.
].
```

In this example, we attach an event handler to the mouseClick event. When the mouse is clicked within the window, the event handler outputs the click position to the Transcript.

Managing Multiple Windows

Often applications require multiple windows to be managed simultaneously. This necessitates handling window focus, positioning, and ensuring windows do not interfere with each other's properties.

```
| window1 window2 |
window1 := Window new extent: 500@300; title: 'Window 1'; open.
window2 := Window new extent: 500@300; title: 'Window 2'; open.
window2 position: (window1 position + (520@0)).
```

In this code, we create two windows, window1 and window2, and position window2 so that it is horizontally offset 520 pixels from window1.

Closing and Disposing Windows

To properly manage resources, it is essential to close and dispose of windows when they are no longer needed. This can be accomplished by sending the close message to the window instance.

```
myWindow close.
```

This command closes myWindow, and should be part of cleanup operations within an application.

Advanced Window Interactions

Advanced interactions may include modal dialogs, nested windows, and custom drawing within a window's canvas.

Modal Dialogs

Modal dialogs are windows that require user interaction before returning control to the parent window.

```
| modalDialog |
modalDialog := DialogWindow new.
modalDialog title: 'This is a modal dialog'.
modalDialog openModal.
```

In the above example, a DialogWindow is created and opened modally, blocking interaction with other windows until closed.

Custom Drawing on Windows

Custom drawing requires access to the window's graphics context. This is typically achieved by overriding the paint method.

```
Window subclass: MyCustomWindow [
  MyCustomWindow>>paint: aGraphicsContext [
    super paint: aGraphicsContext.
    aGraphicsContext
      fillRectangle: (0@0 corner: self extent)
      color: Color blue.
  ]
].
```

In this custom window class MyCustomWindow, we override the paint: method to fill the window's rectangle with blue color.

Understanding the full breadth of window management will be pivotal in developing robust user interfaces. Developers must ensure that all windows behave predictably and engage seamlessly with user interactions. Enthusiastically embracing these methodologies allows for the creation of polished and professional-looking applications in Smalltalk.

8.6 Event Handling and User Interaction

Event handling in Smalltalk is a fundamental aspect of creating reactive and interactive graphical user interfaces (GUIs). Understanding how to handle user-generated events, such as mouse clicks, keyboard strokes, and window resize actions, is crucial for developing responsive applications. Smalltalk provides a robust event-handling model that enables developers to manage and respond to a variety of user interactions.

A typical GUI application listens for events, processes them appropriately, and updates the interface as needed. Events in Smalltalk are managed through the use of event listeners, handlers, and dispatch mechanisms. This section will delve into the intricacies of event handling and how user interactions are managed and processed in Smalltalk.

Event Loop

At the core of event handling in Smalltalk is the event loop. The event loop continuously checks for incoming events, processes them, and dispatches them to the appropriate handlers. The following pseudocode demonstrates a basic event loop:

```
eventLoop
  [ |event|
    [(event := self nextEvent) isNil] whileFalse: [
      self dispatchEvent: event.
    ].
  ].
```

The nextEvent method retrieves the next event from the event queue, and dispatchEvent: routes the event to the appropriate handler based on the event type.

Event Types

Smalltalk defines several types of events, each corresponding to different user actions. Common event types include:

- MouseClick: Generated when a mouse button is pressed.
- MouseMove: Generated when the mouse is moved.
- KeyPress: Generated when a key is pressed on the keyboard.
- WindowResize: Generated when the window is resized.

Each event type carries context-specific information. For instance, a MouseClick event includes the coordinates of the click, while a KeyPress event includes the pressed key.

Event Handlers

Event handlers are methods that respond to specific events. Handlers are usually registered for particular events, ensuring that only relevant parts of the application respond to user actions. Here's an example of registering a handler for a MouseClick event:

```
MyWindow>>initialize
  super initialize.
  self on: MouseClick do: [ :event | self handleMouseClick: event ].

MyWindow>>handleMouseClick: event
```

```
Transcript show: 'Mouse clicked at ', event position printString; cr.
```

In this example, the MyWindow class sets up an event handler during initialization. The handleMouseClick: method processes the event, showing the mouse click position in the Transcript.

User Interaction

Handling basic events such as mouse clicks or key presses often suffices for simple applications. However, more complex user interactions may require advanced handling techniques. These include drag-and-drop, multi-touch gestures, and custom event types.

Drag-and-Drop

Implementing drag-and-drop involves tracking the initiation, continuation, and completion of a drag action. This typically requires handling multiple events in sequence: the mouse press event to initiate the drag, mouse movement events to track the dragged object, and a mouse release event to complete the drop.

```
MyWindow>>initialize
  super initialize.
  self on: MouseDown do: [ :event | self startDrag: event ].
  self on: MouseMove do: [ :event | self continueDrag: event ].
  self on: MouseUp do: [ :event | self endDrag: event ].

MyWindow>>startDrag: event
  self isDragging: true.
  self dragStartPosition: event position.

MyWindow>>continueDrag: event
  self isDragging ifTrue: [
    self moveTo: event position.
  ].

MyWindow>>endDrag: event
  self isDragging: false.
  self finalizeDropAt: event position.
```

In this drag-and-drop example, the MyWindow class manages drag states (isDragging, dragStartPosition), updates object positions on MouseMove events, and finalizes the drop on a MouseUp event.

Multi-Touch Gestures

Handling multi-touch gestures involves processing touch events and recognizing gesture patterns. Each touch event includes information about the touch points and their movements. Gesture recognition can be achieved by tracking these points and analyzing their interactions.

```
MyMultiTouchWidget>>initialize
  super initialize.
```

```
  self on: TouchBegin do: [ :event | self handleTouchBegin: event ].
  self on: TouchMove do: [ :event | self handleTouchMove: event ].
  self on: TouchEnd do: [ :event | self handleTouchEnd: event ].

MyMultiTouchWidget>>handleTouchBegin: event
  self startGestureRecognition: event touches.

MyMultiTouchWidget>>handleTouchMove: event
  self updateGestureRecognition: event touches.

MyMultiTouchWidget>>handleTouchEnd: event
  self finalizeGestureRecognition: event touches.
```

This example involves a multi-touch widget that handles touch events. It initiates gesture recognition on touch begin, updates it on touch move, and finalizes it on touch end.

Custom Events

For applications with unique interaction requirements, custom events can be defined and handled similarly to standard events. Custom event types extend the event class hierarchy and carry specialized data.

```
Object subclass: CustomEvent [
  CustomEvent class>>type
    ^#customEvent.
].

MyWindow>>initialize
  super initialize.
  self on: CustomEvent do: [ :event | self handleCustomEvent: event ].

MyWindow>>handleCustomEvent: event
  Transcript show: 'Custom event triggered with data: ', event data printString; cr.
```

In this example, CustomEvent is defined as a new event type with a data attribute. The MyWindow class registers and handles this custom event.

Effectively managing event handling and user interaction in Smalltalk involves understanding the event loop, recognizing various event types, and implementing appropriate handlers. By properly registering and responding to events, developers can create responsive and interactive user interfaces that enhance the user experience.

8.7 Building Basic User Interfaces

To construct basic user interfaces in Smalltalk, we utilize several fundamental concepts and tools. A user interface generally comprises windows, widgets, layout managers, and event handlers. This section delves into creating elementary user interfaces by establishing a structured and clear approach to each of these components.

Begin by creating a main window that serves as the container for all UI elements. Smalltalk's Window class provides the essential functionality for window creation and management. Here's an example of creating a simple window:

```
| mainWindow |
mainWindow := Window new.
mainWindow label: 'Basic UI Window'.
mainWindow open.
```

The Window instance mainWindow is created and labeled with the title 'Basic UI Window'. The open message makes the window visible on the screen.

Next, introduce widgets such as buttons, labels, and text fields to the window. Smalltalk has a rich set of widgets available through its various UI frameworks. For instance, to create a button inside the main window, you can use:

```
| button |
button := Button new.
button label: 'Click Me'.
button action: [ Transcript show: 'Button clicked';cr ].
mainWindow add: button.
```

In this code, a Button instance is created and labeled 'Click Me'. The action: message assigns a block that writes 'Button clicked' to the Transcript when the button is clicked.

A label can be added similarly:

```
| label |
label := Label new.
label text: 'Welcome to Smalltalk UI'.
mainWindow add: label.
```

Here, a Label instance is created with the text 'Welcome to Smalltalk UI'. It is then added to the mainWindow.

For more complex user interfaces, use layout managers to organize widgets efficiently within the window. Smalltalk provides several layout managers like ColumnLayout, RowLayout, and GridLayout. For example, to use a column layout:

```
| layout |
layout := ColumnLayout new.
mainWindow layout: layout.
```

After setting the layout, add widgets to the window, and the layout manager will arrange them accordingly. Here is an enhanced version demonstrating this concept:

```
| mainWindow layout label button |
mainWindow := Window new.
mainWindow label: 'Layout Example'.

layout := ColumnLayout new.
mainWindow layout: layout.

label := Label new.
label text: 'This is a label'.

button := Button new.
button label: 'Click Me'.
button action: [ Transcript show: 'Button pressed';cr ].

mainWindow addAll: {label. button}.

mainWindow open.
```

In this example, ColumnLayout arranges the label and button vertically in the window.

Additionally, text fields allow users to input data and can be created and added to the window similarly:

```
| textField |
textField := TextField new.
textField contents: 'Type here'.
mainWindow add: textField.
```

The TextField instance is initialized with the text 'Type here' and added to mainWindow.

Understanding event handling is crucial for interactive UIs. Each widget can respond to events like clicks, key presses, or mouse movements. The Button example earlier demonstrates basic event handling with the action: method. Here's an example with a text field changing the label's text upon user input:

```
| mainWindow layout label textField button |
mainWindow := Window new.
mainWindow label: 'Event Handling Example'.

layout := ColumnLayout new.
mainWindow layout: layout.

label := Label new.
label text: 'Enter text and press button'.

textField := TextField new.
textField contents: 'Type here'.

button := Button new.
```

```
button label: 'Update Label'.
button action: [ label text: textField contents ].

mainWindow addAll: {label. textField. button}.

mainWindow open.
```

In this advanced example, clicking the button updates the label's text with the content of the text field. The action: block binds this behavior, illustrating the interactive capabilities of Smalltalk UI components effectively.

By employing these tools and techniques, build and refine fundamental user interfaces in Smalltalk, setting the foundation for more advanced UI development.

8.8 Widgets and Control Elements

Widgets and control elements, often referred to as GUI components, are integral parts of user interface design in Smalltalk. These elements include buttons, text fields, sliders, checkboxes, and other interactive components that allow users to interact with the software application. In this section, we will delve into the specifics of creating, configuring, and managing these elements within a Smalltalk environment.

VisualWorks and Squeak are two popular Smalltalk environments, each offering robust tools for UI development. We will cover both environments, focusing on the nuances that make each unique.

Button Creation and Configuration

Buttons are fundamental to any user interface, serving as triggers for actions or commands. In Smalltalk, buttons can be created and customized with various properties such as labels, colors, and event handlers.

```
| button |
button := PushButton new.
button label: 'Click Me'.
button color: Color red.
button onClick: [ Transcript show: 'Button clicked'; cr ].
button openInWorld.
```

This code snippet creates a button with the label "Click Me" and the color red. When the button is clicked, it prints "Button clicked" to the Transcript, which is a standard output window in the Smalltalk environment.

Text Fields and Input Handling

Text fields allow users to input textual data. They can be configured to respond to various events like focus changes and text modifications.

```
| textField |
textField := TextField new.
textField defaultContents: 'Enter text here'.
textField when: #textChanged do: [ :text | Transcript show: 'Text changed to: ', text;
    cr ].
textField openInWorld.
```

The above code initializes a text field with a default placeholder text and sets up an event handler to capture and print changes to the text field.

Checkboxes and Toggle States

Checkboxes are used for binary choices and can be toggled on or off. They are often used in forms and settings interfaces.

```
| checkbox |
checkbox := CheckBox new.
checkbox label: 'Enable Feature'.
checkbox when: #changed do: [ :checkbox | Transcript show: 'Checkbox state: ', (
    checkbox checked ifTrue: ['ON'] ifFalse: ['OFF']); cr ].
checkbox openInWorld.
```

This code snippet demonstrates the creation of a checkbox with a label "Enable Feature" and sets an event handler to display the checkbox state whenever it is toggled.

Sliders for Range Selection

Sliders allow users to select a value from a continuous range. They are useful for setting parameters like volume control or brightness.

```
| slider |
slider := Slider new.
slider min: 0.
slider max: 100.
slider value: 50.
slider when: #valueChanged do: [ :slider | Transcript show: 'Slider value: ', slider value
    printString; cr ].
slider openInWorld.
```

In this example, a slider is created with a range of values from 0 to 100 and an initial value set to 50. The event handler updates the Transcript with the current value whenever the slider is moved.

Combining Multiple Widgets

User interfaces typically consist of multiple interactive elements. Effective layout management is crucial for a seamless user experience.

We can organize buttons, text fields, checkboxes, and sliders within a single interface using layout containers.

```
| window panel button textField checkbox slider |
window := Window new.
panel := Panel new.

button := PushButton new.
button label: 'Submit'.
button onClick: [ Transcript show: 'Form submitted'; cr ].

textField := TextField new.
textField defaultContents: 'Name'.

checkbox := CheckBox new.
checkbox label: 'Subscribe to newsletter'.

slider := Slider new.
slider min: 1.
slider max: 10.
slider value: 5.

panel add: button.
panel add: textField.
panel add: checkbox.
panel add: slider.

window add: panel.
window open.
```

This script creates a simple form with a button, a text field, a checkbox, and a slider. The Panel element serves as a container for these components, and the Window element displays the assembled interface.

Understanding the properties and event-driven nature of widgets and control elements empowers developers to create sophisticated and user-friendly interfaces. Through customization and combination of these elements, one can build a rich interactive experience in Smalltalk applications.

8.9 Layout Management

Layout management is an essential aspect of user interface (UI) programming. It involves organizing visual components in the user interface to ensure an intuitive and efficient user experience. In Smalltalk, different layout strategies can be employed to control the positioning and sizing of graphical elements within a window or a container. This section will delve into various layout management techniques available in Smalltalk, detailing how to implement and customize them to suit specific interface requirements.

Layout Policies Smalltalk provides several layout policies that define how components are arranged within their parent containers. Some common layout policies include fixed or absolute layout, flow layout, grid layout, and proportional layouts. Each has unique characteristics and use cases.

FixedLayout involves specifying exact coordinates for each component. This policy grants complete control over the position and size but can lead to a non-responsive interface. It is useful in scenarios where the layout does not need to adapt to varying window sizes.

```
"Creating a window with fixed layout"
myWindow := (SystemWindow labelled: 'Fixed Layout Example').
myButton := (PluggableButtonMorph new label: 'Click Me').
myButton bounds: (0@0 extent: 100@30). "Set position and size"
myWindow addMorph: myButton.
myWindow openInWorld.
```

FlowLayout arranges components in a linear sequence, either horizontally or vertically. It is beneficial in creating forms or lists where elements follow a natural order.

```
"Creating a window with flow layout"
myWindow := (SystemWindow labelled: 'Flow Layout Example').
myWindow layoutPolicy: FlowLayout new.

"Adding components"
myWindow addMorph: (PluggableButtonMorph new label: 'Button 1').
myWindow addMorph: (PluggableButtonMorph new label: 'Button 2').
myWindow addMorph: (PluggableButtonMorph new label: 'Button 3').

myWindow openInWorld.
```

TableLayout (or GridLayout) organizes components in a tabular form. It allows for the precise alignment of elements in rows and columns, making it ideal for complex forms and data presentation grids.

```
"Creating a window with table layout"
myWindow := (SystemWindow labelled: 'Table Layout Example').
myTable := TableLayout new.
myWindow layoutPolicy: myTable.

"Setting up the grid structure"
myTable := myTable
    addRow: (Array with: PluggableButtonMorph with: PluggableButtonMorph with:
        PluggableButtonMorph);
    addRow: (Array with: PluggableButtonMorph with: PluggableButtonMorph with:
        PluggableButtonMorph);
    yourself.

myWindow openInWorld.
```

ProportionalLayout arranges components relative to the container's dimensions. This policy ensures that elements rescale adaptively with the window size, maintaining their relative proportions.

```
"Creating a window with proportional layout"
myWindow := (SystemWindow labelled: 'Proportional Layout Example').
proportionalLayout := ProportionalLayout new.
myWindow layoutPolicy: proportionalLayout.

"Adding and configuring components"
myButton := (PluggableButtonMorph new label: 'Resizable Button').
proportionalLayout add: myButton proportion: (0.1 @ 0.1 extent: 0.8 @ 0.8).

myWindow openInWorld.
```

Layout Containers Containers play an essential role in organizing complex interfaces. They serve as parent elements that hold child components, allowing them to be managed collectively.

AlignmentMorph and *BoxLayoutMorph* are examples of such containers. *AlignmentMorph* aligns its children according to specified alignment properties, while *BoxLayoutMorph* allows arranging children horizontally or vertically with configurable spacing.

```
"Using BoxLayoutMorph for vertical layout"
box := BoxLayoutMorph newDirection: #vertical.
box layoutInset: 10.
box horizontalGap: 5.

"Adding components"
(1 to: 3) do: [:i | box addMorph: (PluggableButtonMorph new label: 'Button ', i
    asString)].

box openInWorld.
```

Dynamic Layout Adjustments Adapting the layout dynamically in response to user actions is often necessary for creating a responsive UI. Smalltalk provides hooks and methods to handle layout changes, such as adjusting proportions or repositioning elements when the window is resized.

```
"Responding to window resize events"
myWindow := (SystemWindow labelled: 'Dynamic Layout Example').

"Configure layout policy"
proportionalLayout := ProportionalLayout new.
myWindow layoutPolicy: proportionalLayout.

"Adding resizable components"
myButton := (PluggableButtonMorph new label: 'Resizable Button').
proportionalLayout add: myButton proportion: (0.1 @ 0.1 extent: 0.8 @ 0.8).

myWindow on: #windowResized
    send: #adjustLayout
    to: myWindow.

myWindow openInWorld.
```

Adapting the layout in response to resizing ensures that the user interface remains usable across different display sizes. Properly managing layout is a crucial skill that enhances the usability and appearance of applications, ensuring a positive user interaction experience.

8.10 Customizing and Extending UI Components

Customizing and extending user interface (UI) components in Smalltalk allows developers to create more personalized and feature-rich applications. By leveraging the powerful object-oriented capabilities of Smalltalk, developers can modify existing UI components or create new ones that better fit their application's needs. This section delves into the techniques and best practices for customizing and extending UI components in the Smalltalk environment.

To begin with, let's consider a simple example where we customize a button widget. A button in Smalltalk is often an instance of a ButtonMorph. We can customize its appearance by modifying its properties such as label, color, and border.

```
| button |
button := ButtonMorph new.
button label: 'Click Me'.
button color: Color blue.
button borderWidth: 2.
button borderColor: Color black.
button openInWorld.
```

In this example, a new ButtonMorph is created and customized with a label, background color, border width, and border color. The openInWorld message is then sent to display the button in the main world.

Beyond simple property modifications, developers can extend the functionality of UI components by subclassing existing ones. For instance, we might want to create a specialized button that changes color when clicked. This can be achieved by subclassing ButtonMorph and overriding appropriate methods.

```
ButtonMorph subclass: #ColorChangingButton
    instanceVariableNames: 'defaultColor clickedColor'
    classVariableNames: ''
    poolDictionaries: ''
    category: 'Custom-UI'.
```

After defining our new ColorChangingButton class, we need to implement the necessary methods to handle the color change upon a click event.

```
ColorChangingButton >> initialize
    super initialize.
    defaultColor := Color white.
    clickedColor := Color green.
    self color: defaultColor.

ColorChangingButton >> mouseDown: anEvent
    self color: clickedColor.
    super mouseDown: anEvent.

ColorChangingButton >> mouseUp: anEvent
    self color: defaultColor.
    super mouseUp: anEvent.
```

In the initialize method, we set the default and clicked colors. By overriding the mouseDown: and mouseUp: methods, we can change the button's color when the mouse is pressed and revert it when released.

Customizing and extending UI components isn't limited to visual aspects. Developers can also override event handling methods to alter how a component responds to user interactions. For example, to create a custom text input field that only accepts numeric input, we can subclass TextMorph and override its keyboard event handling methods:

```
TextMorph subclass: #NumericTextField
    instanceVariableNames: ''
    classVariableNames: ''
    poolDictionaries: ''
    category: 'Custom-UI'.
```

We then provide an implementation that filters out non-numeric input:

```
NumericTextField >> keyStroke: anEvent
    | keyValue |
    keyValue := anEvent keyValue.
    (keyValue isDigit or: [keyValue = Character space]) ifFalse:
        [^ self].
    super keyStroke: anEvent.
```

Here, the keyStroke: method checks if the pressed key is a digit or space before allowing the event to propagate. This behavior ensures that only numeric characters are accepted by the text field.

In addition to subclassing and event handling, using Smalltalk's powerful metaprogramming capabilities can greatly enhance UI customization. For instance, dynamically adding methods to a class at runtime enables flexible UI behavior modification. Consider adding a method to an instance dynamically with the compile: message:

```
(MyCustomButton class) compile: 'dynamicMethod
```

```
^ ''This is a dynamically added method'''.

(MyCustomButton new) dynamicMethod.
```

In this code, we dynamically add a method named dynamicMethod to the MyCustomButton class. Calling dynamicMethod on an instance of the class will now execute the newly added method.

Finally, Smalltalk's reflective capabilities allow developers to inspect and modify the behavior of UI components at runtime. This inspection can be useful for debugging and optimizing custom components. For instance, the inspect method provides a window into an object's state:

```
button := ButtonMorph new.
button inspect.
```

By calling inspect on button, developers can view and manipulate its properties interactively.

By combining subclassing, method overriding, event handling customization, dynamic method addition, and runtime inspection, developers can create flexible and powerful user interfaces tailored to their application's requirements.

8.11 Advanced Graphics: Animation and Transformations

Animating graphics and applying transformations in Smalltalk provides a powerful way to enhance user interfaces and create dynamic visual effects. This section delves into the techniques and principles behind animation and transformations, utilizing Smalltalk's robust graphics frameworks.

Animation in Smalltalk typically involves changing some aspect of the graphical representation over time. This might include moving an object, changing its size, rotating it, or altering its color or other attributes. Transformations, on the other hand, refer to the mathematical manipulations such as scaling, rotating, translating, and skewing graphical elements.

Animating Objects: To animate objects, we rely on Smalltalk's ability to repeatedly alter an object's state and redraw it on the screen. This can be accomplished using the step method, which executes at regular intervals. Here is a simple example demonstrating how to move a rectangle across the screen using the Morph class.

```
| rect |
rect := Morph new.
rect width: 100; height: 50; color: Color red.
rect position: 20@20.
World addMorph: rect.

rect step := [
    rect position: rect position + (5 @ 0).
    World doOneCycleNow.
].
```

In this example, a red rectangle is created and positioned at coordinates (20,20). The step method increments the x-coordinate of the rectangle's position by 5 pixels each time it's called, making it look as though the rectangle is moving horizontally across the screen.

Using Timers for Controlled Animation: For more controlled animations, we can use timers to trigger redrawing at precise intervals. Smalltalk's Delay class provides a mechanism for this:

```
| rect timer |
rect := Morph new.
rect width: 100; height: 50; color: Color blue.
rect position: 20@20.
World addMorph: rect.

timer := [
    rect position: rect position + (3 @ 0).
    World doOneCycleNow.
    (Delay forMilliseconds: 50) wait.
] fork.
```

Here, a blue rectangle is created, and a Delay of 50 milliseconds is used to control the speed of the animation. The position update and screen refresh are repeated in a loop.

Understanding Transformations: Transformations in Smalltalk can be easily managed using affine transformations. The Transform class in the GraphicsTransforms package provides methods for creating and applying transformation matrices.

- **Translation:** Shifts an object by a given offset. - **Rotation:** Rotates an object by a specified angle. - **Scaling:** Changes the size of an object by given factors along the x and y axes.

For instance, to rotate a rectangle by 45 degrees, we can use:

```
| rect transform |
rect := Morph new.
rect width: 100; height: 50; color: Color green.
rect position: 200@200.
World addMorph: rect.
```

```
transform := Transform new.
transform rotateByDegrees: 45 around: (200@200).

rect transform: transform.
rect fullBounds: rect bounds transformedBy: transform.
rect changed.
```

This code snippet creates a green rectangle positioned at (200,200), which is then rotated by 45 degrees.

Combining Transformations with Animations: To achieve complex visual effects, transformations can be combined with animations. For example, animating the rotation of a rectangle:

```
| rect timer angle transform |
rect := Morph new.
rect width: 100; height: 50; color: Color yellow.
rect position: 300@300.
World addMorph: rect.

angle := 0.
timer := [
    angle := angle + 10.
    transform := Transform new.
    transform rotateByDegrees: angle around: (350@325).
    rect transform: transform.
    rect fullBounds: rect bounds transformedBy: transform.
    rect changed.
    (Delay forMilliseconds: 100) wait.
] fork.
```

Here, the rectangle's rotation angle is incremented by 10 degrees every 100 milliseconds, creating a continuous rotation effect.

Performance Considerations: When implementing animations and transformations, performance is a key consideration. Efficient redrawing, minimizing unnecessary computations, and optimizing graphical updates are crucial. The Caching technique can be used to store precomputed graphics states to reduce computational overhead.

Combining graphical and computational power, Smalltalk provides versatile capabilities for creating dynamic and visually appealing user interfaces. Leveraging animations and transformations not only enhances user experience but also opens up possibilities for innovative visual interactions.

8.12 User Interface Frameworks in Smalltalk

Smalltalk offers a variety of user interface (UI) frameworks that enable developers to create robust and interactive graphical user interfaces. Understanding these frameworks is essential for effectively developing applications that are both functional and user-friendly. The primary UI frameworks in Smalltalk are Morphic and MVC (Model-View-Controller). Each has its particular strengths and usage scenarios.

Morphic Framework

Morphic is a powerful and flexible UI framework that provides direct manipulation of graphical objects. It supports live interaction with on-screen elements, making it well-suited for highly interactive applications. Morphic's main components are morphs, which are graphical objects that can be manipulated directly by the user.

```
myMorph := Morph new.
myMorph color: Color red.
myMorph position: 100 @ 100.
myMorph openInWorld.
```

In the above example, a new morph is created, its color is set to red, and it is positioned at coordinates (100, 100). The openInWorld message makes the morph visible on the screen.

Morphic uses a hierarchical structure where complex UIs are built by composing simple morphs into larger ones. Each morph can contain other morphs as children, allowing for nested layouts.

```
morph1 (Parent Morph)
 |---- morph2 (Child Morph)
 |---- morph3 (Child Morph)
```

The main advantages of Morphic include its real-time interactivity and ease of constructing graphical objects. However, it can be overkill for applications that do not require complex interactions.

MVC Framework

MVC is a more structured and traditional approach to UI design. It divides the application into three interconnected components: Model, View, and Controller.

- Model: Encapsulates the application's data and business logic.
- View: Responsible for displaying the data to the user.
- Controller: Handles user input and updates the model accord-

ingly.

MVC promotes separation of concerns, making it easier to manage and test each component independently.

```
myModel := MyModel new.
myView := MyView new.
myController := MyController new.

myController model: myModel.
myController view: myView.

myView open.
```

In this example, instances of the model, view, and controller are created. The controller is then linked to the model and the view. Finally, the view is opened to the user.

MVC is advantageous for applications that benefit from clear separation between data handling and user interaction. It is also useful in scenarios where the user interface may need to be dynamically updated based on the underlying data.

Choosing Between Morphic and MVC

The choice between Morphic and MVC depends on the specific requirements of your application. Morphic is ideal for highly interactive, visually rich environments where direct manipulation is a primary feature. MVC is preferred for applications that require a clean separation between the application's data and user interface logic.

Additional UI Frameworks

Apart from Morphic and MVC, there are other UI frameworks in Smalltalk, such as Tweak. Tweak builds upon Morphic, offering an enhanced event-driven architecture and improved performance for building complex user interfaces.

```
tweakWindow := TweakWindow new.
tweakWindow title: 'My Tweak Window'.
tweakWindow open.
```

Using Tweak can be advantageous for applications that require more sophisticated event handling and higher performance.

Underlying all these frameworks is the Smalltalk philosophy of providing powerful tools and libraries to enhance developer productivity. Each framework builds on the core principles of object-oriented programming, enabling rich and dynamic user interface creation. Understanding the strengths and use-cases of these frameworks allows developers to select the most appropriate tool for their application's needs.

Chapter 9

Concurrency and Parallelism

This chapter addresses concurrency and parallelism in Smalltalk. It covers creating and managing processes and threads, using synchronization primitives such as semaphores and mutexes, and ensuring data safety with shared resources. Readers will learn about parallel processing patterns, asynchronous programming, process scheduling, and handling deadlocks and race conditions. The chapter also discusses concurrency in user interfaces and performance considerations for developing responsive and efficient concurrent applications.

9.1 Introduction to Concurrency and Parallelism

Concurrency and parallelism are critical paradigms in Smalltalk programming, especially when dealing with tasks that can be executed simultaneously. These paradigms enable a program to handle multiple tasks at once, improving efficiency and responsiveness. While the terms "concurrency" and "parallelism" are often used interchangeably, they refer to different concepts. Concurrency is about structuring a program so that it can handle multiple tasks at the same time conceptually. Parallelism, on the other hand, is about actual simultaneous execution on multiple processors or cores.

In Smalltalk, concurrency is achieved through the use of Process and Thread classes. These abstractions allow developers to manage tasks that can run independently of each other. Understanding how to create, manage, and synchronize these processes is crucial for building robust concurrent applications.

Processes in Smalltalk are lightweight and managed within the Smalltalk Virtual Machine (VM). Each Process has its own stack and state, but they share the same heap space, making it efficient in terms of memory usage. Processes in Smalltalk are cooperative, meaning they yield control explicitly, allowing for minimal overhead in context switching.

To create a process, you typically use the fork method on a block. The following example demonstrates how to create and start a new process:

```
| process1 |
process1 := [ "Task to be executed concurrently" ] fork.
```

This command creates a new process that runs the block's code concurrently with the main process. The process will run until the block completes execution or is explicitly terminated. It is important to manage processes carefully to avoid issues such as resource contention or deadlocks.

Threads in Smalltalk are similar to processes but are managed by the underlying operating system. They provide a more granular level of control over execution but come with increased complexity and overhead. Threads can be beneficial when interacting with native code or taking advantage of multi-core systems for parallel execution.

Concurrency introduces several challenges, such as ensuring that shared resources are accessed safely. For example, if multiple processes attempt to modify the same variable concurrently, it can lead to race conditions or inconsistent states. To handle this, Smalltalk provides synchronization primitives like semaphores and mutexes. These tools allow developers to control access to shared resources, preventing concurrent modifications from causing problems.

A semaphore is a signaling mechanism that controls access to a shared resource by multiple processes. In Smalltalk, you can create and use a semaphore as follows:

```
| semaphore sharedCounter |
semaphore := Semaphore new.
sharedCounter := 0.
```

```
Process fork: [
    100 timesRepeat: [
        semaphore wait.
        sharedCounter := sharedCounter + 1.
        semaphore signal.
    ]
].
Process fork: [
    100 timesRepeat: [
        semaphore wait.
        sharedCounter := sharedCounter + 1.
        semaphore signal.
    ]
].
```

In this example, two processes increment sharedCounter 100 times each while ensuring that only one process can access sharedCounter at a time. The wait method blocks a process until it can safely enter the critical section, and the signal method releases the semaphore.

Mutexes (mutual exclusion objects) are another synchronization primitive used to ensure that only one process accesses a critical section at any given time. In Smalltalk, the Mutex class provides this functionality. The following example demonstrates how to use a mutex for synchronizing access to a shared resource:

```
| mutex sharedCounter |
mutex := Mutex new.
sharedCounter := 0.

Process fork: [
    100 timesRepeat: [
        mutex critical: [ sharedCounter := sharedCounter + 1 ].
    ]
].
Process fork: [
    100 timesRepeat: [
        mutex critical: [ sharedCounter := sharedCounter + 1 ].
    ]
].
```

Here, the critical: method ensures that the code within the block is executed by only one process at a time, preventing race conditions.

Parallelism in Smalltalk can be more complex due to the global interpreter lock (GIL) in the Smalltalk VM, which can limit the ability to execute processes truly in parallel on multiple processors. However, workarounds and optimizations can be employed to maximize parallel execution, such as dividing tasks into smaller processes that run concurrently and balancing the load across available processors.

By mastering concurrency and parallelism in Smalltalk, developers can build efficient, responsive, and robust applications that handle multiple tasks simultaneously while ensuring data integrity and consistency.

9.2 Understanding Processes and Threads

Understanding the fundamental concepts of processes and threads is critical to mastering concurrency and parallelism in Smalltalk. In this section, we will delve into the definition of processes and threads, their lifecycle, and how they interact within a Smalltalk environment.

A process in Smalltalk represents an independent execution context, which includes its own stack, program counter, and local variables. Processes in Smalltalk are cooperative, meaning that they voluntarily yield control to allow other processes to run. This cooperation is managed through Processor, which schedules and manages these processes.

A thread, often used interchangeably with the term process in other programming languages, also represents a sequence of executable instructions. However, in Smalltalk, threads are more accurately referred to as lightweight processes. They share the same address space and resources but operate independently. Smalltalk's virtual machine manages these threads, ensuring efficient execution.

To illustrate the creation and management of processes in Smalltalk, consider the following simple example where we define two processes:

```
| process1 process2 |
process1 := [ 100 timesRepeat: [ Transcript show: 'A'; flush. (Delay forSeconds: 0.1)
    wait ] ] fork.
process2 := [ 100 timesRepeat: [ Transcript show: 'B'; flush. (Delay forSeconds: 0.1)
    wait ] ] fork.
```

In this example, process1 and process2 are created to repeatedly print the characters 'A' and 'B' respectively 100 times, pausing for 0.1 seconds between each print operation. The fork message is sent to each block, creating a new process.

Processes in Smalltalk belong to a class hierarchy and can be controlled and queried using various methods. For instance, to check the state of a process, we can use the isActive and isTerminated methods:

```
(process1 isActive) ifTrue: [ Transcript show: 'Process1 is active'; flush ].
(process2 isTerminated) ifTrue: [ Transcript show: 'Process2 has terminated'; flush ].
```

The lifecycle of a process involves several stages, from creation to termination. Important states in a process's lifecycle include:

- **New:** The process has been created but not yet started.
- **Running:** The process is actively executing instructions.
- **Blocked:** The process is waiting for some condition or resource before it can proceed.
- **Terminated:** The process has finished execution.

Processes can also be suspended or resumed at any time, allowing for fine-grained control over their execution. This is particularly useful in IO-bound or interactive applications where responsiveness is crucial. Consider the following example to suspend and resume a process:

```
process1 suspend.
"Some operations"
process1 resume.
```

It is essential to manage the suspension and resumption of processes carefully to avoid deadlocks and ensure smooth operation. The suspend message halts the process, and resume restarts it from where it was suspended.

Thread synchronisation is a critical aspect of concurrent programming. Smalltalk provides several constructs, such as Mutex and Semaphore, to facilitate the safe sharing of resources between processes. These constructs help avoid problems like race conditions, where multiple processes attempt to modify shared resources simultaneously.

Consider the following example of using a mutex to protect a shared resource:

```
| sharedResource mutex processA processB |

sharedResource := 0.
mutex := Mutex new.

processA := [ 100 timesRepeat: [
    mutex critical: [
        | temp |
        temp := sharedResource.
        temp := temp + 1.
        sharedResource := temp.
    ]
] ] fork.

processB := [ 100 timesRepeat: [
    mutex critical: [
        | temp |
        temp := sharedResource.
        temp := temp + 1.
        sharedResource := temp.
    ]
```

```
] ] fork.
```

In this example, processA and processB are both incrementing sharedResource. The mutex ensures that these increments are performed atomically, preventing race conditions.

Processes in Smalltalk can also communicate and synchronise using signals and events, which are covered in later sections. Proper understanding and management of processes and threads are foundational skills necessary for building robust concurrent applications.

9.3 Creating and Managing Processes

In Smalltalk, processes are fundamental objects used to manage concurrent execution. Smalltalk provides a simple yet powerful model for creating and managing processes, allowing developers to handle multiple tasks simultaneously, optimizing performance by efficiently using system resources.

A process in Smalltalk is an instance of the Process class. A process can be created using a block of code that specifies the computations to be executed. Let's start by creating a simple process.

```
| process |
process := [1000 timesRepeat: [Transcript show: 'Hello, world!'; cr]] fork.
```

In this example, the block [1000 timesRepeat: [Transcript show: 'Hello, world!'; cr]] represents the task to be executed by the process. The fork message is sent to the block to create and start the process. The process will print "Hello, world!" to the Transcript 1000 times. The fork method schedules the process to run concurrently with other processes in the system.

Managing the lifecycle of processes involves controlling their execution, including suspending, resuming, and terminating them. The suspend method is used to pause a process, and the resume method restarts a suspended process.

```
| process |
process := [1000 timesRepeat: [Transcript show: 'Hello, world!'; cr]] fork.
process suspend.
"Do some other work"
process resume.
```

In this code, the process is suspended immediately after it is started, allowing other operations to be performed before the process is resumed.

Terminating a process is accomplished using the terminate method. This method halts a process permanently and releases any resources it holds.

```
| process |
process := [1000 timesRepeat: [Transcript show: 'Hello, world!'; cr]] fork.
process terminate.
```

Creating processes without proper control can lead to high resource consumption and system instability. Proper management of process priority is essential for maintaining system responsiveness. Each process in Smalltalk has a priority, which determines the order in which processes are scheduled for execution. Process priorities can be set using the priority: method.

```
| process |
process := [1000 timesRepeat: [Transcript show: 'Hello, world!'; cr]] newProcess priority
    : 30.
process resume.
```

Here, the process is created with a specific priority (30). A higher number indicates a lower priority. Adjusting priorities allows critical processes to receive more CPU time than less important ones.

Process creation and management also encompass synchronization to ensure data safety when multiple processes access shared resources. Synchronization primitives such as semaphores and mutexes are instrumental in coordinating process activities to avoid conflicts.

"'latex"'

9.4 Algorithm: Process Creation and Management

Algorithm 5: Algorithm for Creating and Managing Processes

```
Data: Block of code to execute
Result: Managed process execution
Initialize a process with a given block of code;
while process not terminated do
    Execute process code;
    if process needs to be suspended then
        Suspend process;
    if process needs to be resumed then
        Resume process;
    if process needs to be terminated then
        Terminate process;
Set process priority if required;
Register process in system scheduler;
```

To further illustrate process control, consider the following practical example. A process could be used to perform computation-intensive tasks while ensuring that the main user interface remains responsive.

```
| computationProcess result |
computationProcess := [
    | temp |
    temp := 0.
    1 to: 100000 do: [:i | temp := temp + (i * i)].
    result := temp.
    Transcript show: 'Computation finished. Result: ', result printString; cr.
] forkAt: Processor userBackgroundPriority.
```

In this scenario, forkAt: Processor userBackgroundPriority ensures the computation process runs at a lower priority, preserving system responsiveness. This technique is particularly useful in user interfaces where long-running operations must not interrupt user interactions. Background processes can run computations while the main threads continue to handle UI events.

Efficiently managing processes involves recognizing when processes can be suspended or terminated, adjusting priorities based on the workload, and ensuring data consistency through synchronization mechanisms. Careful consideration of these factors ensures optimal application performance and system stability without overloading system resources or causing deadlocks.

9.5 Synchronization Primitives: Semaphores and Mutexes

In a concurrent programming environment, controlling access to shared resources is critical to ensuring data integrity and consistency. Synchronization primitives, such as semaphores and mutexes, provide essential mechanisms to manage resource access and prevent race conditions. This section delves into their utilization within Smalltalk, elucidating their implementation and functionalities.

Semaphores

A semaphore is a synchronization primitive that uses counter values to control access to shared resources. It can be thought of as a signaling mechanism where processes can increase (signal) or decrease (wait) the semaphore value. There are primarily two types of semaphores:

- **Binary Semaphore:** Operates like a mutex, where the counter is either 0 or 1. Binary semaphores ensure mutual exclusion as only one process can access the shared resource at a time.
- **Counting Semaphore:** Uses a wider range of integer values allowing multiple processes limited access to the shared resource based on the semaphore count.

In Smalltalk, semaphores can be easily created and manipulated. The following code snippet demonstrates initializing a semaphore and using it to synchronize access to a critical section:

```
"Creating a semaphore with initial count 1 (binary semaphore)"
semaphore := Semaphore forMutualExclusion.

"Acquiring the semaphore (wait operation)"
semaphore wait.

"Critical section begins"
"Access shared resource here"

"Releasing the semaphore (signal operation)"
semaphore signal.
"Critical section ends"
```

In the above snippet, Semaphore forMutualExclusion initializes a binary semaphore, ensuring that only one process can execute the critical section at any time. The wait message in Smalltalk corresponds to the P operation (or Proberen in Dutch) in semaphore terminology, which decrements the semaphore count. If the count is zero, the process is blocked until another process signals the semaphore. The signal message corresponds to the V operation (or Verhogen in Dutch), incrementing the semaphore count and unblocking waiting processes if any.

To leverage counting semaphores, one can define the initial count to be greater than one, allowing multiple processes to enter the critical section concurrently, as per the count:

```
"Creating a counting semaphore with initial count 3"
semaphore := Semaphore new count: 3.

"Acquiring the semaphore (wait operation)"
semaphore wait.

"Access shared resource here"

"Releasing the semaphore (signal operation)"
semaphore signal.
```

In this context, up to three processes can simultaneously access the shared resource.

Mutexes

Mutexes (Mutual Exclusion) are spinlocks that serve to prevent more than one process from executing a critical section simultaneously. Like binary semaphores, mutexes offer exclusive locks but also provide additional capabilities such as deadlock avoidance and ownership semantics.

Smalltalk allows for straightforward mutex implementation using Mutex objects. A mutex ensures that a single thread can execute the critical section by providing critical: methods, which encapsulates the synchronized code block.

```
"Creating a mutex"
mutex := Mutex new.

"Synchronized block"
mutex critical: [
    "Critical section begins"
    "Access shared resource here"
    "Critical section ends"
].
```

The critical: method only permits one thread to execute the enclosed block at any given time, automatically acquiring the mutex before executing the block and releasing it afterward.

Consider a scenario where two or more processes must concurrently access multiple shared resources. Without careful handling, this can lead to deadlocks. Using mutexes with proper ordering and timeout mechanisms can help mitigate such risks:

```
"Creating mutexes for two resources"
mutexA := Mutex new.
mutexB := Mutex new.
"Process one accessing resources"
mutexA critical: [
    mutexB critical: [
        "Access shared resources A and B"
    ]
].

"Process two accessing resources in the same order"
mutexA critical: [
    mutexB critical: [
        "Access shared resources A and B"
    ]
].
```

Both processes acquire the mutexes in a consistent order, preventing circular wait conditions and reducing the possibility of deadlocks.

When combining semaphores and mutexes, developers can achieve fine-grained control over concurrency, ensuring optimal resource utilization and data integrity. Properly designed synchronization mechanisms enabled by semaphores and mutexes play a crucial role in robust concurrent applications.

9.6 Shared Resources and Data Safety

In concurrent and parallel programming within Smalltalk, safely managing access to shared resources is crucial to maintaining data integrity and system stability. When multiple threads or processes access shared data simultaneously, it can result in inconsistent or incorrect data unless proper synchronization is enforced.

A shared resource can be any entity—such as a variable, an object, or a file—that multiple processes or threads may attempt to access concurrently. To prevent conflicts and ensure data consistency, several techniques and synchronization mechanisms are available.

Understanding Shared Resources In a concurrent environment, a shared resource is an entity accessed by multiple processes or threads simultaneously. A common example is a global variable:

```
SharedCounter := 0.
```

If two processes increment SharedCounter concurrently without synchronization, the final value may not be correct. Ideally, each increment operation should safely lock the resource, perform the update, and then release the lock.

Critical Sections and Race Conditions A critical section is a part of the code that accesses a shared resource and must not be concurrently executed by more than one thread:

```
"Increment the shared counter"
SharedCounter := SharedCounter + 1.
```

If two threads execute this critical section concurrently, a race condition can occur, leading to incorrect results. Race conditions arise when the system's outcome depends on the relative timing of events, causing unpredictable behavior.

Locks and Mutexes Mutexes (mutual exclusions) are synchronization primitives designed to enforce exclusive access to shared resources. A mutex is either locked or unlocked, and only one thread can hold the lock at any point in time:

```
"Create a mutex"
counterMutex := Mutex new.

"Protect the critical section with the mutex"
counterMutex critical: [
    SharedCounter := SharedCounter + 1.
].
```

In this example, the critical: block ensures that only one thread can execute the enclosed statements at a time, thus preventing race conditions.

Semaphores Semaphores are another powerful synchronization primitive. A semaphore typically signals the availability or unavailability of resources and can manage multiple simultaneous accesses depending on its initial count:

```
"Create a semaphore with an initial count of 1 (binary semaphore)"
semaphore := Semaphore forMutualExclusion.

"Wait for the semaphore before accessing the shared resource"
semaphore wait.
SharedCounter := SharedCounter + 1.
semaphore signal.
```

Binary semaphores (count = 1) function similarly to mutexes, where they ensure mutually exclusive access. Counting semaphores can control access to a finite number of resources.

Reentrancy and Deadlocks A lock is reentrant if the same thread can re-acquire it without causing a deadlock. Deadlocks occur when two or more threads are waiting indefinitely for resources held by each other:

```
"A reentrant lock allows the same thread to lock it multiple times"
reentrantLock := ReentrantLock new.

"A sample deadlock scenario"
process1 := [
    lock1 := Mutex new.
    lock2 := Mutex new.

    thread1 := [
        lock1 critical: [
            lock2 critical: [
                "Critical section"
            ].
        ].
    ].

    thread2 := [
        lock2 critical: [
            lock1 critical: [
                "Critical section"
            ].
        ].
    ].

    [ thread1 fork. thread2 fork. ].
].
```

In the given example, thread1 locks lock1 and waits for lock2, while thread2 locks lock2 and waits for lock1, leading to a deadlock.

Avoiding Deadlocks Several strategies can help to avoid deadlocks:

- **Resource Ordering:** Always acquire locks in a consistent order.
- **Timeouts:** Implement timeouts for lock acquisition attempts.
- **Deadlock Detection:** Frequently check for cycles in resource allocation graphs.

For example:

```
"Avoid deadlocks by acquiring locks in a consistent order"
thread1 := [
    lock1 critical: [
        lock2 critical: [
            "Critical section"
        ].
    ].
```

```
].

thread2 := [
    lock1 critical: [
        lock2 critical: [
            "Critical section"
        ].
    ].
].
```

Thread Safety with Atomic Operations An atomic operation completes without interruption, preventing other threads from seeing the operation in an incomplete state. Some Smalltalk environments provide atomic operations for basic types such as integers and booleans, enhancing thread safety without explicit locks.

```
"Atomic increment operation example"
AtomicCounter := 0.
AtomicCounter atomicIncrement.
```

Atomic operations are hardware-supported and usually more efficient than lock-based synchronization for specific tasks.

High-Level Synchronization Constructs High-level synchronization constructs, such as monitors and condition variables, provide more abstract mechanisms for synchronizing thread activities. Monitors encapsulate shared resources, enforcing mutual exclusion and condition synchronization:

```
"A simple monitor implementation"
Monitor := SharedResourceMonitor new.

Monitor critical: [
    "Access shared resource"
].
```

Condition variables allow threads to wait for certain conditions to be met before proceeding, enabling more complex synchronization patterns such as producer-consumer scenarios.

```
"Condition variable in a producer-consumer scenario"
Buffer := SharedBuffer new.

Producer := [
    Buffer write: data.
    Buffer notEmpty signal.
].

Consumer := [
    Buffer notEmpty wait.
    data := Buffer read.
].
```

Each synchronization construct addresses specific concurrency challenges, allowing developers to choose the most suitable approach for a given problem. Proper use of these primitives ensures that shared resources remain consistent and application behavior is predictable, even in highly concurrent environments.

9.7 Using Signals and Events

Signals and events play a crucial role in managing inter-process communication and coordination, especially in concurrent applications. In Smalltalk, signals and events enable processes to communicate asynchronously, triggering actions or responses when certain conditions or states are met. This section delves into the implementation and usage of signals and events within the Smalltalk programming environment, providing detailed examples and best practices to ensure reliable and efficient code.

In Smalltalk, an event can be thought of as a condition that can be awaited by one or more processes. A typical mechanism for handling events is the Semaphore, which we have already touched upon. Semaphores can be used to signal and wait for conditions. The following example demonstrates the use of a semaphore for signaling between processes:

```
| semaphore process1 process2 |

semaphore := Semaphore new.

process1 := [
    "Process 1 is waiting for the signal"
    Transcript show: 'Process 1 waiting...'; cr.
    semaphore wait.
    Transcript show: 'Process 1 proceeding after signal'; cr.
] fork.

process2 := [
    "Process 2 performs some operations"
    Transcript show: 'Process 2 signaling Process 1'; cr.
    (Delay forSeconds: 3) wait.
    semaphore signal.
    Transcript show: 'Process 2 has signaled the semaphore'; cr.
] fork.
```

```
Process 1 waiting...
Process 2 signaling Process 1
Process 2 has signaled the semaphore
Process 1 proceeding after signal
```

In this example, process1 waits on a semaphore and does not proceed until process2 signals the semaphore. This simple synchronization mechanism ensures that process1 only proceeds after process2 completes its signaling action.

Another useful mechanism in Smalltalk for handling events is the use of Events. An Event is a higher-level abstraction compared to a semaphore, and it provides more flexibility and readability in event-driven programming. Here is an example that illustrates the use of Event:

```
| event process1 process2 |

event := Event new.

process1 := [
    "Process 1 is waiting for the event"
    Transcript show: 'Process 1 waiting for event'; cr.
    event wait.
    Transcript show: 'Process 1 received event notification'; cr.
] fork.

process2 := [
    "Process 2 performs operations and then triggers the event"
    Transcript show: 'Process 2 is about to trigger event'; cr.
    (Delay forSeconds: 3) wait.
    event trigger.
    Transcript show: 'Process 2 has triggered the event'; cr.
] fork.
```

```
Process 1 waiting for event
Process 2 is about to trigger event
Process 2 has triggered the event
Process 1 received event notification
```

Key differences between Semaphore and Event include the explicit method names (signal/wait vs. trigger/wait) and the semantics associated with each (semaphores can handle counts, whereas events represent single occurrences). Events provide a cleaner syntax in scenarios where simple notifications are required.

Adding another layer of complexity, Smalltalk also allows for handling multiple signals or events with targeted actions. This is highly effective in scenarios involving event-driven architectures, such as in GUI applications or systems with asynchronous I/O. An example is provided below:

```
| event1 event2 processGUI |

event1 := Event new.
event2 := Event new.

processGUI := [
    [event1 wait. Transcript show: 'GUI Event 1 triggered'; cr] fork.
    [event2 wait. Transcript show: 'GUI Event 2 triggered'; cr] fork.
```

```
    "Simulate event triggering from different parts of the system"
    (Delay forSeconds: 2) wait. event1 trigger.
    (Delay forSeconds: 1) wait. event2 trigger.
] fork.
```

```
GUI Event 1 triggered
GUI Event 2 triggered
```

Here, separate Events are used to handle different GUI signals, showcasing how concurrent processes can effectively manage and respond to multiple asynchronous events.

In addition to Semaphore and Event, Smalltalk's concurrency model supports more advanced constructs such as Announcements and EventQueues for complex event-driven systems. Announcements allow broadcasting events to multiple listeners, while EventQueues support queuing and processing events systematically.

When implementing concurrent systems, it's essential to consider edge cases and ensure that signals and events are handled robustly. Common issues like missed signals, redundant triggers, or deadlocks should be meticulously avoided or managed. Proper testing and use of synchronization patterns are critical in achieving reliable and maintainable concurrent applications.

Properly utilizing signals and events in Smalltalk not only enhances the responsiveness and efficiency of an application but also contributes to a clear and organized code structure, improving overall software quality and performance.

9.8 Parallel Processing Patterns

Parallel processing patterns are essential for designing applications that efficiently utilize the computational power of multi-core processors. In Smalltalk, these patterns help to structure concurrent activities, ensuring that processes run concurrently while minimizing the risk of data corruption and maximizing performance. This section will explore several key parallel processing patterns, explaining their implementations and use cases within the Smalltalk environment.

Fork/Join Pattern

The Fork/Join pattern involves splitting a task into several smaller subtasks that can be processed in parallel. Each subtask is processed independently, and the results are then combined to form the final output. This pattern is particularly useful for tasks that can be naturally divided into smaller, independent units of work.

Input : Large problem P
Output : Solution for problem P

```
if P is small then
    Solve P directly;
else
    Divide P into smaller subproblems P1, P2, ..., Pn;
    foreach subproblem Pi do
        Fork a new process to solve Pi;
    foreach process do
        Join the results of all subproblems;
    Combine results to solve original problem P;
```

In Smalltalk, the Fork/Join pattern can be implemented using the Process class to fork new processes, as shown in the following example:

```
| results processes |
results := SharedQueue new.
processes := (1 to: 10) collect: [:i |
  [| partialResult |
   partialResult := self solveSubproblem: (self subproblemAt: i).
   results add: partialResult] fork].
processes do: [:each | each join].
^self combineResults: results.
```

In this implementation, subtasks are solved in parallel processes, and results are stored in a SharedQueue. Finally, the results are combined using a separate method to obtain the final solution.

Pipeline Pattern

The Pipeline pattern organizes a series of consecutive stages, where each stage performs a part of the task and passes the intermediate result to the next stage. This pattern is useful for applications involving a sequence of transformations or data processing steps.

Smalltalk provides a straightforward way to implement the Pipeline pattern by allowing each stage to execute in its own process. The following example illustrates a simple pipeline with three stages:

```
| stage1 stage2 stage3 input intermediate result |

input := self initialDataset.
stage1 := [intermediate := self processFirstStage: input] fork.
```

Input : Initial dataset D
Output : Processed dataset

Dataset input := D;
foreach *stage* S *in stages* **do**
    Fork a new process to apply S to current input;
    input := Result of applying S to current input;
Return input as processed dataset;

```
stage2 := [intermediate := stage1 value; self processSecondStage: intermediate] fork.
stage3 := [result := stage2 value; self processThirdStage: result] fork.
^stage3 value.
```

Here, each stage is implemented as a separate block, which is forked into a new process. The value message is used to retrieve the result from each process, passing it to the next stage.

MapReduce Pattern

The MapReduce pattern is a model for processing large datasets by parallelizing the map and reduce functions. The map function processes input key-value pairs to generate intermediate key-value pairs, while the reduce function merges all intermediate values associated with the same intermediate key.

Input : Dataset D
Output : Reduced dataset

Map phase;
foreach *input record* r *in* D **do**
    Fork a new process to apply map function to r;
Shuffle and Sort phase;
Group all intermediate key-value pairs by key;
Reduce phase;
foreach *key* k *with intermediate values* $v1, v2, \ldots, vn$ **do**
    Fork a new process to apply reduce function to k and $v1, v2, \ldots, vn$;
Return reduced dataset;

Implementing MapReduce in Smalltalk involves parallelizing the map and reduce phases using processes:

```
| mapper reducer dataset intermediate grouped result |

dataset := self loadDataset.
intermediate := SharedQueue new.
mapper := (dataset collect: [:record |
  [intermediate addAll: (self mapFunction: record)] fork]).
mapper do: [:each | each join].

grouped := self groupByKey: intermediate.
result := SharedQueue new.
reducer := (grouped keys collect: [:key |
  [result add: (self reduceFunction: key values: (grouped at: key))] fork]).
reducer do: [:each | each join].
^result.
```

In this example, mapFunction: and reduceFunction: are methods that implement the map and reduce logic. Intermediate results are grouped by key and subsequently reduced.

Parallel processing patterns such as Fork/Join, Pipeline, and MapReduce enable efficient utilization of computational resources. Understanding and correctly implementing these patterns in Smalltalk are crucial for developing high-performance applications capable of leveraging modern multi-core processors.

9.9 Asynchronous Programming

Asynchronous programming is a crucial concept in concurrent systems, designed to improve the efficiency and responsiveness of applications. It enables a system to perform other tasks while awaiting the completion of an operation. This can prevent an application from becoming unresponsive, especially in user-interface-intensive environments or when dealing with I/O-bound operations.

Implementing Asynchronous Methods

In Smalltalk, asynchronous programming is implemented typically using blocks, promises, and futures. A block represents a segment of code that can be delayed for later execution. Promises and futures, on the other hand, manage the representation of results that will be available at some future point.

```
"Declare a block to be executed asynchronously"
asyncBlock := [ :a :b | Transcript show: (a + b) asString ; cr ].

"Fork a new process to execute Block asynchronously"
Process fork: [ asyncBlock value: 5 value: 10 ].
```

In this example, asyncBlock is a block that takes two arguments, a and b, and prints their sum to the Transcript. By forking a new process, we execute the block asynchronously without blocking the main thread.

Promises and Futures

Promises and futures in Smalltalk handle asynchronous results smoothly. A promise is an object that functions as a proxy for a result that is initially unknown. Futures complement promises by allowing interaction with these results when they become available.

```
"Create a Promise and obtain the corresponding Future"
promise := Promise new.
future := promise future.

"Block handling long-running task"
[ (Delay forSeconds: 5) wait.
  promise resolve: 'Task Completed'] fork.

"Handling Future outcome"
future then: [:result | Transcript show: result; cr].
```

In this example, we initiate a Promise and retrieve its Future. The promise is eventually resolved by the delayed block, simulating a long-running task. The then: message attached to the future specifies the action to perform upon successful resolution of the promise.

Error Handling in Asynchronous Contexts

Error handling in asynchronous code is crucial to maintain robust applications. In Smalltalk, error handling can be incorporated into promises to ensure that exceptions do not propagate unnoticed.

```
"Create a Promise and obtain the corresponding Future"
promise := Promise new.
future := promise future.

"Block raising an error"
[ promise reject: (Error new: 'Something went wrong!') ] fork.

"Handling both success and error"
future
    then: [:result | Transcript show: result; cr]
    catch: [:error | Transcript show: error messageText; cr].
```

This demonstrates creating a promise which intentionally raises an error. The catch: message applied to the future will handle the exception, allowing us to manage errors gracefully without crashing the application.

Concurrent programming often involves ensuring that multiple asynchronous tasks complete, which can be managed using the Promise when:all:then: construct.

```
"Create multiple Promises"
promise1 := Promise new.
promise2 := Promise new.

"Fork processes to resolve Promises after reaching completion"
[ (Delay forSeconds: 2) wait.
  promise1 resolve: 'First Task Completed' ] fork.

[ (Delay forSeconds: 3) wait.
  promise2 resolve: 'Second Task Completed' ] fork.

"Handling all Promises resolution"
Promise
    when: (Array with: promise1 future with: promise2 future)
    all:
    then: [:results |
        results do: [:result | Transcript show: result; cr]].
```

This example creates two promises, each resolved after different delays. The Promise when:all:then: ensures that all specified promises are resolved before proceeding, enabling synchronization of multiple asynchronous tasks.

Efficient asynchronous programming enhances the responsiveness and efficiency of an application by allowing it to handle other tasks while awaiting the completion of background operations. Proper understanding and usage of blocks, promises, and futures form the cornerstone of asynchronous programming in Smalltalk, providing a solid foundation for building responsive and high-performance applications.

9.10 Process Scheduling and Prioritization

In any concurrent system, the ability to manage the execution of processes efficiently is crucial for performance and reliability. Process scheduling and prioritization determine how processes are allocated CPU time and resources, ensuring that the system remains responsive and efficient. Smalltalk, like many other programming languages, provides mechanisms to control process scheduling and prioritize certain tasks.

Process Scheduling

Process scheduling in Smalltalk is managed by the underlying system's scheduler, which determines the order in which processes are executed. The scheduler uses a variety of algorithms to make these decisions, often balancing the need for fairness (ensuring all processes get a chance to execute) with the importance of responsiveness (ensuring high-priority or time-sensitive processes are executed promptly).

The key concepts involved in process scheduling are:

- **Time Slicing**: This technique allows multiple processes to share the CPU. The CPU time is divided into small time slices, and each process is given a slice in turn. This creates the illusion of parallelism by rapidly switching between processes.
- **Scheduling Algorithms**: These algorithms define how the scheduler assigns CPU time to processes. Common algorithms include round-robin, first-come-first-served, and priority-based scheduling.
- **Context Switching**: The act of saving the state of a currently running process and loading the state of the next process to be executed. Efficient context switching is vital to minimize the overhead and maintain system performance.

Here is an example of how Smalltalk can handle simple process scheduling:

```
"Creating Processes"
process1 := [[10 timesRepeat: [Transcript show: 'Process 1 executing'; cr. (Delay
    forMilliseconds: 500) wait]]] fork.
process2 := [[10 timesRepeat: [Transcript show: 'Process 2 executing'; cr. (Delay
    forMilliseconds: 500) wait]]] fork.

"Setting Process Priority"
process1 priority: 5.
process2 priority: 10.
```

In the above code, two processes are created, each repeating an action ten times with a delay of 500 milliseconds between actions. process2 is given a higher priority, meaning it is more likely to be scheduled before process1. This can be observed in the output window where process2 outputs are more frequent.

Process Prioritization

Process prioritization allows the developer to influence the scheduling of processes. Each process in Smalltalk can be assigned a priority, an integer value indicating its importance relative to other processes. By adjusting process priorities, critical tasks can be given more CPU time, while less critical tasks receive less.

The Smalltalk environment uses these priority levels:

- **User Background**: Processes that perform non-urgent tasks. Generally assigned lower priority values.
- **User Interactive**: Processes that handle user interactions. Require quick responses, so they are assigned higher priority values.
- **System Background**: Background system processes that need to run regularly but are not time-critical.
- **System Interactive**: High-priority processes that ensure the system remains responsive.

The priorities can range from 1 (lowest) to 100 (highest), with default priorities often set around 50. To set a process priority, the priority: message is used, as shown in the code example above.

To manage multiple processes of varying priority and ensure responsive operation, the system scheduler enforces policies such as:

- **Preemptive Scheduling**: Higher-priority processes can preempt lower-priority ones, ensuring critical tasks are not delayed.
- **Aging**: Long-running processes may have their priority adjusted over time to prevent starvation.

Consider complex scenarios where priority adjustments might be necessary for enhanced control. For instance, in user interfaces, interactive processes handling user inputs must operate with higher priority to ensure responsiveness:

```
"Interactive Process Example"
uiProcess := [[10 timesRepeat: [Transcript show: 'UI Process executing'; cr. (Delay
    forMilliseconds: 100) wait]]] fork.
backgroundProcess := [[10 timesRepeat: [Transcript show: 'Background Process
    executing'; cr. (Delay forMilliseconds: 1000) wait]]] fork.

uiProcess priority: 80.
backgroundProcess priority: 20.
```

In the above example, uiProcess is given a higher priority than backgroundProcess, ensuring that the user interface remains responsive. This prioritization is critical in applications where user satisfaction depends on the quick response time.

Efficient process scheduling and prioritization are vital components of developing robust and responsive concurrent applications in Smalltalk.

By understanding and leveraging these mechanisms, developers can ensure that high-priority processes receive the necessary resources while maintaining overall system performance and fairness.

9.11 Handling Deadlocks and Race Conditions

Deadlocks and race conditions represent critical issues in concurrent programming. Understanding and mitigating these problems is essential for creating robust and efficient Smalltalk systems.

A *deadlock* occurs when a set of processes becomes permanently blocked, each waiting for a resource held by another process in the set, creating a cycle of dependencies with no possible resolution. Conversely, a *race condition* arises when the outcome of processes is dependent on the sequence or timing of uncontrollable events, causing inconsistent or erroneous results.

Deadlock Detection and Resolution

In Smalltalk, deadlock detection can be challenging due to the dynamic nature of objects and processes. A typical method for deadlock detection involves constructing a *wait-for graph* where nodes represent processes and edges denote resource allocation and request. Deadlock is identified if this graph contains a cycle.

Consider the following Smalltalk example illustrating basic deadlock detection:

```
| process1 process2 resourceA resourceB |

resourceA := Semaphore new.
resourceB := Semaphore new.

process1 := [[resourceA wait. resourceB wait. "Do Work" ensure: [resourceA signal.
        resourceB signal.]]] fork.
process2 := [[resourceB wait. resourceA wait. "Do Work" ensure: [resourceB signal.
        resourceA signal.]]] fork.
```

In this code, process1 and process2 attempt to acquire resourceA and resourceB in opposite orders, creating a potential for deadlock.

Deadlock Prevention

To prevent deadlocks, one must enforce certain strategies:

- **Resource Ordering**: Impose a global ordering on resource acquisition. Processes request resources in increasing order based on predefined priorities, ensuring that circular wait conditions do not form.

- **Hold and Wait**: Ensure processes do not hold onto resources while waiting for others. Processes should request all required resources at once or release them if they must wait.
- **Preemption**: Allow resources to be forcibly removed from processes holding them.
- **Resource Hierarchies**: Structure resource acquisition hierarchically to prevent cyclic dependencies.

```
process1 := [[OrderedSemaphore new acquire: {resourceA. resourceB} do: ["Do Work"]].
process2 := [[OrderedSemaphore new acquire: {resourceA. resourceB} do: ["Do Work"]].
```

In this refined approach, OrderedSemaphore ensures that resources are acquired in a consistent order, mitigating deadlock risks.

Handling Race Conditions

Mitigating race conditions requires careful synchronization to control the sequence of actions in concurrent environments. Race conditions can manifest in various scenarios, such as shared counters, buffer storage, and resource allocation.

Consider a shared counter example prone to race conditions:

```
| counter processes |

counter := 0.
processes := (1 to: 100) collect: [[:i | [counter := counter + 1] fork]].
processes do: [:process | process join].
```

In this scenario, the final counter value may not be 100 due to simultaneous updates by multiple processes. Addressing this requires synchronization:

```
| counter mutex processes |

counter := 0.
mutex := Mutex new.
processes := (1 to: 100) collect: [[:i | [mutex critical: [counter := counter + 1]] fork]].
processes do: [:process | process join].
```

Here, the use of Mutex ensures that increments on the counter occur atomically, preventing race conditions.

Another essential pattern for avoiding race conditions is the use of *atomic operations* where supported. These are low-level operations that execute as indivisible steps, eliminating intermediate states visible to other processes:

```
| counter processes |

counter := 0.
processes := (1 to: 100) collect: [[:i | [Smalltalk atomicWrite: [counter := counter + 1]]
    fork]].
processes do: [:process | process join].
```

By leveraging atomic operations, we ensure that even with interleaving of process execution, the shared data's integrity remains intact.

Deep understanding and strategic handling of deadlocks and race conditions are fundamental to mastering concurrency in Smalltalk, contributing to the development of resilient and efficient applications. Employing synchronization primitives judiciously and adhering to well-founded design patterns can significantly alleviate risks associated with concurrent computations.

9.12 Concurrency in User Interfaces

Concurrency in user interfaces (UIs) is crucial for providing a responsive and efficient user experience, especially in complex applications where time-consuming tasks are executed. In Smalltalk, managing concurrent operations within a UI involves creating and handling processes, ensuring smooth interaction, and updating the UI without freezing or creating unresponsive states. This section will explore best practices, techniques, and tools available in Smalltalk for effective concurrency management in user interfaces.

To begin with, it is essential to understand the fundamental concept of decoupling long-running tasks from the main UI process. By doing so, we can prevent the UI from becoming unresponsive. Typically, the main UI process should handle user inputs, render updates, and execute quick operations, while separate worker processes handle more time-consuming tasks.

Consider the following example where a long computation task is decoupled from the main UI thread:

```
longComputationProcess := [
    | result |
    result := self performLongComputation.
    [ self updateUIWithResult: result ] forkAt: Processor userBackgroundPriority.
] fork.
```

In this example, the method performLongComputation is separated from the UI updating code by forking it at the background priority. This ensures that the lengthy computation does not block the main UI process, keeping the user interface responsive. The computed result is then used to update the UI from another forked process.

When updating the UI from a background process, it is vital to ensure thread safety. Smalltalk supports several synchronization primitives that we have covered in previous sections, but it is particularly important to make sure that UI updates are performed in the main UI thread to avoid inconsistencies. One approach to ensure this is using UIProcess defer: or Application current perform:.

```
result := self performLongComputation.
UIProcess defer: [ self updateUIWithResult: result ].
```

UIProcess defer: schedules the provided block to run in the UI process, ensuring thread safety for UI updates. This guarantees that the UI can be safely manipulated without running into race conditions or inconsistencies caused by concurrent operations.

Another common scenario in concurrent UIs is handling user input while background tasks are running. In such cases, signaling mechanisms can be employed to notify the UI process about the completion of background tasks, prompting it to update relevant interface elements. Smalltalk's signaling primitives, such as semaphores and signals, are useful for this purpose.

```
taskCompletedSignal := Signal new.

longComputationProcess := [
    | result |
    result := self performLongComputation.
    taskCompletedSignal signal: result.
] fork.

"Handle the signal in the main UI process"
taskCompletedSignal wait.
taskCompletedSignal value: result [
    self updateUIWithResult: result.
].
```

In this example, a Signal is used to synchronize the completion of a background task with the UI update. The main UI process waits for the signal, which carries the computation result, and subsequently updates the UI with this result.

To enhance the responsiveness and usability further, employing Progress Bars and Task Cancelation mechanisms can significantly improve user experience. Showing progress indicators keeps users informed about the ongoing tasks' status, preventing them from feeling uncertain about the application's state. Similarly, enabling task cancellation allows users to abort long-running operations if they decide to stop the task.

```
progressBar := ProgressBarMorph new.
progressBar openInWorld.

longComputationProcess := [
    (1 to: 100) do: [:each |
        (Delay forSeconds: 0.1) wait.
        progressBar value: each.
    ].
    progressBar delete.
] fork.
```

The above example demonstrates creating a ProgressBarMorph, updating it incrementally within a forked process, and removing it after the task completion. This approach ensures users are aware of the ongoing process status.

Finally, recognizing that concurrency in user interfaces often introduces complexity in debugging and troubleshooting, adopting structured logging and monitoring tools is advisable. These tools can capture the state of various concurrent operations, thus aiding in identifying and resolving issues that arise from concurrent interactions.

Effective concurrency in user interfaces is achieved by balancing responsiveness with accuracy in handling concurrent tasks, ensuring that long-running processes do not hinder the user experience. Through careful management of processes and synchronization, Smalltalk provides robust capabilities to create efficient and responsive user interfaces.

9.13 Performance Considerations in Concurrent Applications

Managing performance in concurrent applications entails understanding both the theoretical and practical implications of concurrent execution. Key factors influencing performance include task granularity, load balancing, the overhead of context switching, synchronization costs, and avoiding contention. This section provides a detailed examination of these factors and offers strategies to optimize performance in Smalltalk concurrent applications.

Task Granularity

Task granularity refers to the size of the tasks into which work is partitioned. Fine-grained tasks have a small computational load, whereas coarse-grained tasks carry larger computational loads. The overhead associated with scheduling and managing tasks must be balanced against the computational effort required for each task. In Smalltalk, this can be managed by composing tasks that have minimal interdependencies and by chunking work into appropriately sized units.

```
| task1 task2 task3 taskScheduler |
taskScheduler := TaskScheduler new.
task1 := [1000 timesRepeat: [Transcript show: 'Task 1'; cr]].
task2 := [1000 timesRepeat: [Transcript show: 'Task 2'; cr]].
task3 := [1000 timesRepeat: [Transcript show: 'Task 3'; cr]].
taskScheduler addTask: task1.
taskScheduler addTask: task2.
taskScheduler addTask: task3.
taskScheduler start.
```

TaskScheduler manages the execution of tasks, balancing granularity to achieve effective parallel execution. For maximum performance, tasks should perform sufficiently substantial amounts of work relative to the cost of task management.

Load Balancing

Load balancing ensures all processors or cores are utilized effectively to prevent scenarios where some processors remain idle while others are overloaded. In Smalltalk, we can distribute tasks across multiple Processor instances. Dynamic load balancing adapts to runtime conditions, redistributing tasks as needed to achieve optimal usage.

```
| processorCount taskSchedulers tasks |
processorCount := Processor systemProcessorCount.
taskSchedulers := (1 to: processorCount) collect: [:i | TaskScheduler new].
tasks := (1 to: 1000) collect: [:i | [Transcript show: 'Task ', i printString; cr]].

tasks do: [:task |
    (taskSchedulers at: (Random new nextInt: processorCount) + 1) addTask: task
].

taskSchedulers do: [:scheduler | scheduler start].
```

Here, tasks are randomly assigned to different processors, enabling effective load distribution across available computational resources.

Context Switching

Context switching is the process of storing and restoring the state of processes so that execution can be resumed from the same point at a later time. Frequent context switching introduces overhead, hindering performance. Minimizing unnecessary context switches is critical. Smalltalk's cooperative multitasking environment can reduce context switch overhead by managing when tasks yield control.

```
Processor yield: [
    "Critical section of code that performs significant work"
    1000 timesRepeat: [ self heavyComputation ].
].
```

The Processor yield: method directs a process to yield control, allowing essential tasks to complete before switching contexts.

Synchronization Costs

Synchronization mechanisms such as mutexes and semaphores, essential for data integrity in concurrent execution, introduce delays. These delays, often termed synchronization costs, must be minimized by limiting critical sections and using lock-free data structures when feasible.

```
| mutex sharedResource workerBlock |
mutex := Mutex new.
sharedResource := 0.

workerBlock := [
    1000 timesRepeat: [
        mutex critical: [sharedResource := sharedResource + 1]
    ]
].

fork: workerBlock.
fork: workerBlock.
```

This ensures that sharedResource is safely incremented without incurring excessive synchronization overhead.

Avoiding Contention

Contention occurs when multiple processes compete for the same resource, leading to bottlenecks. Minimizing contention involves reducing shared resources and employing scalable algorithms tailored for parallel execution.

```
| sharedResources workerBlock |
sharedResources := Array new: Processor systemProcessorCount withAll: 0.

workerBlock := [:index |
    1000 timesRepeat: [
        (sharedResources at: index) withSemaphore: [:res |
            res value: res value + 1
        ]
    ]
].

(1 to: Processor systemProcessorCount) do: [:i | [workerBlock value: i] fork].
```

This distributes work across multiple shared resources, each guarded by a semaphore to reduce contention.

Efficient concurrent programming in Smalltalk requires careful consideration of task granularity, load balancing, context switch overhead, synchronization costs, and contention avoidance. By employing these strategies, developers can significantly improve the performance of their concurrent applications. Understanding the nuances and trade-offs through practical implementation patterns ensures robust, high-performing concurrent systems.

Chapter 10

Testing and Debugging in Smalltalk

This chapter focuses on testing and debugging techniques in Smalltalk. It includes writing test cases using the SUnit framework, running and managing tests, and embracing test-driven development (TDD) practices. The chapter explores the basics of the debugger tool, setting breakpoints, inspecting variables, tracing code execution, exception handling, and leveraging logging for debugging. Readers will also learn about automated testing and continuous integration, as well as refactoring code to improve debugging efficiency.

10.1 Introduction to Testing and Debugging

Testing and debugging are critical aspects of software development in Smalltalk, ensuring that code behaves as expected and identifying issues to maintain program integrity. In this section, we delve into the importance of rigorous testing and effective debugging strategies, establishing a foundation for the detailed techniques covered in the subsequent sections.

The process of testing involves systematically checking whether the software meets specified requirements. This often includes verifying that functions provide the correct output for a given input, the program handles exceptions gracefully, and the integration of various components operates smoothly. Debugging, on the other hand, is the process of finding and resolving defects or problems within the software, ensuring it runs efficiently and correctly.

Benefits of Testing and Debugging:

- Ensuring software reliability and robustness by identifying errors early.
- Facilitating the maintenance of code by making it easier to understand and modify.
- Increasing confidence in the software, allowing for smoother releases and updates.
- Encouraging good programming practices and clean code structure.

Smalltalk places a significant emphasis on the quality of software, and this is reflected in its robust tools and frameworks designed for testing and debugging.

Essential Concepts in Testing:

- Unit Testing: Focuses on individual units of source code to validate their correctness.
- Integration Testing: Ensures that combined parts of the application work together without errors.
- System Testing: Tests the entire system's compliance with its specified requirements.
- Acceptance Testing: Conducted to confirm if the system meets business requirements.

Key Components of Debugging:

- Breakpoints: Useful for pausing program execution at specific points to examine the state of the program.
- Variable Inspection: Allows observation of variable values at certain points during execution.
- Code Tracing: Involves following the execution path to understand the flow of the program.

- Exception Handling: Deals with managing and logging exceptions to prevent crashes and unexpected behavior.

The choice between various testing strategies and tools often depends on the specifics of the project and the development environment. In Smalltalk, the SUnit framework stands out as a vital tool for unit testing. Inspired by JUnit in Java, SUnit provides a structured way to write and manage test cases in Smalltalk.

```
TestCase subclass: MyTestCase [
    MyTestCase>>testExample [
        self assert: (1 + 1 = 2).
    ]
]
```

Executing this simple test case using SUnit helps developers ensure that fundamental mathematical operations perform as expected within their environment. The output of running this test is typically formatted to provide clear feedback on the success or failure of the tests.

```
MyTestCase
Run: 1 tests, 1 passed, 0 failed, 0 errors
```

Debugging in Smalltalk leverages an interactive debugger tool that integrates smoothly with the development environment. This debugger allows for real-time inspection and modification of running code, which is a powerful feature not commonly found in many other programming languages.

The Smalltalk debugger is typically invoked when an error occurs, providing a detailed stack trace and an interactive interface to navigate through the code. This interface helps developers identify the exact location and the nature of the issue, making it easier to implement a fix. For example, placing a breakpoint in a critical function ensures that the debugger halts execution at this point, allowing the developer to inspect the program state.

The following snippet demonstrates setting up a breakpoint in Smalltalk:

```
Object subclass: MyClass [
    MyClass>>myMethod [
        " Setting a breakpoint in myMethod "
        self halt.
        ^ 'Hello, World!'.
    ]
]
```

When myMethod is invoked, the program execution will pause, and the debugger will activate, offering tools to inspect variables, trace through the code, and modify execution flow if necessary.

Understanding and utilizing these testing and debugging tools effectively forms the cornerstone of successful Smalltalk programming, providing a clear path towards high-quality, reliable software development.

10.2 Writing Test Cases in Smalltalk

In software development, writing test cases is an essential practice to ensure the correctness and robustness of code. In Smalltalk, test cases are typically written using the SUnit framework, which is a Smalltalk port of the popular JUnit framework from the Java programming ecosystem. Here, we delve into the process of writing test cases in Smalltalk, exploring the core principles, conventions, and practical steps involved in the process.

When writing test cases, it is crucial to understand the basic structure and purpose of a test case. A test case in Smalltalk is essentially a method that verifies a specific aspect of the code. Test cases are grouped in test classes, which in turn extend the SUnit framework's TestCase class.

To begin, consider a simple class Calculator with basic arithmetic operations. Here is the definition of this class:

```
Object subclass: Calculator [
  | value |

    Calculator class >> new [
        ^super new initialize.
    ]

    Calculator >> initialize [
        value := 0.
    ]

    Calculator >> add: aNumber [
        value := value + aNumber.
    ]

    Calculator >> subtract: aNumber [
        value := value - aNumber.
    ]

    Calculator >> value [
        ^value.
    ]
]
```

The next step involves writing test cases for the Calculator class to verify its functionality. We start by creating a subclass of TestCase, often with a naming convention that appends Test to the class being tested, here CalculatorTest.

```
TestCase subclass: CalculatorTest [
    | calculator |

    CalculatorTest >> setUp [
        calculator := Calculator new.
    ]

    CalculatorTest >> testAddition [
        calculator add: 5.
        self assert: calculator value = 5.
    ]

    CalculatorTest >> testSubtraction [
        calculator add: 10.
        calculator subtract: 3.
        self assert: calculator value = 7.
    ]

    CalculatorTest >> testInitialValue [
        self assert: calculator value = 0.
    ]
]
```

Each test method verifies specific functionality of the Calculator class:

- testAddition: This method verifies that the add: method correctly adds a number to the current value.
- testSubtraction: This method checks the behavior of the subtract: method.
- testInitialValue: This method confirms that the initial value of the calculator is zero.

The setUp method is executed before each test method, ensuring a fresh instance of Calculator for each test. This isolation is critical to prevent side effects between tests.

Writing effective test cases requires a few key practices:

- **Isolate Tests**: Each test should be independent of others. Reset the state before each test method, using setUp.
- **Clear Assertions**: Use self assert: to verify the expected outcomes of the test. Assertions should be granular and cover different scenarios.

- **Descriptive Naming**: Test methods should clearly indicate what functionality they are verifying. For example, testAddition is more descriptive than test1.
- **Single Responsibility**: Each test method should verify one aspect of the behavior. This makes tests easier to read and maintain.

The benefits of these practices become apparent as the codebase grows. Properly isolated and clearly named test cases facilitate easier identification of issues and maintenance of both the test code and the application code.

Additionally, leveraging test fixtures such as tearDown can help manage resource cleanup after each test:

```
CalculatorTest >> tearDown [
    calculator := nil.
]
```

The tearDown method is executed after each test, ensuring that any resources or state used during the test are appropriately cleaned up, preventing any unintended interactions between tests.

A complete workflow for writing and running tests in Smalltalk typically follows a cycle of writing a test that fails (since the functionality may not yet exist), writing the minimal code to pass the test, and then refactoring the code while ensuring all tests pass. This practice aligns with test-driven development (TDD), which emphasizes writing tests before the actual code.

Writing test cases in Smalltalk, encapsulated in the SUnit framework, involves creating TestCase subclasses, defining test methods using descriptive names, and employing efficient setup and teardown methods. These principles and practices, when adhered to diligently, contribute significantly to maintaining high code quality and facilitating easier debugging and maintenance.

10.3 Using the SUnit Framework

The SUnit framework is an integral component of the Smalltalk environment, widely adopted for developing unit tests. It facilitates writing, organizing, and running tests, enhancing code reliability and maintenance. In this section, we delve into the foundational aspects of utilizing the SUnit framework effectively.

Creating a Test Class

In SUnit, a test class is a subclass of TestCase. This inheritance provides methods that define test cases and life-cycle hooks to set up and tear down any necessary state. Start by subclassing TestCase and naming your test class descriptively to reflect the class or functionality being tested.

```
Object subclass: TestMyFunctionality [
    TestMyFunctionality superclass: TestCase.

    TestMyFunctionality class >> setUp [
        "Code executed before each test"
    ]

    TestMyFunctionality class >> tearDown [
        "Code executed after each test"
    ]
]
```

Writing Test Methods

Each test method in SUnit should begin with the prefix test to ensure automatic detection by the framework. A test method typically includes an assertion to verify expected outcomes against actual results.

```
TestMyFunctionality >> testMethodBehavior [
    | result expected |

    "Arrange"
    expected := 5.

    "Act"
    result := MyClass new performOperation.

    "Assert"
    self assert: result equals: expected.
]
```

In the example above, the testMethodBehavior verifies that the method performOperation yields the expected result.

Assertions in SUnit

Assertions are crucial for validating code behavior. The SUnit framework provides a variety of assertion methods beyond assert:equals:, such as:

- self assert:description:
- self deny:

- self should:raise:
- self shouldnt:raise:

Assertions help confirm that the system under test meets specified conditions. For instance, self should:raise: ensures that a block of code generates the expected exception.

```
TestMyFunctionality >> testExceptionRaised [
    self should: [ MyClass new triggerError ] raise: Error.
]
```

Running Tests

To execute tests in SUnit, use a test runner to load and run all test cases. Smalltalk IDEs typically include a test runner interface for convenience. Alternatively, tests can be programmatically executed using:

```
(TestRunner new buildSuiteFrom: TestMyFunctionality) run.
```

This command initiates the TestRunner to discover and run all tests in TestMyFunctionality.

Test Suite Aggregation

Tests can be grouped into test suites for collective execution. This aggregation simplifies running a logical collection of tests and is beneficial for managing large test sets.

```
Object subclass: MyTestSuite [
    MyTestSuite superclass: TestCase.

    MyTestSuite class >> suite [
        ^TestSuite new
            addTest: TestMyFunctionality;
            addTest: AnotherTestClass;
            yourself.
    ]
]
```

Here, the suite method builds a TestSuite containing multiple test cases, facilitating consolidated execution.

Handling Setup and Teardown

SUnit's setUp and tearDown methods manage resource initialization and cleanup, executed before and after each test method, respectively. Proper use of these methods ensures that each test runs in a controlled and predictable state.

```
TestMyFunctionality >> setUp [
    super setUp.
```

```
    "Initialize code before each test"
]

TestMyFunctionality >> tearDown [
    "Cleanup code after each test"
    super tearDown.
]
```

These methods help manage dependencies and shared resources, promoting test independence and reliability.

Exploring Advanced SUnit Features

Beyond basic assertions and test organization, SUnit offers advanced features such as:

- Parameterized Tests: Creating a single test method to run against multiple sets of data.
- Mocks and Stubs: Simulating object behavior for components not under test.
- Test Coverage Analysis: Measuring the extent to which codebase is exercised by tests.

These features enhance the robustness of the testing process and support comprehensive verification of complex behaviors. By mastering SUnit, developers can significantly improve code correctness and resilience.

10.4 Running and Managing Tests

Executing and overseeing tests in Smalltalk forms an essential part of the development process, ensuring code reliability and robustness. In Smalltalk, tests are primarily executed using the SUnit framework, which offers comprehensive capabilities for managing test cases. Understanding how to run tests efficiently and manage the results will enhance your productivity and facilitate quicker identification of errors.

Running Individual Tests

Invoking tests in Smalltalk can be done at various granularity levels: individual tests, entire test classes, or test suites comprising multiple classes. To execute an individual test case, you'll typically select the test method within the Smalltalk browser and use the SUnit framework commands.

```
MyTestClass new testMethod.
```

Executing the above command runs the specific test method testMethod defined in MyTestClass.

Running a Test Class

To run all test methods within a specific test class, the framework provides convenient methods to invoke the entire class rather than individually selecting each test method.

```
MyTestClass run.
```

The command MyTestClass run initiates all test cases defined in the class.

Test Suites

For managing larger sets of tests, SUnit allows the creation of test suites. A test suite is a collection of related test classes designed to be executed together, facilitating comprehensive testing across multiple components.

A test suite can be defined by creating a subclass of TestSuite and overriding the suite method:

```
TestSuite subclass: MyTestSuite [
  MyTestSuite class >> suite [
    | suite |
    suite := TestSuite new.
    suite addTest: MyTestClass1 suite.
    suite addTest: MyTestClass2 suite.
    ^suite.
  ]
]
```

In this example, MyTestSuite includes all test methods from MyTestClass1 and MyTestClass2. Running MyTestSuite run will execute every test across both classes.

Managing Test Results

Upon executing tests, SUnit provides useful feedback, including counts of passed and failed tests, and detailed error messages. These results can be managed programmatically to enhance debugging efforts.

Capturing test results programmatically:

```
| result |
result := TestResult new.
MyTestClass suite run: result.
```

The variable result now holds detailed information about the test outcomes, facilitating further analysis.

Continuous Testing

Embracing continuous testing practices is crucial for maintaining high code quality throughout the development cycle. Continuous integration (CI) tools can be configured to run your Smalltalk tests automatically every time changes are pushed to the repository.

Integration with CI tools, such as Jenkins, GitLab CI/CD, or Travis CI, can be achieved by adding scripts to execute Smalltalk test suites, ensuring immediate feedback on potential code issues. The automated test execution process can be scripted as follows:

```
#!/bin/bash
gst-boss -f TestRunner.st
```

Here, gst-boss -f TestRunner.st is a command that runs a script file TestRunner.st, which is designed to execute the desired test suites within the GNU Smalltalk interpreter.

Interpreting Test Output

Understanding the output of test runs is essential for diagnosing issues. SUnit outputs a summary indicating the number of tests run, the number of failures, and the number of errors.

```
10 run, 8 passes, 2 failures, 0 errors
```

The above output signifies that out of 10 tests, 8 passed successfully, 2 failed, and none encountered errors. Failed tests are typically due to assertions not meeting expectations, whereas errors are exceptions raised during test execution.

Implementing Test Suites in CI

For seamless integration with CI tools, a test runner script can be implemented to invoke the necessary test suites, capture results, and report back to the CI system.

```
| result |
result := TestResult new.
MyTestSuite suite run: result.
Transcript show: result runCount.
Transcript show: result failureCount.
```

This script runs the test suite and outputs the counts of total tests and failures to the transcript, which can then be parsed by the CI tool to determine the build status.

Mastering the execution and management of tests in Smalltalk ensures that your code remains clean, reliable, and maintainable throughout its lifecycle.

10.5 Test-Driven Development (TDD) Practices

Test-Driven Development (TDD) is a software development methodology where test cases are written before the code that needs to be tested. This approach helps ensure that code is thoroughly tested and meets desired specifications. In Smalltalk, TDD practices can be seamlessly executed using the SUnit framework.

The key steps in TDD include:

- Writing a test case
- Running the test, which should initially fail
- Writing the minimum code necessary to pass the test
- Running the test again to confirm it passes
- Refactoring the code while ensuring that tests still pass

Writing a Test Case: Begin by writing a test case for the functionality you are about to implement. In Smalltalk, a test case is created by subclassing TestCase and defining methods that perform assertions. Consider that you are going to implement a method add:to: in a class Calculator. First, you write a test case as follows:

```
CalculatorTestCase subclass: TestCase [
  CalculatorTestCase >> testAddition [
    | calculator result |
    calculator := Calculator new.
    result := calculator add: 3 to: 4.
    self assert: result equals: 7.
  ]
]
```

Running the Test: Execute the test. Since the method add:to: has not yet been implemented, the test should fail. In an IDE supporting SUnit, you can run the tests by selecting the test class or method and initiating the test runner. Alternatively, in a workspace or script, you can use:

```
(TestCase named: 'CalculatorTestCase') run
```

Implementing the Method: Now, write the minimal amount of code required to make the test pass. Implement the add:to: method in the Calculator class.

```
Calculator subclass: Object [
    Calculator >> add: aNumber to: anotherNumber [
        ^aNumber + anotherNumber
    ]
]
```

Verifying Test Pass: Rerun the test case to check whether it passes with the new implementation.

```
Test run: 1 assertions, passed: 1
```

The test should now pass, indicating that the implementation meets the requirements specified by the test case.

Refactoring: After the implementation passes, you may refactor the code for improved readability, performance, or maintainability. Ensure that the refactoring does not break the tests by running them again. If the tests still pass, the refactor is considered safe.

```
Calculator >> add: aNumber to: anotherNumber [
    ^aNumber + anotherNumber
]
```

Refactoring in TDD involves constant testing, thus minimizing the risk of introducing defects while improving code quality.

Writing More Tests: Continue by writing more test cases for other functionalities or edge cases. For example, adding test cases to handle zero or negative numbers ensures comprehensive coverage.

```
CalculatorTestCase >> testAdditionWithZero [
    | calculator result |
    calculator := Calculator new.
    result := calculator add: 0 to: 5.
    self assert: result equals: 5.
]

CalculatorTestCase >> testAdditionWithNegativeNumbers [
    | calculator result |
    calculator := Calculator new.
    result := calculator add: -3 to: -4.
    self assert: result equals: -7.
]
```

By writing these additional tests and following the TDD cycle, you ensure robust code. Each new test follows the same sequence: writing the test, verifying it fails, implementing the code, running the test, and refactoring.

TDD encourages the development of high-quality, maintainable code. An essential principle is to keep each test as simple and atomic as possible, focusing on one aspect of the functionality. This makes identifying the cause of a test failure easier, leading to more efficient debugging.

Through the repeated application of the TDD cycle, developers can achieve cleaner designs, better compliance with requirements, and a thorough suite of tests that safeguard against regressions. This practice ultimately contributes to a reliable and maintainable codebase.

10.6 Debugging Basics: The Debugger Tool

Debugging is an essential process for any software developer, and the debugger tool in Smalltalk is a powerful ally for diagnosing and resolving software issues. Understanding how to utilize the debugger effectively can greatly enhance your ability to identify and correct errors in your code. This section delves into the fundamental aspects of using the debugger tool in Smalltalk, providing the knowledge required to navigate through code execution, inspect variables, and understand the program flow.

The debugger in Smalltalk is invoked automatically when an exception occurs, or it can be called manually to examine the state of a program at any given point. When an exception is raised, the debugger provides an interactive environment where the developer can inspect the call stack, view local and instance variables, and even modify code on the fly.

To manually invoke the debugger, one might insert a breakpoint in the code using the self halt message. This will pause execution at the desired point and open the debugger. Here is an example of how to insert a halt in Smalltalk code:

```
MyClass>>myMethod
    "This is an example method in MyClass"
    self doSomething.
    self halt. "Inserting a breakpoint"
    self doSomethingElse.
```

When myMethod is executed, the program will halt at the breakpoint, and the debugger will open, allowing for inspection and interaction.

The debugger window consists of several crucial sections:

- **Call Stack:** Displays the sequence of method calls that led to the current execution point. This allows the developer to trace back through the method calls to understand the flow of execution.

- **Source Code:** Shows the source code of the currently selected method in the call stack. This is where the developer can read and understand the context of the code being executed.
- **Variables:** Provides access to local and instance variables. This section is essential for inspecting the current state of data and verifying that variables hold the expected values.
- **Execution Controls:** These include buttons for stepping through the code (Step Over, Step Into, Step Out), resuming execution, or terminating the debugging session.

Here is a closer look at the call stack and its importance. The call stack shows the list of methods that were called in order to reach the current state. Each method call in the stack can be selected to view its source code and the variables in scope at that call frame. This backtracking capability is indispensable for understanding how a particular state or error was reached. Consider the following example:

```
MyClass>>methodA
    self methodB.

MyClass>>methodB
    self methodC.

MyClass>>methodC
    self halt. "Breakpoint here"
```

When methodC is executed, the program will halt at the self halt breakpoint, and the debugger will display the call stack showing methodC, called by methodB, which in turn was called by methodA. Selectable frames in this call stack allow developers to navigate through the sequence of method calls seamlessly.

Stepping through code is another vital feature of the debugger. The execution control buttons provide granular control over code execution.

- Step Over advances the execution to the next line within the same method, effectively skipping over method calls.
- Step Into drills down into the method calls, allowing the developer to see the execution inside called methods.
- Step Out completes the execution of the current method and returns to the calling method.

For example, consider the need to debug a method to understand its flow:

```
MyClass>>calculateSum: a b: b
    | sum |
    sum := a + b.
    self print: sum.
    ^sum
```

Using the debugger, you can place a breakpoint on the sum := a + b line and step through each line of code. This level of control helps verify that each operation performs as expected and that variables maintain the correct values through the execution.

Inspecting variables in the debugger is straightforward. When a breakpoint is hit, the variables section lists all local and instance variables in the current context. Developers can expand these variables to see their contents. Suppose you were debugging the previous calculateSum: b: method and wanted to verify the sums computed:

```
self halt. "Insert halt in the method"
a := 5.
b := 10.
sum := a + b.
```

When the execution pauses, you can inspect a and b to ensure they hold the correct values, and sum to verify it is correctly computed as 15. This inspection capability is crucial for complex data structures where nested elements may require detailed examination.

Additionally, Smalltalk's runtime being highly dynamic, offers the ability to alter code directly within the debugger. This unique feature permits hot-fixing bugs and testing solutions without restarting the application. For example, if a method is identified to contain a flaw, it can be edited within the debugger, and execution can proceed with the updated code immediately.

Debugging in Smalltalk involves utilizing these tools and techniques to gain a comprehensive understanding of the program's execution and identify the precise location and cause of errors. Familiarity with the debugger and its features—call stack navigation, execution control, and variable inspection—empowers developers to dissect and resolve issues efficiently.

10.7 Setting Breakpoints and Inspecting Variables

In the process of debugging, breakpoints are essential tools allowing developers to pause the execution of a program at specified points. This pause provides an opportunity to inspect the state of the application, including the values of variables. In Smalltalk, setting breakpoints and inspecting variables can be seamlessly achieved using the built-in debugger tool.

The Debugger in Smalltalk is invoked automatically when an error occurs during program execution. Additionally, developers can manually initiate the debugger at specific points in the code by using the self halt method. Here is an example:

```
MyClass>>myMethod
  "This method does some computations"
  self halt. "Set a breakpoint here"
  "Further computation and logic"
```

When the program execution reaches self halt, it will pause, and the Debugger interface will appear. At this point, the state of myMethod can be examined.

Within the Debugger, developers can inspect variables, evaluate expressions, and step through the code. The main interface typically displays the current stack trace, local variables, instance variables, and temporary variables.

Inspecting Variables

In the Debugger, right-clicking on a variable name provides the option to inspect it. This action opens an Inspector window displaying the current value of the variable. For example, consider the following code snippet:

```
MyClass>>computeSum: a b: b
  | sum |
  sum := a + b.
  self halt. "Breakpoint set after initialization of sum"
  ^sum
```

Upon invoking computeSum: 3 b: 4, and reaching the self halt line, the Debugger allows us to inspect the value of sum, which will be displayed as 7.

To evaluate expressions within the current context, the Debugger interface provides a workspace where expressions can be typed and evaluated. This feature is useful for deeper inspection and analysis, such as evaluating more complex expressions involving current variables.

Using Watchpoints

Smalltalk's Debugger also supports watchpoints, which are similar to breakpoints but specifically designed to monitor changes in variable values. A watchpoint can be set by providing an expression that, when evaluated to true, triggers the debugger. For instance:

```
MyClass>>loopUntilZero: aNumber
  | counter |
  counter := aNumber.
  [ counter > 0 ] whileTrue: [
    counter := counter - 1.
    self halt: counter = 0. "Watchpoint set to halt when counter is zero"
  ].
```

In this example, the debugger will be invoked when counter reaches zero.

Step Execution

Another feature of the Debugger is its ability to step through code line-by-line or statement-by-statement. The Debugger typically provides several step execution commands:

- Step - Executes the next Smalltalk statement.
- Over - Steps over the next statement, executing it in entirety without entering into any calls.
- Into - Steps into the next statement, entering any called methods.
- Return - Completes execution of the current method and returns to the caller.

Using these commands, developers can methodically traverse through the code, observing the effects of each line and identifying where issues might arise.

Setting Conditional Breakpoints

Smalltalk allows setting conditional breakpoints that will trigger only if a specified condition is met. This can be particularly useful for debugging loops or large code blocks where stopping at every iteration would be inefficient. For example:

```
MyClass>>processArray: anArray
```

```
anArray do: [ :element |
    self halt: element > 10. "Conditional breakpoint"
    "Further processing"
].
```

In this case, the Debugger will be invoked only for array elements greater than 10, facilitating more focused debugging.

Advanced Variable Inspection

For complex objects, the Inspector window provides a detailed view, often allowing navigation through object properties and relationships. This feature aids in understanding the internal state of more intricate objects and their interactions.

```
MyClass>>complexMethod
    | user |
    user := User new.
    user name: 'Alice'; age: 30.
    self halt. "Inspect the user object"
    "More operations involving user"
```

When the Debugger halts at `self halt`, inspecting `user` reveals its attributes and their values, facilitating comprehensive debugging of the object's state.

Understanding and effectively utilizing breakpoints and variable inspection in Smalltalk significantly enhances the debugging process, making it more efficient and precise.

10.8 Tracing Code Execution

Tracing code execution in Smalltalk is an essential skill for understanding program flow and identifying errors or performance bottlenecks. This section will cover various methods and tools available in Smalltalk for tracing code execution. We will explore how to utilize the built-in debugger to step through code, inspect the state of objects, and understand the sequence of method calls.

The primary tool for tracing code execution in Smalltalk is the debugger. The debugger allows you to pause the execution of a program at specific points, called breakpoints, and step through the code line-by-line or method-by-method. This granular control over code execution provides deep insights into how programs operate and facilitates the identification of issues.

To start tracing code execution, consider the following example. Assume we have a simple Smalltalk method that processes a list of numbers:

```
processNumbers: aCollection
  aCollection do: [:each |
    self processNumber: each].
```

This method iterates over a collection, processing each number by calling another method, processNumber:.

To trace the execution of processNumbers:, open the debugger and set a breakpoint at the start of the method. Here's how to do this:

- Select the method processNumbers: in the browser.
- Right-click on the first line of the method and choose set breakpoint.

Run the part of the program that calls processNumbers:. The execution will pause at the breakpoint, allowing you to examine the current state and stack. In the debugger window, you can see the call stack, the current method, and the values of variables.

Next, step through the code using the commands available in the debugger toolbar:

- Step - Executes the next line of code.
- Over - Steps over the current line, executing it entirely before pausing again.
- Into - Steps into the method call on the current line.
- Out - Steps out of the current method, resuming execution in the calling method.

Using these commands, you can trace through each iteration of the collection and dive into the processNumber: method for detailed inspection. Here is an example of the processNumber: method:

```
processNumber: aNumber
  aNumber isEven
    ifTrue: [self handleEvenNumber: aNumber]
    ifFalse: [self handleOddNumber: aNumber].
```

Set breakpoints within the processNumber: method to investigate the code paths for even and odd numbers. This deeper level of tracing helps detect logical issues or unexpected behavior.

Another useful tracing technique involves conditional breakpoints, which trigger only when a specific condition is met. This feature is particularly valuable for debugging complex programs where you only want to pause under certain circumstances. To set a conditional breakpoint:

- Right-click on the line where you want the breakpoint.
- Choose set conditional breakpoint.
- Enter the condition expression, such as aNumber > 100.

When the program runs, execution will only pause if the condition evaluates to true. This selective tracing significantly reduces the noise in the debugging process, allowing you to focus on critical issues.

Sometimes, you need to trace code that involves callbacks or asynchronous operations. In such cases, logging can complement the interactive debugger. Use the Transcript or other logging mechanisms to capture important events and data for later analysis. Here's an example:

```
processNumber: aNumber
   Transcript show: 'Processing number: ', aNumber printString; cr.
   aNumber isEven
      ifTrue: [self handleEvenNumber: aNumber]
      ifFalse: [self handleOddNumber: aNumber].
```

In the Transcript window, you will see a log of each number being processed, which can help trace asynchronous flows or repetitive issues.

Algorithm 6: Tracing Code Execution in Smalltalk

```
Input  : Method to trace, condition for breakpoints (optional)
Output : Step-by-step insight into method execution
Open the debugger;
Set breakpoints at the start of the method;
Run the program section calling the method;
while execution is paused at a breakpoint do
    Inspect variables and call stack;
    if further tracing is required then
        Step through the code using Step, Over, Into, and Out
          commands;
    else
        Adjust breakpoints or resume execution;
    if using conditional breakpoints then
        Set condition expression for the breakpoint;
        Continue executing the program;
Add logging statements if needed to capture additional data;
```

This methodical approach ensures comprehensive understanding and effective debugging of Smalltalk programs. By combining interactive debugging, conditional breakpoints, and logging, you can accurately trace and diagnose issues within complex codebases.

10.9 Handling Exceptions and Errors

In Smalltalk, exception handling provides robust mechanisms to manage runtime errors gracefully. This capability is critical for writing resilient and dependable applications. Proper exception handling can prevent abnormal termination, manage unforeseen conditions, and offer meaningful feedback to users or developers. Understanding and utilizing these mechanisms effectively requires knowledge of core concepts, including exception classes, signaling exceptions, and handling or resuming execution.

Smalltalk employs a class-based model for exceptions, with the Exception class serving as the root. Derived exception classes represent specific types of errors, such as Error, Warning, and Notification. Developers can also define custom exceptions tailored to their application's needs.

To signal an exception, the signal method is invoked on an instance of an exception class. For example, to signal a generic error, one might write:

```
Error new signal: 'An unexpected error occurred.'
```

In the above code, Error new creates a new instance of the Error class, and signal: raises the exception with the provided message. Once an exception is signaled, Smalltalk's runtime system searches for an active handler capable of managing the exception.

Exception handlers are installed using the on:do: method. This method takes two arguments: the first is the exception class to handle, and the second is a block of code to execute if the exception is raised. For instance:

```
[ criticalOperation ] on: Error do: [ :ex | Transcript show: 'Error occurred: ', ex
    messageText ]
```

In this example, criticalOperation represents a block of code that may raise an error. Should an Error occur, the handler block will be executed, and the exception object ex will be passed as an argument. The messageText method can be used to retrieve the exception's message.

Handling specific exceptions involves refining the exception class in the on:do: method. For example:

```
[ riskyOperation ] on: ZeroDivide do: [ :ex | Transcript show: 'Division by zero
    attempted.' ]
```

Here, the handler specifically targets ZeroDivide exceptions, which occur when a denominator is zero during division.

In some cases, it is desirable to manage exceptions and resume normal execution instead of terminating the operation. The resume method allows this:

```
[ criticalOperation ] on: Error do: [ :ex | Transcript show: 'Error encountered, resuming
    operation.' . ex resume ]
```

By invoking ex resume, the exception handler effectively skips over the error, allowing the program to continue execution. This technique is useful for non-fatal errors where a fallback mechanism is available.

For more fine-grained control, handlers can use the retry method to re-execute the protected block:

```
[ criticalOperation ] on: Error do: [ :ex | Transcript show: 'Retrying operation.' . ex
    retry ]
```

This approach instructs Smalltalk to run criticalOperation again, potentially with modified conditions.

When dealing with multiple exception types, nested handlers or combination handlers can be employed. Nested handlers are established by wrapping one on:do: block within another:

```
[ criticalOperation ] on: Warning do: [ :warn | Transcript show: 'Warning issued,
    continuing.' ] on: Error do: [ :err | Transcript show: 'Error occurred, handling.' ]
```

Combination handlers use the on:do: method at different points within the code block to address multiple exception types:

```
[
    [riskyOperation] on: Warning do: [ :warn | Transcript show: 'Warning handled.' ].
    criticalOperation
] on: Error do: [ :err | Transcript show: 'Error occurred, handling.' ]
```

Beyond signaling and handling, Smalltalk supports the creation of custom exception classes. This involves subclassing from an appropriate base class, typically Exception or one of its subclasses. Custom exceptions allow specific error conditions to be represented clearly:

```
CustomException subclass: #MySpecificError
    instanceVariableNames: ''
    classVariableNames: ''
    poolDictionaries: ''
    category: 'MyApplication-Exceptions'
```

Once defined, the custom exception can be raised and handled similarly to built-in exceptions:

```
[ riskyOperation ] on: MySpecificError do: [ :ex | Transcript show: 'Handled
    MySpecificError.' ]
```

Integrating effective exception handling in Smalltalk applications enhances reliability and maintains user trust. Employing these techniques judiciously ensures that applications can gracefully recover from errors, provide informative diagnostics, and continue operating under adverse conditions.

10.10 Refactoring for Better Debugging

Refactoring is a software engineering practice that involves altering the structure of code without changing its external behavior. The primary goal of refactoring is to make the code more maintainable, understandable, and easier to debug. By improving the clarity and reducing complexity, refactoring ultimately contributes to more efficient debugging and enhances overall code quality.

Several strategies can be implemented during refactoring to facilitate better debugging in Smalltalk.

- **Modularization:** Break down large methods and classes into smaller, more manageable, and cohesive units. Small methods and classes are easier to test and understand.
- **Naming Conventions:** Use descriptive and consistent naming for variables, methods, and classes. Clear names provide insight into the functionality and aid in tracking errors.
- **Code Duplication:** Eliminate duplication by abstracting common patterns into reusable methods or classes. This not only reduces potential sources of errors but also saves time when debugging similar issues.
- **Single Responsibility Principle:** Ensure that each class and method has a single responsibility or concern. This makes the code more predictable and easier to trace when issues arise.
- **Coupling and Cohesion:** Minimize tightly coupled code and strive for high cohesion. Loose coupling and high cohesion increase the modularity of the code and simplify identifying and isolating the source of bugs.

Here are examples demonstrating refactoring techniques in Smalltalk. Consider an initial snippet of a poorly structured method:

```
saveUserData: aUser
    | fileStream |
    fileStream := FileStream newFileNamed: 'userdata.txt'.
    fileStream nextPutAll: ('Name: ', aUser name, ' Address: ', aUser address).
    fileStream close.

    Transcript show: 'User data saved successfully.'
```

This method performs multiple responsibilities: handling file operations and interacting with the transcript. For better debugging, refactor it into smaller, more focused methods:

```
saveUserData: aUser
    self writeDataToFile: aUser.
    self notifyUser.

writeDataToFile: aUser
    | fileStream |
```

```
    fileStream := FileStream newFileNamed: 'userdata.txt'.
    fileStream nextPutAll: self createUserString: aUser.
    fileStream close.

createUserString: aUser
    ^'Name: ', aUser name, ' Address: ', aUser address

notifyUser
    Transcript show: 'User data saved successfully.'
```

Refactoring the original method into writeDataToFile:, createUserString:, and notifyUser ensures each method has a single responsibility. This approach isolates file handling, string creation, and user notification. Reducing method size and responsibility makes issues easier to isolate when debugging.

Consistent naming conventions enhance code readability:

```
writeDataToFile: aUser
    | fileStream |
    fileStream := FileStream newFileNamed: 'userdata.txt'.
    fileStream nextPutAll: self createUserStringFrom: aUser.
    fileStream close.

createUserStringFrom: aUser
    ^'Name: ', aUser name, ' Address: ', aUser address
```

In this revision, method names explicitly describe their functionality, aiding both understanding and debugging. Additionally, consolidating code that interacts with the same entities and ensuring descriptive names guide the developer through code behavior.

Addressing code duplication is essential. Consider the following example:

```
displayUserDetails: aUser
    Transcript show: 'Name: ', aUser name; cr.
    Transcript show: 'Address: ', aUser address; cr.

logUserDetails: aUser
    Logger log: 'Name: ', aUser name.
    Logger log: 'Address: ', aUser address.
```

This code contains duplicated logic for displaying and logging user details. By refactoring duplicated code into a single responsibility method, the code becomes more maintainable and easier to debug:

```
displayUserDetails: aUser
    Transcript show: (self userDetailsString: aUser); cr.

logUserDetails: aUser
    Logger log: (self userDetailsString: aUser).

userDetailsString: aUser
```

```
^ String streamContents: [:stream |
    stream nextPutAll: 'Name: ', aUser name; cr.
    stream nextPutAll: 'Address: ', aUser address; cr ]
```

Creating userDetailsString: eliminates duplication and consolidated the logic for user detail formatting, thus simplifying revisions and debugging.

Adopting the single responsibility principle ensures methods and classes remain focused. For instance, in a class handling user authentication:

```
authenticateUser: username password: password
    | user valid |
    user := self findUserByName: username.
    valid := user notNil and: [user password = password].
    valid ifTrue: [self logSuccessfulLogin: user]
        ifFalse: [self logFailedLoginAttempt: username].
    ^ valid
```

Here, authenticateUser:password: is responsible for user lookup, validation, and logging. By refactoring these concerns into separate methods:

```
authenticateUser: username password: password
    | user valid |
    user := self findUserByName: username.
    valid := self validateUser: user withPassword: password.
    self logAuthenticationAttempt: user isValid: valid.
    ^ valid

validateUser: user withPassword: password
    ^ user notNil and: [user password = password]

logAuthenticationAttempt: user isValid: valid
    valid
        ifTrue: [self logSuccessfulLogin: user]
        ifFalse: [self logFailedLoginAttempt: user username].
```

This enhances modularity and simplifies each method's responsibility, facilitating debugging and testing.

Ultimately, refactoring is an ongoing process essential to maintaining high code quality and efficiency in debugging. Enhanced readability, improved structure, and reduced complexity lead to a more maintainable and robust codebase, allowing for rapid identification and resolution of issues.

10.11 Using Logging for Debugging

Logging serves as an instrumental technique in debugging and understanding the behavior of your applications during runtime. By inserting log statements at strategic locations in your Smalltalk code, you can record messages, variable values, and execution flow, which are invaluable for identifying issues and gaining insights into application performance.

In Smalltalk, logging can be achieved by utilizing the Transcipt, a predefined class for writing textual output. The following details provide a structured overview of employing logging effectively:

- **Transcripts and Messages**: The Transcript class offers a centralized point for writing messages. These messages can assist in tracking the execution sequence, recording variable states, and noting error occurrences.

```
Transcript show: 'This is a log message'; cr.
```

  The show: method writes the specified string to the Transcript, while cr appends a carriage return, ensuring that subsequent messages appear on new lines.

- **Logging Variable States**: To keep track of variable values at different execution points, incorporate log statements that output these values. This practice helps verify data integrity and trace how variables evolve.

```
| a b c |
a := 10.
b := a + 20.
c := b * 2.
Transcript show: 'Value of a: ', a printString; cr.
Transcript show: 'Value of b: ', b printString; cr.
Transcript show: 'Value of c: ', c printString; cr.
```

  The printString method converts numerical values to strings, making them suitable for logging with the show: method.

- **Conditional Logging**: Sometimes, logging everything may clutter the Transcript, particularly in loops or frequently executed sections. Apply conditional logging to focus only on significant states.

```
| x |
x := 0.
1 to: 100 do: [ :i |
    x := x + i.
```

```
    (i \\ 10 = 0) ifTrue: [ Transcript show: 'Current sum at step ', i printString,
          ': ', x printString; cr ].
].
```

Here, only every tenth iteration's sum is logged, reducing verbosity and highlighting relevant information.

- **Error and Exception Logging**: Logging errors and exceptions immediately when they arise aids in quickly identifying failure points and understanding the context.

```
[ 1 / 0 ] on: ZeroDivide do: [ :ex |
    Transcript show: 'Error: Attempted division by zero.'; cr.
    ex return: 0.
].
```

The error message is logged to the Transcript, and the exception handling logic ensures that such events are both detected and recorded.

- **Timestamping Logs**: Timestamping log entries can significantly enhance the debug information by providing a temporal context.

```
Transcript show: Time now asString, ': Execution started'; cr.
```

Attaching the current time to log entries helps track the sequence and duration of operations.

- **Advanced Logging with External Libraries**: For comprehensive logging requirements, external libraries such as Log4Smalltalk offer advanced features like category-based logging, different log levels (debug, info, warn, error), and formatted output.

```
| logger |
logger := Logger named: 'MyLogger'.
logger info: 'Informational message'.
logger error: 'Error message with context: ', context printString.
```

Using such libraries can modularize and standardize logging across extensive Smalltalk projects, improving maintenance and readability.

- **Configuring and Managing Logs**: Efficient logging also involves managing log output sizes, rotating log files, and selectively enabling logs.

```
LoggerRoot new
    level: LoggerLevelInfo;
    addHandler: (LoggerFileHandler new fileName: 'app.log'; build).
```

Here, logs are written to app.log with an information level threshold, meaning only messages of info and higher severity are recorded.

Employing these logging practices facilitates robustness in your debugging strategy, allowing for thorough examination and timely resolution of issues. Fine-tuning the granularity and scope of your log entries optimizes both their completeness and conciseness. Additionally, leveraging sophisticated logging frameworks can significantly enhance the manageability and scalability of your logging system.

10.12 Automated Testing and Continuous Integration

In contemporary software development, automated testing and continuous integration (CI) play crucial roles in ensuring code quality and reliability. Smalltalk, with its dynamic nature and interactive programming environment, provides robust tools and practices that align well with these paradigms. This section delves into methodologies for automating tests in Smalltalk and the practical aspects of setting up a continuous integration pipeline.

Automated testing refers to the practice of using software tools to perform tests on codebases automatically. The goal is to minimize human intervention, enhance test coverage, and identify defects early in the development lifecycle. Smalltalk's integration with the SUnit framework facilitates the creation and execution of automated tests efficiently.

SUnit test cases, which were discussed in earlier sections, lay the foundation for automated testing. Once tests are written, they can be executed automatically on each code change, ensuring that new changes do not break existing functionality. Below is an example of how to write a simple SUnit test case in Smalltalk:

```
TestCase subclass: MyFirstTest [
    MyFirstTest >> testAddition [
        self assert: (1 + 1) = 2.
    ]
]
```

The next step involves running these tests automatically. Tools and scripts are used to invoke test runs without manual intervention. The following snippet demonstrates how to run tests programmatically:

```
| result |
result := TestRunner runAll.
Transcript show: result.
```

To establish continuous integration, a CI server such as Jenkins or Travis CI is employed. These tools continuously build and test software projects, allowing teams to detect problems early. Setting up a CI pipeline involves the following key steps:

- **Version Control:** Ensure that the code is stored in a version control system like Git. The CI server will monitor this repository for changes.
- **CI Server Configuration:** Set up the CI server to check out code, build the project, and run tests automatically on each commit or at scheduled intervals.
- **Build Scripts:** Create build scripts that detail the steps for building and testing the project. In our Smalltalk environment, the build script would likely involve running SUnit tests.

Consider a configuration file for Jenkins to automate a Smalltalk project:

```
pipeline {
    agent any

    stages {
        stage('Checkout') {
            steps {
                git 'https://github.com/your-repo/smalltalk-project.git'
            }
        }

        stage('Test') {
            steps {
                sh './run-tests.sh'
            }
        }
    }

    post {
        always {
            junit '**/test-results.xml'
        }
    }
}
```

The script run-tests.sh might look like the following to run SUnit tests:

```
#!/bin/sh
gst -f runTests.st
```

And runTests.st would be:

```
ObjectMemory snapshot: true andQuit: false. "Prepare a clean state"
| results |
results := TestRunner runAll.
results storeOn: 'test-results.xml'.
```

Additionally, CI systems provide feedback mechanisms, keeping developers informed about the build status. Successful builds can be deployed automatically, or failed builds can trigger alerts for immediate attention. Email notifications, dashboards, and integration with communication tools like Slack or Microsoft Teams are common feedback channels.

In practice, automated testing and continuous integration foster a culture of continuous improvement and collaboration. By integrating these practices, teams can achieve higher development velocity, maintain code quality, and reduce the time to market for new features.

Upon encountering a failing test, detailed reports and logs generated by CI servers assist in diagnosing issues. Advanced CI setups may employ additional stages, such as static code analysis, performance testing, and deployment automation, further enhancing the robustness of the development pipeline.

Overall, automated testing and continuous integration form the backbone of modern software engineering practices in Smalltalk, ensuring that code remains clean, functional, and maintainable.

Made in the USA
Monee, IL
07 November 2026

67911519R10164